FOREVER FLY FREE

ONE WOMAN'S STORY OF RESILIENCE AND THE POWER OF HOPE AND LOVE

JENNY BRANDEMUEHL

A REGALO PRESS BOOK
ISBN: 979-8-89565-030-1
ISBN (eBook): 979-8-89565-031-8

Publishing Team:
Founder and Publisher – Gretchen Young
Editorial Assistant – Caitlyn Limbaugh
Managing Editor – Madeline Sturgeon
Production Manager – Kate Harris
Production Editor – Rachel Paul

Phoenix Society for Burn Survivors is the leading nonprofit organization dedicated to empowering people affected by a burn injury. Phoenix Society serves burn survivors, loved ones, burn care professionals, researchers, and anyone else committed to supporting the burn community and building a safer world. The organization sees a future where no one facing the life-changing effects of a burn injury is forced to journey through healing alone. For more information, visit: www.phoenix-society.org.

This book, as well as any other Regalo Press publications, may be purchased in bulk quantities at a special discounted rate. Contact orders@regalopress.com for more information.

All people, locations, events, and situations are portrayed to the best of the author's memory. While all of the events described are true, many names and identifying details have been changed to protect the privacy of the people involved.

Regalo Press
New York • Nashville
regalopress.com

Published in the United States of America
1 2 3 4 5 6 7 8 9 10

To Mark, whose love and belief in me was my true north
To Wesley and Adrian who are the future
To Robert, our magical love carries me forward everyday

~

CONTENTS

PART 1
HEROES

PART 2
THE ROLLERCOASTER

PART 3
SURVIVAL

PART 4
HOPE AND HEALING

PART 5
LOVE IS ALL THERE IS

Part 1

HEROES

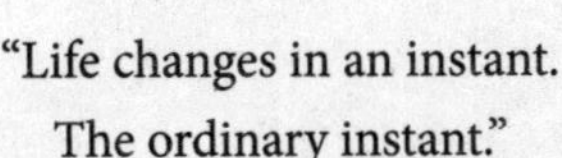

"Life changes in an instant.
The ordinary instant."

—Joan Didion,
The Year of Magical Thinking

Chapter 1

THE PHONE CALL

I'm hiding in an empty conference room, trying to respond to urgent emails before my next meeting. Amanda, the head of recruiting on my team, slips into the room.

"You're not going to believe what Justin wants—hire thirty engineers in Berlin, India, and Santa Clara in four weeks." She exhales loudly, shaking her head as she paces in front of me. "We all *know* it takes at least three months lead time in the current market to hire even one engineer."

"Geez, Justin is running so fast. As my kids used to say, he's cuckoo for Cocoa Puffs." I twirl my forefinger by the side of my head, spinning it the way my sons, Wesley and Adrian, used to do as little kids, hopping back and forth on their two feet like bouncy, midget marsupials.

Amanda chuckles. "And I say four weeks is great if we're hiring sixty sales clerks for Petco."

My phone rings suddenly. On cue, Amanda waves to me as she steps out of the room.

It's not a number I recognize, so I don't answer, turning my attention back to reading my emails. My phone rings again for a while until it goes silent. Probably someone trying to sell me something or recruit me for a job. The phone rings again. Same number, 602 area code. *Boy—these people are persistent!* I think. I Google the area code. *Phoenix. Crap. Mark's in Scottsdale flying back to Lake Tahoe today.*

I immediately pick up the phone, feeling instant remorse that I hadn't picked up earlier.

"Jenny, it's Mark."

"Hi, Mark, sweetie." I'm glad to hear from my husband. *But why isn't he calling me from his phone?*

"The plane's gone."

He sounds so calm.

"I've been in an accident and I'm at the hospital."

Hospital. Accident. Oh, no.

"The doctors tell me I'm in for a very…long recovery." He emphasizes *long.*

"Are you okay? Are you injured?" I feel dizzy, off balance. The room is spinning.

"I love you, Jenny."

Why isn't he answering my question? What happened?

"I love you too, Mark…. What happened?"

"I'm handing you to the doctor," Mark says in his no-fuss voice. Maybe he didn't hear my question.

A professional, self-assured man's voice comes on the phone. He introduces himself as Dr. Reese, the attending physician at Maricopa County Hospital in Phoenix.

The doctor explains several medical facts about Mark's condition, but I have no idea what he's saying. At all. His words are so technical. I catch key words here and there, but they slip away before I can ask questions. Fluid bolus therapy. Hemodynamic stability. *Stability, okay—I got that. But wait. What's "hemodynamic"?* Crystalloid. It's so technical and he doesn't pause for questions. I'm gripping the phone so tightly that my hand hurts. I slowly stretch my fingers out. I'm not following what he's saying about Mark's condition. He finally pauses. I should be all over him with my questions. After all, I'm the executive. *Get more information.* But instead, I'm overwhelmed. I don't know where or what to begin to ask because I don't understand him, starting from his first sentence. So I ask, "What happened to the plane?"

"I don't actually know."

What? How can he not know? I stop my mental torrent of questions, thinking that Mark and I are the kind of people who say to each other and others, "There's nothing to worry about until we have more information. Why get worked up until we know more?"

"So I assume his plane was in an accident?" *What a lame question!* I realize it the minute I blurt it out.

"Yes," he replies.

"And you can't tell me any details about how it happened?" Somehow I think knowing what happened to Mark's plane will tell me more clearly what happened to him. I'm fidgeting with my pen, clicking it up and down. *Click, click. Click.*

"That's right."

I drop my pen onto the floor. I stare at it, feeling paralyzed and unable to pick it up.

"Okay..." I take a deep breath. "I didn't understand anything you just said earlier." I close my eyes, in my desperate need to focus. "I just need to know this, Dr. Reese. Bottom line—are his injuries life-threatening?"

"Yes, they are."

"Okay, that's all I need to know." A rock seems to have dropped into my stomach. It feels so heavy. "I'll catch the first flight I can to get there."

"Of course."

"Thank you."

I brush the heavy feeling aside. Something instantly switches on. I will myself to feel calm. Deep breathing. In, out, in, out. *Just breathe*, they always say in my meditation app.

After a few deep breaths, I kick into high gear now that I know Mark's life is at risk. I run to my desk, attempting to find everything I need to pack up in my backpack. All I can think about is, *How fast can I get to Phoenix? How fast? How fast?* I grab my purse out of my drawer. Debra, one of the leaders on my team, walks by. I pull her aside.

"Debra, Mark's been in a terrible plane accident."

"Oh, no!" she exclaims, wide-eyed. Her mouth drops open.

Seeing her troubled expression is jarring, because in my attempt to control my whirlwind of emotions, I see how obviously terrible the news is. And I didn't even explain what the doctor just told me.

"In Phoenix. I've gotta go." I nervously glance at my watch. "Like now." I put my laptop in my backpack. *Where's the mouse? Oh, wait. I need my notebook, don't I?*

"What can I do for you, Jenny?"

I shrug helplessly. *I don't know*. I grab my power cord. *I need that.*

"Okay. No problem. You need to go home and find a flight to Phoenix. I'll take care of everything here." She mentions something about letting our CEO, Dan, and my team know.

I need my pen. I grab it and zip up my backpack. Barely looking at Debra, who's hovering, I pick up my backpack and purse and race out the door. *Where's my car? Where did I park?* I'm searching frantically in the parking lot. I spot my car, two rows from the lobby. Thank God—I had gotten in early enough to find a parking space close to the building.

The drive home is a blur.

Arriving home, I park the car and sit in the driveway thinking about how horrible the news is. *How do I explain this to our boys? I need to stay calm. Calm.* Wesley's my kid even though he's twenty-six years old, a strapping big guy like his dad. *I need to protect him from whatever is happening. Don't rattle him.* Wesley's sensitive and occasionally suffers from panic attacks.

Wesley is lying in his familiar spot on the couch in the family room. His contract job wrapped up recently and he's been applying for jobs online.

"Hi, Mom!" He's surprised to see me at this time of day. I never get home before six o'clock.

I carefully put down my backpack and purse, composing my thoughts.

"Wes, I have some bad news."

His mouth is slightly open as he stares at me.

"What?"

"Dad's been in a plane accident." I work hard to keep my voice even.

"Oh, no." Wesley's face crumples. He gets up from the couch.

"He's in the ER. I talked with the doctor just now."

"How is he?" Wesley approaches me, standing close, facing me.

"Not good, Wesley. I didn't understand what the doctor said—but it's not good."

Wesley hugs me. I hug him back but I feel like a robot, going through the motions. My body feels stiff and awkward.

"I've gotta get to Phoenix today. Can you help me out while I pack?" I ask.

"Sure, Mom."

"Check the next available flights from San Jose to Phoenix, will you?" I briskly climb the stairs to my bedroom. Wesley follows me.

"Will do," Wesley replies and disappears to find his iPad.

Okay, focus Jenny. I need to quickly pack in case Wesley finds me a flight that leaves soon. I pull out my suitcase, place it on the bed, and begin looking for any summer clothes I can find. *It's hot in Phoenix, right?* I start haphazardly throwing anything that looks as if it's for summer into my suitcase. Shorts, short-sleeved tops. I picture Mark lying on a gurney at the hospital calling me. *Stop. Don't go there. I need to pack. I can't miss the next available flight. I just can't.* My neck feels hot, panicked at the thought of missing a flight. I move faster, conscious of my jerky movements as I continue packing, literally throwing everything into the suitcase.

The suitcase is half full before I think to Google the weather in Phoenix. *I might be there for a while.* Ninety-five to ninety-nine all week. *Hot.* I start digging around my closet for my sandals. *Shoot. Where are they?* I pull out a bunch of shoes to find sandals in my closet. Shoes pile up around me—it's a mess but I don't care. The first pair I find I toss into the suitcase.

It suddenly occurs to me that I need to let Mark's family know—his brother, his sisters, his cousin. Between throwing in my sandals and more clothes, I send texts to Mark's family in the Midwest. His youngest sister is farthest away in New York. Since I don't know much about Mark's condition, all I can tell them is what I know—that Mark's been in a bad plane accident and it's serious, though I don't really know what that means when his sister Rene immediately responds, asking for details. I tell her I don't know. I'm flying to Phoenix ASAP and promise to send an update when I know more.

I have no idea what I've packed, but I zip up my suitcase after I text them. It makes me feel better to know Wesley and I aren't the only ones close to Mark who know what's happened. I don't know why but it does.

Wesley manages to get me on a flight leaving at 6:15 p.m. It gives me enough time to get to the airport. I'm relieved.

I start hauling my suitcase down the narrow stairs.

"Mom, let me get that," Wesley calls from behind me.

"It's okay, honey—I got it," I reply, continuing my march down the stairs with my luggage. It's heavy.

"Are you sure? I can get that for you," he calls again, with a mixture of concern verging on impatience.

"No, no!" I wave him off. "I've got it!" I continue lugging my heavy bag down the stairs.

I want so badly to keep him at a distance, not to involve him yet. It's a way of protecting him from all this. This—I don't even know yet what *this* is really.

"I'll drive you," Wesley insists, grabbing his keys.

In the car a text pops up from Sue Tessman, a friend who had moved to Phoenix from Madison, Wisconsin, with her husband a few years ago. She mentions that Steven, Mark's brother, updated her about Mark. She asks for my flight information so she can pick me up at the airport and take me straight to the hospital to see Mark. I'm grateful she's there because I don't know anyone else in Phoenix.

Wesley and I ride in tense silence while he drives me to San Jose airport. I text my sister in LA and my close Wellesley friend, Suzie, in Denver, who is our boys' godmother. I feel like command central. I've let everyone who needs to know, know. It feels good to do something. A welcome distraction.

When I get to the airport I check in. My phone rings as I'm walking to the gate. Another 602 area code. Phoenix again. I pick up. It's a professional, smooth-sounding man's voice asking if I'm Jenny Brandemuehl. He mentions that he's from some aviation company at Scottsdale Airport. I confirm my identity and yes, I'm Mark's wife. He asks me questions about Mark and the plane. I snap to attention. This must be part of the process of filing an accident report by the airport.

While I talk with him, I continue my purposeful stride to the gate. *I can't miss this flight.*

"Tell us what happened," he says.

What? Don't they know? They're at the airport.

"*You* tell *me* what happened," I reply aggressively. "You're there at the airport, aren't you?" I'm exasperated—and really annoyed.

"He was flying a Mooney, right?"

"Yes." *Why don't they know this already?*

He asks me more questions. I have no answers for almost all of them.

"I don't know anything," I said. "I only just spoke with the doctor at the hospital."

"How *is* Mark doing?"

Why would they want to know his condition? Aren't they just collecting facts about the plane accident? It hits me suddenly. *This guy's got to be a reporter!*

My face feels flush as a tide of anger bursts through. "I can't talk to you anymore." I abruptly hang up. I hate them. *These reporters will stop at nothing to get information.* For a moment I lose track of where I am at the airport. I feel blood pounding in my ears and all I see is a blur of people walking by me. I step aside to escape the flow of people walking, close my eyes and take a deep breath. *Ah, yes—I'm going to Gate 12.* My legs have a will of their own and I start walking again.

When I reach the gate, I text Sue my flight arrival information. She tells me she's trying to get into the hospital to see Mark. When I find a seat in the crowded gate area, I sit down. It's only then that it occurs to me that I should Google to see if there's a news update about what happened to Mark. I read a 12News article:

> *Pilot in critical condition with severe burns after plane crash in Deer Valley*
>
> *The cause of the crash Tuesday afternoon near North 31st Avenue and Deer Valley Road is under investigation.*
>
> *PHOENIX—A man has severe burns after a plane he was piloting crashed and caught fire near North 31st Avenue and Deer Valley Road, according to the Phoenix Fire Department. Phoenix Fire said the 50-year-old man was the only passenger in the plane.*
>
> *The plane nearly hit at least one driver during the crash, firefighters said. According to crews, a bystander pulled the pilot from the plane as flames engulfed the aircraft.*
>
> *The pilot was rushed to the hospital and remains in critical condition. Phoenix Fire said the man suffered 2nd- and 3rd-de-*

gree burns. Firefighters said the man was awake and talking when he was taken to the hospital.

It is unknown what caused the crash.

The Federal Aviation Administration says the plane was a single-engine Mooney M20. The plane burst into flames again as crews dismantled and towed the wreckage from the scene.

The FAA and National Transportation Safety Board will handle the investigation. It typically takes the NTSB a year or more to determine a probable cause of an accident.

Deer Valley Road was closed between 31st Avenue and 35th Avenue for an extended period of time, Phoenix PD says.

Severe burns. I can't stop staring at those words. *Fuck.* A string of profanities pour into my mind. I want to scream. I look around the gate area. People are sitting quietly, reading their phones, listening to music. A woman is feeding her baby. *How did this happen to Mark? My beautiful, beloved husband. How did this happen? I'm shouting silently in my mind in a private bubble that no one around me can hear.* The world goes blurry again. I wipe away tears that I'm barely aware of until I realize that my face is wet.

My flight's being called. Hastily I put my phone away and get into the boarding line.

The flight to Phoenix is only a couple hours long. I resist the urge to use the in-flight Wi-Fi and look up "second-degree burns" and "third-degree burns." I promise myself I'll do that when I get to Phoenix. I need to stay calm and wait until I talk with the doctors. I don't want to get wound up before I get an update from Mark's physician.

It's dark outside when I step out the door with my baggage at Sky Harbor International. A wall of dry heat hits me immediately. No matter how hot the day is at home, it's always chilly at night. *So this is Phoenix.*

I quickly spot Sue in her red Cadillac SUV. I hug her and hold onto her a little longer than usual. She's a familiar and reassuring presence. Once she starts driving, she explains that she visited Mark briefly at the hospital before she came to pick me up. Sue works at a life sciences start-up and sounds very knowledgeable about all things medical.

"So I talked to a Dr. Hale."

I'm confused. *Who is he?* I had pictured Dr. Reese from my phone call earlier. I stay quiet, wanting to know what was shared with her.

"He said that they put Mark into a medically induced coma because the burns are so traumatic and painful. The sedation helps him with his condition as well as the treatment."

"Did he say what type of treatment Mark will receive?"

Sue shook her head. "Only that for tonight they're giving him fluid intravenously and monitoring his vitals closely."

"So you saw Mark?"

"Yes."

"And how did he look?"

"You should know that he's completely wrapped up in bandages."

"Oh." I'm trying to imagine it while digesting the fact that he's in a coma. "So I can't talk to him?" I think of the brief call he and I had.

"I'm so sorry, Jenny. They sedated him pretty quickly after he arrived in the ER."

So they must have sedated him after he called me. I see him lying on a gurney again.

I don't see much of Phoenix on our drive because it's dark out. Maricopa County Hospital, where the Burn Center is located, is near the airport. Sue parks close to the brightly lit emergency room sign at the entrance. As we walk through the parking lot in the warm evening, it occurs to me that the only times Mark and I have been at a hospital at night were when our boys were born. This is new.

A police officer is behind the check-in counter in the ER. It strikes me as odd that it's not a regular receptionist. We make our way to another lobby with a security entrance to the Burn Center. Sue presses the intercom button to let them know who we are and the name of the patient we're visiting.

Once inside the burn unit, Sue and I follow the instructions posted on the wall. It's quiet except for the steady hum of machines in the individual patient rooms. Everyone has his or her own private room and a square two-foot by two-foot peephole window to the right side of each door. Sue shows me the visitor protocol. We put on yellow hospital gowns and wash our hands thoroughly with soap and warm water. Next we pull on blue latex gloves. Sue explains that the nurses told her the environment has to be super clean for burn patients to prevent any possibility of infection.

Sue leads the way to Mark's room, which is quiet and dimly lit. I glance at the clock. 8:30 p.m.

Mark is lying on the bed, wrapped in white bandages. Sue had told me he would be bandaged up, but nothing prepares me for seeing him this way. He's a huge mummy. His chest and legs look big because of the dressing layers. Mark's already a big man. *Is he really in there somewhere?* I look at his face, where the white coverings look sticky. His face is fully bandaged as well, except for his eyes, which are closed. Mark is hooked up to a machine that's rhythmically breathing. In and out, in and out. Otherwise, it's completely silent in the room.

It doesn't yet fully occur to me how bad things are because he's wrapped up in these pristine white bandages. I'm not sure what Mark looks like underneath. I would be afraid to look.

A nurse walks in and examines a machine with a screen. From the screen reading I can see she's checking his heart rate and blood pressure.

"Does everything look okay?" I ask her, hesitant because I'm a little afraid to hear her answer.

"His blood pressure's a little low but that's normal in burn patients," she explains matter-of-factly. "We'd worry if there's a severe drop in pressure, which can be an indication of septic shock."

I nod, taking it in. With a start, I realize I should introduce myself, which I do. She is Linda, Mark's night nurse tonight. Linda has a kind-looking face. She bustles about in a competent manner.

I introduce Sue.

I watch silently as Linda checks the breathing apparatus. "What's that machine for?" I ask.

"It's Mark's respiratory machine. The good news is that he didn't suffer a lot of smoke inhalation, which can damage the lungs. We get a lot of patients who suffer from that, and you can die from it."

"So *that's* good."

"Yes. But because your husband is in a medically induced coma, he needs help breathing."

"Where exactly are his burns?"

"Let me check." She pulls out Mark's chart and looks through it. After a few minutes, she says, "Okay, his arms, his chest, his torso, his back… um, both legs and feet."

"My goodness. Where is he *not* burned?"

"His right butt cheek. Not his left. His lower stomach wasn't burned either."

"What about his face?" Sue asks.

Linda looks at the chart again. "His face is burned but not as badly as the rest of his body."

"Why are the bandages so sticky on his face?" I ask.

She explains that they use medical-grade honey on less severe burn wounds. It sterilizes and helps the skin heal and regenerate with minimal to no scarring.

Sue and I marvel at how something organic and natural can have such healing properties. She and I go on and on about this. We enthusiastically clamor around this fact, grabbing a lifeline in our desperate attempt to find something positive to hang onto.

I ask Linda if there are any doctors around for me to speak to. She explains that the doctors have left for the day and that only an intern is around. She's quick to mention that Dr. Williams, the head of the Burn Center, will definitely be in touch to meet with me.

The room is quiet again except for the respiratory machine. It's a strangely comforting indication that Mark is breathing and alive.

When Linda leaves the room, Sue and I decide there's nothing more we can do. I stare one last time at Mark before we leave. It's just so much to digest. I've never seen anyone in a coma, never mind knowing that it's Mark in there somewhere in this silent mummy body. I can't talk to the man I've had animated conversations with almost every day for thirty years. Mark, the man who loved a good debate—is now unconscious and silent.

When we get back in Sue's car, I feel very tired. All I want to do is crawl into bed as soon as I check into my hotel room. Sue tells me that the Arizona Burn Center is among the best in the country. They take care of burn patients not just from Arizona but also from New Mexico, Southern California, and northern Mexico. She says that luckily this facility wasn't far from Mark's crash site. I nod. "That *is* good." But my own words ring hollow. It's such a small consolation when Mark's so horribly injured.

I'll plan to come back tomorrow. My text alerts keep pinging. Mark's brother, Steven, and his sisters, Rene and Michelle, are working on flights to get to Phoenix tomorrow.

When Sue drops me off at my hotel in downtown Phoenix, I'm impatient as the receptionist rattles off breakfast hours, the fitness center, blah blah blah. I just want to get into my room and climb into bed. I desperately want to turn my mind off.

Should I call Adrian now to let him know what's happened? Adrian, our twenty-three-year-old son, is in graduate school at ETH Zurich, in Switzerland. I glance at my watch. Nine-fifteen here. Phoenix is nine hours behind Zurich. Six-fifteen in the morning there. He'll be asleep for a few more hours on a student schedule, which means he won't be up until eight or nine. Adrian needs a lot of sleep; he has ever since he was a little kid. There's not much he can do now anyway. Best to catch him first thing tomorrow morning, which would be afternoon for him. That's soon enough for him to find flights to Phoenix. I pass out in bed without noticing what time it is.

Sometime after I fall asleep, my phone rings. *What time is it? Midnight. Who would be calling this late?* Groggily, I look at my phone. *Adrian Brandemuehl.*

"Mom?"

"Hi, Adrian," I croak.

"Someone reached out to me on Facebook just now."

"Uh-huh."

"She asked if Mark Brandemuehl is my dad."

"What?"

"Mom, what's going on?" I can hear an edge of near-panic in his voice.

It's those crazy reporters. I'm suddenly wide awake. The sheer audacity of them to contact Adrian. *Poor Adrian. So this is how he'll find out.*

"I was going to wait until the morning, Adrian, but your dad's been in a bad accident with his plane."

"What happened?"

"I don't really know yet. The doctors don't even know."

"How bad is it?"

"He's in a medically induced coma because he has severe burns. Apparently the plane must've caught on fire."

"Oh, no." I can picture the shocked expression on Adrian's face. I feel terrible sharing the news with him. There's a part of me that desperately wants to protect our boys from all this.

"The doctor told me his injuries are life-threatening. I'll know more tomorrow."

There's a pause. "I'll look into flights to Phoenix," he replies finally, in a subdued voice.

"Yes, that would be good."

Adrian sounds unnaturally calm, even for him. Wesley's the excitable one in our family. The rest of us tend to be fairly composed, including Mark. But the reality of this situation hits me hard. The snapshot of my beloved husband in mummy form is jarring. It is unbelievable that he was conscious enough to call me from the ER earlier.

"I'll let you know what flights I'm able to get, Mom."

"Okay, honey."

What a horrible way for Adrian to find out! It'll be important for me to protect our privacy as a family. Agitated, I thrash around in bed for a while after our call ends. It takes me a long time to fall back asleep after the call.

Chapter 2

PROGNOSIS

Steven, Mark's younger brother from Michigan, is the first to arrive. He's the runner, Mark's the football player. Their voices have the same timbre and cadence when they speak, the one giveaway that they're brothers. This morning we have a meeting with Dr. Williams, the head of the Arizona Burn Center.

Dr. Williams looks as if he's in his late forties or early fifties, with some gray in his hair and wire-rim glasses. He has a genial face with a self-assured air about him that causes me to feel immediate calm. Soft-spoken and firm at the same time, he has a combination that creates instant confidence that we're in good hands, most importantly for Mark. Dr. Williams introduces himself and waves us into his private office. With the door shut behind us, Steven and I sink into the deep leather couch. When Dr. Williams begins speaking, the room seems to close in on us. I feel hyperaware of everything he starts to say, as if a bright spotlight is on the three of us. When the doctor mentions that he's originally from Ohio and did his residency at the University of Wisconsin-Madison, Steven mentions how wonderful Wisconsin is and how their family is from a small town there. Steven feels an instant kinship with people who attend UW or who grew up in a small town.

Dr. Williams smiles and continues. "After my residency, I did my fellowship at the University of Washington in Seattle and moved to Phoenix very soon after."

Steven nods attentively.

"I've been in Arizona now for more than twenty years. I really love it here and consider Phoenix my home. I've raised my family here."

Dr. Williams moves on from our initial pleasantries. My mouth feels dry as he starts discussing Mark's condition.

"Mark suffered third-degree burns on the majority of his body," he says quietly. "Severe and serious burns like this impact a person differently depending on their age. A young man in his twenties will have a significantly higher rate of survival than someone older, like Mark. The mortality rate increases significantly with every decade."

Steven and I are silent as we digest this statement. Mark's such a tough guy. Since he had grown up on a farm, I never thought of him as anything but sturdy, strong, and a sheer force of nature. When Mark and I were first dating, a young woman who worked on my team in New York laughingly described what it was like to run into Mark on the coed soccer field. "When I ran into Mark, it was like hitting a brick wall." And this came from a woman who was five feet ten inches tall and physically tough in her own right.

Dr. Williams continues. "The work before us is to aggressively debride his burned skin and treat his body with strong antibiotic ointment."

"What do you mean, 'debride'?" I ask.

"Remove his burned skin layer. We do it continuously to prevent infection."

That's so tough on his body. Poor Mark. So this is what he's in for. I'm suddenly relieved that he's in a coma and will be spared knowing what's happening to him.

"Time will tell how Mark will do, especially in the next two weeks."

It seems good to have a time frame to focus on. I glance at Steven. He looks pensive, his mouth in a tight grip. He spent so much time as a kid with Mark running around playing and working on their family's farm. This is so hard for him too. He and Mark are close in spite of the physical distance between them over the years—Mark in California, Steven in Michigan. Steven used to tell me that very few people understood what it was like growing up in a small town. Many more people know cities and suburbs. It was part of the special bond he felt with Mark.

Dr. Williams's calm voice breaks through my thoughts. "Debriding involves surgery. Mark will be in multiple surgeries in the next couple weeks. We have to keep things clean to prevent an infection."

"Our skin is our body's largest protective covering," Dr. Williams explains. "Think about how massive that is. When a burn patient's natural barrier is gone, they're vulnerable to infection."

"How much of Mark's body is burned?" Steven asks.

"Around 80 percent."

I search Dr. Williams's face for clues about whether we should be seriously concerned, but his face is neutral.

"What are his chances?" Steven asks. I'm glad he doesn't come out and say it more explicitly. *Will Mark survive this?* I suddenly don't feel ready for that discussion. I stare at the bookshelves behind Dr. Williams, fighting an overwhelming desire to escape the room. It feels claustrophobic. It takes all my attention to stay focused on staying put on the couch as my gaze shifts to the door. I take a long, deep breath.

"If a twenty-five-year-old is 90 percent or 80 percent third-degree burned, they have a better chance than someone Mark's age. He's what, fifty-nine years old?"

I nod. He's just shy of sixty. I cling to this fact, as if his being fifty-nine and not sixty will give him some extra advantage in the survival numbers game. His birthday is July 4, and today is June 12.

"But he's so healthy," I insist. "He was just at the Mayo Clinic and received a clean bill of health, including his heart. It's why he flew here on his plane from Carson City."

"That's good to know," Dr. Williams replies. "If it's okay with you, I'd like to get your permission to have access to Mark's health records from Mayo. It would be helpful to us."

I nod. "Of course."

"Burn patient survival rates correlate more with age although good health can help. But the most important factor is simply age," Dr. Williams pronounces in a gentle but firm tone.

Steven has a few more questions about Mark's condition and burn trauma in general. When he's done, Dr. Williams looks straight at me and asks, "What do you want for Mark? Do you want us to keep him alive at all costs?"

"Yes." My answer is immediate, but then I realize I'm not sure what it means in terms of Mark's condition.

"He may be handicapped." Dr. Williams has already anticipated my question.

My mind goes to Mark's legs. He's an avid hiker and skier. There isn't a mountain that he hasn't wanted to hike or ski.

"What about prosthetics?" Steven asks. "For his legs." He's a step ahead of me. "Like that Olympic South African runner, Oscar Pistorius. Aren't they making amazing advances in prosthetics?"

"It's possible. We just don't know yet at this early stage," Dr. Williams replies.

I'm sure Adrian knows someone in the biomedical PhD program at ETH Zurich who's working on advanced prosthetics.

"He might lose the use of his hands. We don't know yet but it's a possibility," Dr. Williams continues in a soft voice.

"That would be hard," I reply. "He loves to bake, cook, grill, work on his cars."

"But his mind would be intact," Dr. Williams adds.

"He loves to debate." I look at Steven. His brother knows what I mean, although Steven would describe Mark as "argumentative."

"Mark has a formidable intellect." I hear the passion in my voice. I'm proud of who my husband is.

"He could read," Dr. Williams offers. "Books, the internet."

Suddenly it's all so clear. "You know what? Even if he can't do the more active things he loves, he would want to see our boys grow up and live their lives." I'm on the verge of tears thinking of how much Mark loves our boys and what a great dad he is. I hear my voice cracking. "And he could use his big brain. And he could socialize and debate with friends. And drink beer and eat. He loves food." I'm impassioned as I ramble. "So yes. Please do everything you can to save his life."

"Do you have any other questions?" I ask Steven. "Because I don't. I think I've heard all that I can absorb for now."

Steven shakes his head and silently mouths, "No." He has a furrowed brow.

We stand up and thank Dr. Williams. Before we end our meeting, he tells us that they structure the care for burn patients around three-week segments. Every three weeks they rotate the doctor who takes the lead. The next three weeks will be led by Dr. Jameson.

Later, when I'm in Mark's room, a text pops in from a friend mentioning that he Googled the Arizona Burn Center and discovered it's one of the top burn centers in the country. The fire department chief who was in charge of Mark's rescue and transport to the facility told me that they rushed Mark to the ER within fourteen minutes. It was important to him to impress upon me how fast they were in getting Mark to medical treatment. How fortunate we are that Mark's crash site was so close! It was only eleven miles. Between feeling reassured that Dr. Williams is more than competent and how fast the first responders acted, I'm grateful. In this high-stakes game of survival, it makes me feel that both factors could give Mark a fighting chance.

A nurse appears in the room and looks carefully at Mark's vitals. Appearing satisfied, she turns to introduce herself to me as Alyssa.

"I was here the day that Mark came into the ER," she says.

She has my instant and full attention. *What was Mark's physical condition, having survived the plane crash?* I have no idea since he's fully bandaged up like a mummy. I've studiously avoided reading the news articles about the accident because Sue said there were photos. I couldn't stomach looking at them. I had asked Sue to describe what the articles said about the day of the crash. I knew that Mark got burned when the right wing of his plane clipped two light poles and caught fire.

"Reaching you on the phone was all Mark could talk about. He was insistent about calling you."

I think about Mark with his third-degree burns.

"How is it possible that he had the presence of mind to call me when he was so burned?" I ask. I am now educated on that by Dr. Williams.

"When a person has third-degree burns, their nerve endings are gone and their skin looks white," Alyssa explains. "Mark felt no pain. He probably didn't fully understand how bad his burns were because he just saw white skin. The skin doesn't get dark from the burn until later."

Her explanation is both a relief and a shock, a relief that Mark mercifully didn't feel pain but a shock that his nerve endings were burned off. Dr. Williams hadn't mentioned that.

"We had to remove his wedding band when he checked into the Burn Center from the ER. But don't worry. I'll personally make sure they give it to you."

I shudder at the image of a hospital attendant sliding the ring off Mark's ghostly white, burned finger.

A man in scrubs enters the room and introduces himself. His name is Dylan and he is Mark's respiratory therapist. He's here to check the respiratory machine several times during his shift. It's what keeps Mark breathing while he's in a coma.

"You're Mark's wife?" he asks.

I nod.

"Your husband is something else," he says with admiration in his eyes. "When he arrived in the ER, he asked, 'Doc, where am I burned?' Dr. Reese replied, 'Your arms, your legs, your back, your chest. Oh, and one butt cheek.' Your husband asked, 'Which one?' Dr. Reese said, 'Your left. Your right butt cheek didn't get burned.' Your husband said, 'Oh, great! That's my good side.'"

Mark has always been spirited, but what Dylan relates makes me appreciate that much more how incredible my husband is.

"In all the years I've worked, I've never had a patient make a joke in the ER like that!" Dylan exclaims. "What an amazing guy! That he could be so funny and have the presence of mind to say something like that given what had happened to him!"

I feel a little choked up and look away for a moment while Dylan busies himself with printing out Mark's respiratory chart.

"I can tell how much you and Mark love each other," Alyssa says. "The way he insisted on reaching you before he was sedated."

"We're soulmates," I say simply. There's no need for any more words to describe our marriage and who we are to each other.

"How long have you been married?" Alyssa asks.

"Thirty-one years come July 2. We've had so many wonderful years together." I feel tears coming on.

It's quiet while Alyssa takes a reading from Mark's blood pressure monitor. Steven shows up, having taken some calls in the waiting room.

"What made you decide to become a burn nurse?" I ask, trying my best to keep it together.

"My dad was burned badly from a fire in our backyard," she replies.

"What happened?" Steven asks.

"He was trying to get a fire started in the backyard and poured some gasoline and it exploded. He had second- and third-degree burns on 70 percent of his body. That was fifteen years ago, so the treatment and skin graft technology weren't as advanced as they are today. He still has a lot of pain from his burn injuries."

She carefully swaps out Mark's blanket with a clean one, efficiently folding up the one she took off him.

"It's why I became a burn nurse. After what my dad went through, I wanted to help other burn patients. I know what it's like for them and their families."

I know I should be curious about what her dad's disabilities are as a result, but I can't go there right now.

Chapter 3

EYEWITNESSES

Our families visit over the next few days. The Burn Center visitor policy restricts guests to two at a time in Mark's room, but because they know our families are not local to Phoenix, they make an exception and allow three people. It's cramped in Mark's room when we rotate three people, along with the two nurses' constant presence and the respiratory and physical therapists who show up at regular intervals. Mark's hooked up to a plethora of machines surrounding his bed. His large respiratory machine is on wheels next to him by the window. There is barely room for two visitor chairs, so the third person has to stand. We've put up photos all over the one bare wall showing the smiling faces of Mark, his family, and his friends. A green-and-yellow Green Bay Packers flag hangs high on the wall near the ceiling.

During my rotation into Mark's room with Mark's sister Rene and my friend Suzie, I notice an email that Patty, our real estate agent in Lake Tahoe, has sent me with an escrow document to sign and a request to make a payment. Mark and I had planned to retire in six months and move to Lake Tahoe full time. We were excited about a house we planned to buy. Mark was flying to Carson City from Phoenix on the day of his plane crash. That following Friday he planned to pick me up in San Jose and together we would fly to Truckee to look at the house. Caught up with what was happening to Mark, I completely forgot about the house.

What do I do? Should I keep going with the house purchase? Do I keep our retirement dream alive? What would Mark want me to do? I feel a sudden heaviness in my chest. Mark and I knew how to think our way through just about anything in our lives, if we could just thoughtfully talk about it. For the first time, I don't know what to do. I feel alone in this decision and stressed by the time pressure of funding the escrow payment to keep things moving forward.

I look up from my phone at Rene and Suzie standing near me.

"I've just received the request for escrow payment on the Tahoe house," I blurt out to them. They both know about the house and our Tahoe retirement plan. "What do I do? Do I keep going?" I ask them. "Wouldn't Mark want me to keep going with it?" *Letting go of the Tahoe house means letting go of our plans.*

"Maybe buying the house now isn't the right timing," Suzie replies quietly. Rene's looking at me attentively. *Does she agree?*

"Yeah, but maybe Mark would want me to buy the house," I say. "He was so excited about moving to Tahoe."

Suzie hesitates a bit and says, "Things are so uncertain right now with Mark's condition. Are you sure you want to commit to the house? You can always look for another house when Mark recovers."

Suzie's right. I send the realtor a note explaining that we need to cancel and why. She promptly replies, saying how shocked and sorry she is about Mark's accident and that, of course, she'll take us out of the process. She hopes that Mark will be okay. My entire body relaxes from the relief of making the decision.

I watch the flood of emotions Mark's brother and sisters are going through. I see it on their faces and in their bodies. Rene has an air of resigned sadness. She's quiet. Michelle sits upright with her forehead furrowed a lot. Steven paces and doesn't sit still. He's always talking to someone or out in the hallway on a call. I know they're feeling the full range of emotions I'm feeling, from disbelief—*I can't believe this happened to Mark*—to worry. *He's so badly burned. Will he be okay?*

Reporters have somehow gotten my phone number and are trying to call me. They want to know how Mark's doing. I've learned in just a few days not to answer the phone if it's a local number that I don't recognize. The only local friends I have are Sue, her husband Neal, and Jeff, Mark's high school friend who was the last to see Mark before he took off from Scottsdale Airport. I knew they had had dinner together the night before because he had texted me a photo of the two of them at a restaurant in Scottsdale. A couple of high school buddies catching up on old times. Mark looked so happy.

Larry, the burly, friendly receptionist at the Burn Center, lets me know he's screened a couple of journalists trying to reach me at the hospital. But there is one note he passes through to me. It's from the guy who pulled Mark out of his plane. He came by and asked Larry to pass on the note to me. When I'm ready, he wants to tell me what happened that day.

I look at the note. It just has his name, Thomas Hunnicutt, and his phone number. I tuck it into my purse just as a call comes in from my friend Showa.

"Oh, my God, Jenny. What happened to Mark? I just saw your Facebook post." Her voice is higher pitched than usual. I had forgotten in the blur of the first few days that I had posted an update. A flood of responses showed up and I ran out of time and energy to read them all.

After I explain everything to Showa, she asks what day it happened. When I tell her it was June 12, she goes silent for a few seconds and then tells me she had a dream a couple of days before that in which Mark was in a plane crash.

My heart skips a beat.

"Remember how Mark said he would fly you and me somewhere nice for a lunch to celebrate our June birthdays? So maybe that dream was just my feeling a little afraid of getting in a small plane. "

Maybe. Or was it a premonition?

I spend the rest of our call explaining his condition and the uncertainty regarding his prognosis.

Suzie secures a two-bedroom Airbnb for me. The boys and I have been staying at a hotel in downtown Phoenix and it's clear that I'll be here for a while. Suzie's my super competent friend from our college days at Wellesley, a former Wall Street executive and a whirling dervish on all practical matters. She's also Wesley and Adrian's godmother.

The condo she finds for me is only twenty minutes from the Burn Center, which is part of the Maricopa County Hospital complex on Roosevelt Avenue.

A few days later my sister, Teresa, and Suzie leave. Mark's brother and sisters, Steven, Rene, Michelle, and our boys, Wesley and Adrian, remain. No one's sure how long they will stay. We're taking it a day at a time right now.

I pull out Thomas Hunnicutt's phone number and text him. He wants to meet us as a family to explain what happened on the day of the accident. I decide it's a good idea to arrange a meeting while enough of our family is still here. I coordinate with him that he and his partner, Jakki, will come by the hospital on Saturday morning. The nurses suggest some semi-private rooms near the main hospital entrance for our meeting.

Rotating three at a time, Adrian, Rene, and I arrive in Mark's room a couple days after Mark's hand debridement surgery. Olivia and Dani introduce themselves as Mark's nurses for the next three days. I've learned that the Burn Center nurses work three-day, twelve-hour shifts so the patient can have continuity of care during that time. Olivia tells Adrian and me that Mark's temperature spiked and has been elevated for almost two days.

"We had hoped his fever would resolve itself within forty-eight hours," Dani explains while Olivia bustles in and out of the room and now sits at a computer station right outside Mark's room.

"So what does it mean for Mark?" I ask.

"Most likely he has an infection that requires antibiotics, which we've started him on."

"What kind of infection does he have?" Adrian asks.

"We don't know. It could be in his lungs or elsewhere. Dr. Jameson ordered lab tests this morning. Once we get the results, we can be more targeted with the antibiotics."

"How long does it take to get results?"

"Around one to two days."

Good—it's fairly quick.

"Let's just hope it doesn't negatively affect Mark's kidney functioning. He's been doing so well without needing kidney dialysis," Dani says. "Antibiotics can affect the kidney. Mark suffered renal failure when he first arrived at the Burn Center. We put him on kidney dialysis for a while but took him off recently."

I vaguely recall one of the nurses explaining that Mark was suffering kidney failure when he was admitted but seems to be doing well without it now. There had been so much else to absorb and deal with that I hadn't paid much attention to this detail.

Olivia steps into Mark's room looking for me.

"Jenny, there's a woman in the lobby named Cynthia who wants to meet you."

I'm immediately on guard. She must be a reporter. "Is she a reporter?"

"I don't know. Why don't you ask Larry?" She points to the guy behind the reception desk. I walk out to where Larry sits.

"I've been screening out the journalists for you."

"Thank you, Larry. I really appreciate it. Is this Cynthia person another journalist?"

"No, she told me that she's an eyewitness who was at the scene of Mark's accident."

"Oh." I'm torn. On the one hand I want to know what she saw. But I'm also afraid it would be too painful to hear the details.

I could always tell her no, that I'll see her some other time, when I'm ready. *But will I* ever *be ready? I'll need to be ready this Saturday when we meet Thomas Hunnicutt.*

"Larry, tell her I'll talk to her."

"Are you sure?" He raises his eyebrows with concern.

"Yes. Tell Cynthia I'll meet her in the lobby."

I let Adrian and Rene know what's going on. Before I leave, Adrian says, "Wait." He shows me an online article from a local news channel about Mark's plane crash.

"I think she's legit, Mom. She's quoted as an eyewitness in this article. She told the reporter that Dad almost hit her and two other drivers on Deer Valley Road, but he pulled up to avoid them."

"Okay, I'll go talk to her now."

Once I'm in the lobby, a friendly-looking woman gets up from her chair and approaches me, introducing herself. It's Cynthia. We take a seat next to each other in a quiet corner of the lobby.

"I'm so sorry about your husband. How is he doing?" she asks, her lips drawn with concern.

"He's in a coma. He's fighting for his life."

"I'm sure he is. I'm glad he's still alive. I came today because I wanted to thank him for what he did that day."

"What happened?"

"I was driving home from work when I saw him flying his plane directly at me and two other cars behind me. I saw his face in the cockpit, the nose of his plane headed toward me. I thought I was going to die—when he saw me and pulled his plane up to avoid hitting me and the other drivers. All I saw next was that his plane crashed on the side of the road and there was a huge fireball. I pulled over and ran toward the plane." She stops to take a breath. "The fuel was pouring out of the plane where one of the wings had ripped off. I knew the plane was going to explode any minute. I thought your husband was going to die then and there."

My head is throbbing. *My God—it all sounds insane what happened, that Mark went through all that.*

"Then all of a sudden I heard your husband yelling for help. Another woman had also run up close to the plane. She tried to help while everyone else, a crowd of people, were filming everything on their phones. Then out of nowhere, a gentleman stepped in and yanked your husband out of the plane."

That must have been Thomas Hunnicutt. He and a couple of motorcycle mechanics carried Mark across the road to safety. I read about that in one of the articles.

"The accident could've been so much worse. There were easily five people who could've died in those few minutes, but your husband's split-second decision saved our lives."

Her eyes well up. "When your husband wakes up, can you please thank him for me? I'm praying for him and your family."

I nod, mute.

"If you or your husband need any help, don't ever hesitate to call me. Here's my phone number. That day changed my life. I'll never forget what happened. Your husband's a hero. I'm glad he's survived so far, and I hope one day I can meet him to thank him personally."

"Thank you. Thank you for coming by today."

"Bless you all," she says. "I'll be praying for Mark."

While she described the scene that unfolded, I was watching it with her in my mind. The fireball, Mark screaming for help. I've never seen Mark panic, scream, or cry. He was always so calm and collected. *Poor Mark.* I never use expressions like that to describe him. He was always so tough both physically and mentally. But I do now. Because he went through the unimaginable. What was it like for him to realize that his plane failed shortly after takeoff? If I were in his shoes, I'd be panicked and paralyzed by fear.

After I explain to Adrian and Rene what happened, I look at Mark's mummified body on the bed, and all I feel is an uncontrollable desire to wrap my arms around his broad chest. To hug him. But I can't. Instead, I pull my chair up to his bedside as close as I can get and stare at him. I suddenly feel like screaming because he can't talk to me. The room's quiet with the gentle, rhythmic whooshing of the respiratory machine. I listen to Mark breathe. In and out, in and out. In my mind, I say, *Mark! How did this happen? I can't believe you survived. Thank God you're alive.*

Chapter 4

THE COURAGE OF A STRANGER

Up to this point I had avoided reading detailed news updates about the plane crash. I finally made Sue describe the sequence of events for me. Mark had reported a rough-running engine seven minutes after takeoff from Scottsdale Airport. At eleven minutes he declared an emergency. While the tower directed him to Deer Valley Airport, he apparently knew he wasn't going to make it. So he attempted an emergency landing on Deer Valley Road, which is just two lanes wide. Because there were three cars on the road, he swerved the plane to the right to avoid hitting the drivers. The plane lost its balance. It careened, and the right wing clipped two light poles and caught on fire. The plane then hit a concrete barrier near the road and flipped upside down.

It's so hard to listen to what happened. I shudder inwardly when I think back to the fireball that Cynthia described. I still can't bear to look at the photos, scrolling past them quickly. Sue said that the news story pictures showed the plane wreckage in flames by the side of the road. Never, ever did I think that Mark or I would suffer anything so violent happening to us. It's the kind of thing you read about happening to other people. Not us.

The next morning at the condo, Adrian says to me, "I read in one of the articles that Dad's considered a hero by Cynthia and other drivers on Deer Valley Road. Like Cynthia said, Dad turned right and pulled the plane back up instead of landing. That's what put his life at risk, because by turning, his right wing clipped the light poles and caught on fire, since the fuel tanks are in the wings. The plane went out of control because he lost engine power. They said that he was doing everything he could to save lives."

I nod as I take it all in. I'm not surprised Mark's considered a hero. He's the type of person who would be there for you in a pinch no matter what. I remember one of my first impressions of him when we were first dating. On a road trip from New York to Montreal, we encountered a guy stranded on the side of the road with motorcycle problems. Mark made me pull over so he could help. What happened with Mark's plane is so much bigger. There were lives at stake. He did the unselfish thing, which may now cost him his life. Knowing Mark, even if he knew the consequences to himself, he wouldn't have done anything different. I'm convinced of that.

Before Wesley, Adrian, and I leave for the burn center, I receive an online note from another witness who mentions how she saw Mark shouting and waving for help. She didn't know what to do but to pray for him and soon after, noticed that his seat belt had melted off him.

It's the first time I realize that Mark was strapped in and unable to get out. I'm grateful to this woman for praying for Mark.

A little while later, Thomas, Jakki, and their young daughter arrive, right on schedule.

"How is Mark doing?" Thomas asks. I explain the extent of Mark's burns and that we are hoping and praying he survives. Thomas nods solemnly. "I wanted to meet you to tell you about what happened."

"Jakki and I"—he glances at Jakki, who squeezes his hand—"were driving on Deer Valley Road. Normally I'd have no reason to drive in that neighborhood on a Tuesday afternoon. I'm a cell phone tower technician so I'm usually working in the field all over greater Phoenix. We were there at that exact moment only because we were on our way to our first couples counseling appointment."

Thank God Thomas was there.

"We saw the fire from the plane and I pulled over. Someone had called 911. The crowds were standing around filming—but no one was helping the pilot. I was so angry. I thought, *If no one helps the pilot now, he's going to die*. So I go running toward the burning plane."

"And I was screaming at Thomas to come back—I was so afraid for him," Jakki interjects, wide-eyed. "Thomas was in a T-shirt, shorts, and flip-flops, headed to a plane on fire."

"Right when I got up close to the cockpit, which was cracked open, I noticed that Mark's seat belt melted away in that instant." Thomas pauses and looks at us.

A miracle. I think of the woman who prayed for Mark.

"Luckily, the entire cockpit window was broken open. I was able to reach in on one try and pull Mark out of the plane. He was on fire inside the cockpit, but when I pulled him out, the flames went out."

I cringe, picturing Mark engulfed in flames. My vision gets blurry. That must have been when he started yelling for help, as the praying woman and Cynthia described. My chest is pounding. My face feels hot.

"We were near a motorcycle mechanic school. Two guys from the school ran over to help me carry Mark to the other side of the road to safety. Mark's clothes had melted off of him completely."

I feel slightly shaky and grab hold of the armrest of my chair. Rene, who's sitting across from me, has a pained look on her face, her mouth tight. I can't handle looking at anyone else. Instead, I bring myself back to my own feelings. I feel my chest sinking and then my mind goes blank. *Am I in shock?*

Thomas quietly continues. "I found a blanket in the car and covered him. I also took out our windshield sun protector and covered him with that too. And then a few minutes later, the plane exploded."

I didn't know that. None of the news articles mentioned the explosion.

If Thomas hadn't been there, would anyone else have had the courage to run out to Mark's burning plane to rescue him? Probably not, given what he just described. Everyone was filming. I feel a surge of anger but it disappears quickly because Thomas, the one brave person who mattered the most, was there at exactly the right time.

"Then the Deer Valley fire department and EMT arrived. They took Mark straight to the Burn Center. I stayed for a while because the police wanted to talk to those of us who were eyewitnesses. The reporters showed up after that."

"It's amazing that you managed to pull Mark out on your first try," I say. Thomas looks as if he's about five-nine. Mark's almost six-foot-two and weighs 210 pounds.

"It must've been adrenaline," Jakki comments. "Thomas is a local jujitsu champion."

That explains it.

"Did you get burned anywhere, Thomas?" I ask, remembering that he was wearing shorts, a T-shirt, and flip-flops. *Talk about brave.*

"Not much," he says with a look of surprise. "Just the tops of my feet."

How is that possible?

"It's amazing you weren't more burned."

Thomas shrugs. "I guess I was lucky."

After we chat for a few minutes more, Thomas stands up. "I really want to help Mark," he says with an intense gaze. "I know right now it's up to the doctors. One day, when Mark's ready for rehab, I want to help him."

"Thank you so much, Thomas. We'll stay in touch."

I promise to keep Thomas updated on Mark's progress. We ask Adrian to add Thomas and Jakki to our Lotsa Helping Hands online community.

I wonder who the two motorcycle mechanics were that helped Thomas carry Mark to safety. I mentally say a quick thank-you to them both. I'll be forever thankful to these three men.

Chapter 5

STANFORD CLASSMATES

I wake up with cold feet, shivering and wishing I had gone to bed in socks. I'm not used to how cold the air conditioning is in the condo. I suddenly recall that last night at 3:00 a.m. I found myself in a strange, semiconscious state in which I was convinced that I, too, was burned. I touched every part of my body. My feet. My calves. My thighs. My stomach and my arms. I don't know how long I lay there in that state, but eventually I fell back into a deep, dreamless sleep.

When I'm up having my coffee, I check my emails while Adrian's on a call with classmates for a project at ETH Zurich, where he's getting his master's in robotics. He'll need to stay back to do some classwork this morning. Kathy, our neighbor and Mark's Stanford business school classmate, emails me to say that she's been providing updates to their class on their online alumni community forum. She forwards to me a compilation of their comments. I quickly scroll through and scan pages and pages of posts.

I take a deep breath and Google local news articles that show the wreckage of Mark's plane. Although I already knew the sequence of events described to me by Sue and later Thomas, I had avoided looking at the photos. I now want to see what Mark's Stanford classmates have viewed before they posted to their online community. The first photo is of his charred plane lying upside down, surrounded by a white pool of chemicals from the fire extinguishers they used to put out the fire. Another picture shows a huge smoke-tinged orange fireball when his plane exploded. *How did Mark survive this?* I quickly close the tab. It's unbearable to see what happened. I want to throw up.

At the Burn Center, I learn that Mark's vitals are good. I pass a prisoner in an orange jumpsuit waiting in the lobby with a guard. It reminds me I'm at a county hospital. Alyssa had mentioned that they treat prisoners here. The police officer behind the ER counter buzzes me through.

When I arrive in Mark's room, I pull up a chair as close as I can get to him, but it's hard because he's surrounded by monitors and machines. The big respiratory machine is still on the side by the window. At least Mark is near some natural sunlight, unlike the windowless, dungeon-like cafeteria with its harsh fluorescent lights. A music player sits on a shelf. Knowing Mark's love of music, Adrian had asked the nurses to find one for his room. With my help, he created some Spotify playlists with Mark's favorite songs.

"Hi, Mark, sweetie!" I call out cheerfully, forcing a smile on my face. I have to make the effort. He may not know what I'm saying, but I hope he can feel it's me. My energy.

After I update friends and family that Mark is in an induced coma, a Stanford business school classmate of Mark's sends me a note mentioning that people in a coma can feel the energy of their loved ones in the room. He described that when his mom was in a coma in the hospital, his sister had been in the room extremely agitated about their mother's condition. When she came out of her coma, his mom spoke of feeling the anxiety and negative energy around her when she was in that coma state. He tells me not to underestimate how much Mark can feel our energy in the room even if he isn't consciously aware of what's going on.

I now imagine that Mark at some level can feel the energy of the nurses and me.

"Do you ever see expressions on his face—to know he's feeling something?" I ask Lindsey, one of the nurses.

Lindsey has a pleasant and deliberate style of speaking. She nods, "Yeah."

I wait.

"He was grimacing today during the morning dressing change."

It hurts me to hear that, to know he's suffering. I know the nurses painstakingly remove his dressings and put fresh ones on him. Every single morning. They raise the temperature in the room so it's like a sauna to keep Mark warm, because burn patients without skin have poor temperature regulation. By the time they're done three hours later, the nurses' scrubs are soaked through with sweat. It's a grueling job.

"So, Mark—Adrian's on the ETH car team," I announce brightly. "They've entered a competition with entrants from many of the robotics grad schools across Europe."

I pause, searching Mark's face for any sign that he's heard me. His face is wrapped in bandages, oozing and sticky-looking because of the medical honey they're treating his face with. Layers of gauze are wrapped around his head and chin, tubes in his nose. His eyes are stitched shut. It was jarring at first to see his eyes forcibly closed this way. The nurses tell me it's to protect them and to allow them to heal from the smoke of the fire. The voice in my head repeats the reason, as if by telling myself over and over again I can convince myself that this is okay. I reason to myself that he would keep his eyes closed anyway, being in a coma. He's got two soft splints under his chin to keep his head in position so it doesn't roll.

"The competition's in September. Adrian's learning so much technically. And you'd be glad to know he's learning a lot about leadership and how to motivate people." Mark had been a leader of people from the earliest days of his career.

Mark's face is still. *Can he hear me? I don't know.* I keep talking.

"Can you believe he's reading Dale Carnegie's book, *How to Win Friends and Influence People*?" I chuckle out loud. "I bet you'd have a lot to teach Adrian. He's learning how to work with the Swiss and the Germans especially." I relate Adrian's quote about the Swiss being more German than the Germans because they're such sticklers for process and rules.

I decide to keep talking even though I don't see anything registering on Mark's face.

"Adrian says the Americans want to win as badly as the Germans and Swiss. But they want to have fun doing it instead of being so grim about everything."

It's quiet in the room now except for the sound of the machines humming. Lindsey has stepped out and is working on something at the computer station outside Mark's room.

I stand up to get closer to Mark's bedside. "I think Adrian's trying to be a bridge-builder between the Swiss and German team members and the rest of the team. Darling, you'd be so proud of him," I say softly, hovering near him, examining his bandaged face and arms. I remember how much I loved holding his solid, muscular arms and big elbows. It reminds me of the strength of his physical presence before he was wrapped up like this. I feel a momentary tremor and then it's gone.

After a while I sit back down in my chair. It's noticeable how quiet it is. Where's his music playlist? They must have turned it off to do the dressing change. That's okay. The nurses have told me that they have to sedate Mark more heavily so he doesn't suffer so much during the change. When I picture what the process must be like, I feel a stab of pain in my stomach. I brush it out of my mind. *Get busy. Do something useful.* I walk over to the music player to turn on his rock playlist. The Black Keys' latest album starts playing. Mark would love it. We're going to miss their concert in San Francisco in July. A spasm of sadness passes through me again. Live music and skiing were the two things Mark and I are equally passionate about. It makes me giddy just remembering how much we enjoyed the New Year's show in downtown Long Beach last year. They had a lineup of up-and-coming bands playing on four different stages outdoors. I held Mark's hands tightly in mine as we rocked to the music on that festive night. And now I want to hold his hand so badly but I can't.

There's nothing I can do about it. Remembering the posts Kathy sent, I decide to read them as a welcome distraction. I scroll through the posts. They're wonderfully supportive and loving. I read some of them out loud to Mark.

"Mark, honey. Listen to what your fellow GSBers [graduate students of business] are saying about you…

> *I am very saddened by the news. EVERY interaction I've had with Mark, during school or post-graduation, has been a pleasant one. He was always genuine, kind, thoughtful and engaging. This is so sad. He's a really good guy.*

"Okay, here's another post.

> *Thank God Mark is at a great facility with cutting edge care. He's a tough son of bitch, too. So he will fight hard to get a wonderful recovery.*

These classmates are from what, twenty-nine years ago? I marvel at how their simple words strike a chord because they so aptly capture the essence of who Mark is. Good, genuine, thoughtful, tough. I've always known him to be such a principled, good person, and having grown up on a farm, he knows how to take care of the practical things in life. He's the kind of guy you want on your team if you're stranded on a desert island. Resourceful, smart, and empathetic. High IQ doesn't always correlate with high empathy, but it does in Mark. And like a classmate expressed it, Mark's a fighter. Their love flows through me like water spilling over the rock and crevices, the parts of my heart that have become jagged from everything I've been through in the last few weeks. It's deeply satisfying to read these emails and to know his classmates recognize this in him the way I know him.

I keep reading aloud to Mark.

> *I had chills reading about the accident, thinking that Mark may have had a better chance of landing his plane safely, but he did all he could to avoid hitting those cars. Truly heroic....It's inspiring to see how the best of people's character comes out in times of tragedy. He's a very brave man.*

After I read each post, I mention to Mark which classmate wrote it, searching his face to see if there's any flicker of recognition. His face doesn't move and he's silent. Suddenly a wave of something I can't even describe rolls through my body. I realize that I desperately miss his voice.

I continue reading to him.

> *What happened brings tears to my eyes. It's inspiring and sobering to consider how Mark may have made his own situation worse by trying to avoid harming those drivers. His selflessness at the most critical instant of his life is inspirational.*

"They think you're a hero," I pronounce. "Not just Thomas Hunnicutt."

These posts remind me of Cynthia's eyewitness chat with me, thanking Mark for taking quick action to avoid hitting her and the cars behind her. Thomas's courageous and dramatic actions of that day, which dominated the news media, had made me forget that Mark was a hero in his own right. His Stanford classmates certainly think so.

I replay the movie in my mind of Mark trying to land his plane on that two-lane road in the blistering Arizona heat. Jeff, Mark's high school friend, said that one of the eyewitnesses mentioned watching Mark's descent and that he would have made a near-perfect landing if it hadn't been for the cars on the road. Instead, he jerked the steering wheel, making a hard right to avoid hitting Cynthia and the other drivers. I can't see because my vision goes blurry and my face feels hot. I feel a stormy ocean churning furiously inside me. It's a feeling of pride for how good and courageous Mark is, but I'm also mad at him for acting so selflessly in that moment. There's no way of knowing whether Mark would have fared any better if he hadn't swerved, but there's absolutely no doubt that in doing so he saved the lives of others.

I don't want Mark to witness my breakdown. I have to be strong for him. I get up and stand by the window, staring outside at the cluster of hospital buildings shimmering in the heat.

A few days later, Will, the Stanford classmate who suggested that Mark could feel our energy even in a deep coma, emailed me to share that Mark's accident had prompted their GSB class to discuss spiritual things. He mentioned that this was unprecedented and that typically their online forum was used for inquiring and sharing information about consultants, business resources, and other practical topics that are on the minds of MBA alumni from a top school. Will said it prompted some people to share their own scary health issues over the years and how it forced them to think about the spiritual side of life. It drew them closer together as a community—and it was Mark's plane crash that was the catalyst.

Mark's Stanford classmates give generously to the Arizona Burn Foundation when I suggest it to our Lotsa Helping Hands community. Kathy said people are constantly asking her how they can help. They start sending me all sorts of gifts in the mail, everything from inspirational books about hope and resilience to a cute teddy bear, food baskets, and cards with handwritten, beautiful, heartfelt messages.

I lose count of how many people mention that they are praying for us along with their church and synagogue communities. They pray for Mark's recovery. They pray for my continued strength, resilience, and wisdom. They pray for our boys. People who don't typically pray say that they'll now join their classmates to pray.

I'm in awe of the blanket of love I feel from this community, some that I know well and many others that I didn't know as well from our time as a newly married couple living at Stanford many years ago. And yet it's jarring to realize that for all the gushing accolades, Mark's a mummy in a coma, in intensive care—the devastating result of his courage. It makes me want to scream, *It's not fair!*

From that day on, I'm determined that Adrian and I will read any cards and additional GSBer posts aloud to Mark—to keep up positive energy in the room. I want to believe that all these Stanford posts and the many well wishes in the cards I read to Mark will help him. He is in the fight of his life and he needs every little bit of positivity he can get.

Part 2

The Rollercoaster

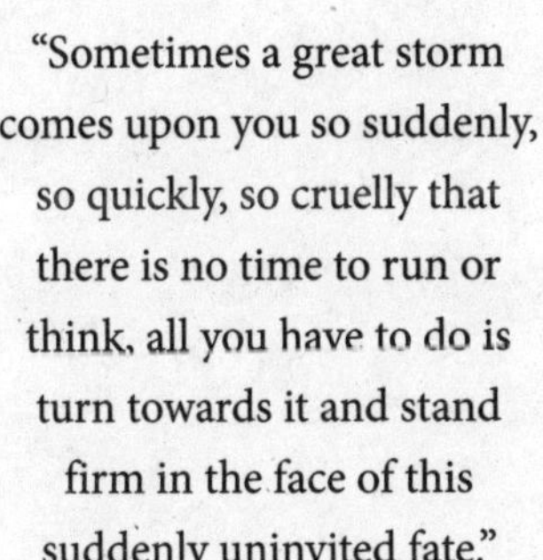

"Sometimes a great storm
comes upon you so suddenly,
so quickly, so cruelly that
there is no time to run or
think, all you have to do is
turn towards it and stand
firm in the face of this
suddenly uninvited fate."

—Mehmet Murat Ildan,
@ildanmmi, December 19, 2022

Chapter 6

BAD NEWS

I wake up in the middle of the night seeing the flash of a bright orange fireball. It's the photo from the news story I read yesterday. It's dark out and the noise from the air conditioner kicks in, sputtering loudly. I grab my phone and navigate to my go-to sleep meditation on Headspace. Listening to it relaxes me, but after a few minutes I'm still awake. This time it doesn't help me sink back into a deep sleep. Instead, I drift in and out, and I'm not sure how long I'm in this in-between state.

I take naps at the condo on the days the interns need to change out Mark's lines. What sounded simple to me the first time they came in to do this turned out to be a several-hour affair. I've learned to go to a cafe or back to the condo for a break. On those afternoons the ocean guided meditation becomes my constant companion. The sound of ocean waves fills my senses and lulls me into a welcome state of oblivion. I love the feeling of being on the precipice of passing into a dark state of unconsciousness. It gives me the excuse to stop thinking. For half an hour I can forget that my husband and soulmate is catastrophically burned and lying in a coma, a mummy at the Burn Center. But it also puts off the inevitable, which is that every time I wake up, it's a jolt of reality to remember why Adrian and I are in Phoenix. If I were home I would have my daily routines, familiar places, and friends to distract me from remembering. But living in an unfamiliar city, I find that every waking minute I'm reminded why I'm here. There's no escape.

I've learned not to look at my watch when I wake up in the night. It just stresses me out. When I give up hope that I'll fall back asleep, I finally glance at my watch: 4:45 a.m. A knot of worry starts to grow. I hope I won't be dragging today. I hate that murky, underwater feeling when I'm exhausted. My body feels as if it's moving in slow motion, dragged down by the water, my mind in a fog. Thank goodness Adrian's here. He can drive. I don't trust myself behind the wheel when I'm tired. I had already scraped the right corner of my rental car trying to squeeze it into a small parking space at the condo in a middle-of-the-night stupor, having fallen asleep in Mark's room.

When I remember Adrian's smart and competent presence, my anxiety floats away. It occurs to me how much he's like Mark in this way—a rock in the churning, chaotic water that feels like my life right now.

At dawn I drag myself out of bed. I give up. My mind can't allow sleep to fully take over. I must be too wired from the jumble of thoughts floating in my brain, triggered by pictures of the wreckage of Mark's plane. I envision Mark waking up like Lazarus, demanding to know, "What on earth happened to the plane?" He would be angry. God knows—we all want to know.

I'll need some really strong coffee this morning, so I add an extra heaping spoonful in the coffeemaker. Once I feel the start of a caffeine buzz from my first cup, I pull out my laptop to update our Lotsa Helping Hands community. The crash is being investigated but there's nothing to share until the investigation is completed.

Each morning I call the Burn Center to ask when they'll start and finish Mark's daily morning dressing change. By then the night shift nurses will have already updated the day nurses, giving them time to deal with the first order of the day—their patient's daily dressing change. It's critical in the continual battle against the spread of infection.

Today, Adrian's up and working on recovering the hard drive on Mark's laptop, which was damaged in the fire. It had all our financial and retail account passwords stored in the Chrome browser, which I urgently need. I had lost track a long time ago of saving the password to Mark's password manager app, never thinking I would be in this very situation.

Adrian's been faithfully accompanying me to the Burn Center every day. I used to joke with Mark that when we were old and in wheelchairs, our boys would take care of us in their own unique ways. Adrian, "Mr.

Organized," would call Medicare and our doctors to persist in getting whatever we needed. Wesley, who has a big heart, would hug us and push our wheelchairs. Never in a million years did I think that I would be experiencing what I had joked about this soon.

I feel okay driving this morning and use our time in the car to have a lighthearted conversation with Adrian, plying him with a variety of questions about his social life at ETH. He tells me his international community of friends is from a medley of countries, ranging from Mexico and Indonesia to France and Egypt. His only American friend is a guy from Sacramento. When we arrive in Mark's room, we enthusiastically greet him. It's become our daily habit when we arrive.

"Mark! It's me and Adrian here!" I say in a loud voice above the din of the machines humming around his bed.

"Hi, Dad!" Adrian announces.

"How's your day been so far?" I ask.

Mark is silent.

"I love you, sweetheart," I whisper, standing as close to Mark as I can near the tangle of cords and monitors. Still, no matter what we say or how animated we are, nothing stirs on his face. We keep hoping for some sign that he hears us. It's been a bit more than three weeks and still nothing.

"How's Mark doing today?" I ask Lindsey, who's still on her three-day shift with Mark.

"Well, the night nurses reported that his temperature spiked last night. It's still high."

"What is it now?" I ask.

"103.5 degrees."

The knot of worry returns. Adrian's brows furrow with concern.

"The doctors have already sent out lung and blood cultures to the lab to see what type of infection he has."

"How long will it take?" Adrian asks.

"A couple days."

"Why so long?" I ask in a voice more demanding than I intend, impatient with worry.

"They need the cultures to grow for two to three days in order to identify them," Lindsey patiently explains. "Once we know what type of infection he has, the doctors can be more targeted about the antibiotics we give Mark."

"What about in the meantime?" Adrian asks. He's read my mind.

"Oh, we've already had him on general antibiotics since the middle of the night, when his temperature increased," Lindsey explains in a pleasant, soothing voice.

"Oh, that's good." Adrian nods. He glances at me.

That makes me feel better and I relax a bit in my chair.

Ginger, Lindsey's nurse partner on this shift, walks in, catching the tail end of our conversation.

"Hopefully it doesn't negatively affect Mark's kidney functions. He's been doing so well without needing dialysis," Ginger says. "Antibiotics can affect the kidney. As you know, Mark suffered renal failure when he first arrived at the burn center."

I nod, remembering that the nurses had mentioned this before. I ask Lindsey and Ginger for an update on the skin grafts Dr. Jameson ordered. They explain that it will take another two weeks for them to ship from Boston. Until then, the doctors have covered Mark's burned areas with allografts, which are pig skin, and xenografts, which are cadaver skin. It's the only way they can protect the areas of his body where his burned skin had to be debrided. The doctors have to change them every five days to keep his body clean and to prevent infection. This debriding and laying down of allografts and xenografts will be a continuous cycle.

The nurses provide a concise rundown of Mark's vitals. They're all good other than his elevated temperature. They remind me that Mark's going into the operating room (OR) this afternoon. Dr. Williams will assess him and do more debriding where needed.

A couple of attendants show up to work with Ginger and Lindsey to get Mark ready to go into the OR. It's a little earlier than I expected and I'm glad they're here. Anything is good when it's the medical attention Mark needs.

Once Mark's in the OR, Adrian and I head back out to the waiting room since they'll need his room to be empty when he returns. We're not sure how long the surgery will be. It'll depend on what they find and what they need to do.

I suddenly remember today is June 24, the day before my birthday. Jeff, Mark's best friend from high school, and his friend Traci have reserved a table for us tomorrow at an Italian restaurant because they know how much Mark and I love Italy. I'm looking forward to it. I want to be surrounded by the love that Mark and I share for food in Italy with all the happy memories of family time there. It's also simpler than that. I want to enjoy an evening out with friends. To laugh again. To eat good food. To feel for one night that life is normal.

When I'm comfortably settled in a waiting room chair, I notice that my dear friend Laurie in London has sent me a text.

> *"Dr. Williams is quite an impressive doctor, Jenny. It's very good that Mark is at such a fine burn center. Take a look at this article about what he did for this little girl named Isabella McCune."*

He includes a link to a Phoenix news story from six months ago.

I click on the link and start reading. Isabella McCune, an eight-year-old girl in Phoenix, was badly burned when her dad built a firepit in their driveway, poured gasoline on it, and ignited it. Bella, as she's known, was standing nearby and was immediately engulfed in flames. It was a horrible accident that undoubtedly her father would torture himself about for the rest of his life. Little Bella had third degree burns on 65 percent of her body—her torso, buttocks, and legs. She would undergo 109 surgeries and procedures in nine months. Like Mark, she was immediately put in a medically induced coma but later she asked Dr. Williams to take her off intubation. She didn't like being unconscious, wanting to be awake no matter what she was in for. When the doctor finished her daily dressing change and she gradually came out of anesthesia, Bella would softly sing Taylor Swift songs.

They harvested skin cells from her unburned back for grafts, then used an experimental procedure to apply it, spraying the skin over a fishnet-like mesh that covered the burned parts of her body. Bella never complained, her confidence in Dr. Williams unwavering before every surgery.

This little girl had the courage to always ask for the truth about her condition from Dr. Williams. But then an infection resistant to antibiotics set her back for two months. Infections prevent skin grafts from "taking." Instead of letting it weigh her down, she adjusted to life in the hospital, receiving stars for achieving physical therapy milestones. After 276 days, Bella left the hospital, and while she was in for a long period of rehabilitation and physical therapy, she would eventually go back to school and to her beloved gymnastics.

What a heartbreaking accident! And what extraordinary courage and resilience this little Bella had! 109 surgeries! How is that possible? How does a human body handle that? My hand feels shaky holding my phone. *So this is what Mark's in for?* It's a struggle for me to look at the photos in the article. Especially the one where they show Bella's new skin cells being prepared in the operating room to be sprayed on her body. I'm horrified and intrigued at the same time, imagining it's Mark's body instead of that of this brave little girl.

Bella's courage gives me courage. She and Mark possess an indomitable spirit. *Mark can do this—I know he can. And will.* A hard kernel of determination sprouts inside me. It'll be difficult every step of the way, but if a resolute little girl can do this—we can too.

When Mark is back resting in his room, the nurses let me know that Dr. Williams wants to meet with me tomorrow. I wonder if something worrisome has come up but brush the thought aside. He's a busy man and may have run out of time to talk with me. Most likely he had back-to-back surgeries today.

The next morning, Dr. Williams stops by and says hello. I'm reminded from the first meeting Steven and I had with him what a pleasant bedside manner he has. Remembering the article about Bella, I also know how impressive he is in what must be one of the hardest medical jobs in the world.

After initial pleasantries, he tells me that they're freeing up one of the patient rooms for us to meet in. Suddenly I feel off balance and queasy. He's never allocated a room just for us to talk. Typically we've chatted inside Mark's room or in the waiting room. When Adrian and I make our way to the room that's set up, there's a crowd of hospital staff in the room. We recognize most of them—Matt, one of the traveling nurses; Jillian, another nurse on staff; Dylan, the respiratory therapist; and Dr. Williams. There are a couple of other people I don't recognize. And then Dr. Williams delivers a crushing blow.

"We're going to need to amputate Mark's legs," he says quietly.

I clutch Adrian's arm.

"I think you know the tibia bones in his calves are badly burned." Dr. Williams pauses with a gentle look in his eyes. "They are the bones closest to the surface and vulnerable when burned. Mark's calf muscles are permanently damaged and can't control his feet."

I picture the huge calf muscles he had as a young man on the soccer field. He had Popeye legs.

Adrian and I reach out to hold each other. My mind shuts down and all I know is that my body is shaking terribly and I'm crying. I can't stop. We cling to each other, unable to let go.

The hospital staff surrounding us are professionals. They have the kindest expressions on their faces and Matt grabs a Kleenex box and puts it into my hands. My vision's blurry, but I can see that Dr. Williams looks grave and kind at the same time.

A few minutes later I'm able to compose myself. I gather the strength to speak.

"So where would you amputate?" I ask. "Would it be below the knee?"

"No, we'd have to amputate above the knee."

"Why?" I demand.

"It's because we need a four-inch flap with good blood circulation to close the amputated site," he explains. "The knee is in the way since we need to amputate the entire calf." He gestures toward his own leg.

"What about prosthetics?" Adrian asks. He's the robotics engineer. He's been texting his biomedical engineering friends at ETH. One friend is doing research on "intelligent" prosthetics.

"They're a possibility."

I nod, thinking of photos I've seen of people doing adaptive skiing.

I feel a sudden wave of exhaustion. I don't ask more questions like I normally do. All I needed to hear was Dr. Williams's reassurance that Mark wouldn't be in a wheelchair for the rest of his life.

"I looked at Mark's hands. His left hand looks okay but we'll need to amputate the fingertips. As you know, he was more badly burned on his right side. We'll need to remove his right ring and pinkie fingers."

Ah, yes, because it was the right wing of his plane that caught on fire first, clipping the light poles. It's not good news, but it's a relief that as long as he has his hands, he can manage. To hold things. A fork to eat. A spatula or big wooden spoon to cook with over the stovetop. He can still bake a pie. Type on his laptop. There are so many things he can still do. These thoughts flash through my mind quickly.

"The fact that Mark has made it this far is remarkable," Dr. Williams says. "I didn't expect his vitals to do so well."

"Mark's a fighter," I declare proudly. Outwardly I'm saying the words but inside there's a heaviness.

Dr. Williams nods. "It'll help him. I can tell you're a great family and he has a lot of support."

I remember a nurse who told me that not all patients do. I'm proud that Mark is surrounded by us. His loving family.

"We need to do the amputations very soon or his calves will become infected and the infection will spread."

I nod. I don't ask about logistics as I normally do like, *How soon? Both amputations at the same time? Recovery process?* I need time to digest this. It's such difficult news.

The meeting ends. Everyone quietly files out of the room while Adrian and I remain sitting. The tears return and I cover my face with tissues for a long time before we head back to Mark's room.

That afternoon I ask Adrian if we can go to dinner early and back to the condo. I can't handle staying at the hospital tonight. After dinner at the condo, I read the last of the latest Stanford GSB posts. It's from one of the GSBers who was a doctor before business school.

> *Read on if you are interested in the realities of burn injuries. While my experience was limited to only a handful of severe burn patients, taking care of them required all the mental fortitude one could muster. Indeed, there was no complaining/moaning and black humor (fairly common otherwise) among the surgical interns about the rotation they served in the burn unit. One could readily see why. Burn injuries are devastating in all respects; in short, the suffering is beyond that of any disease I have witnessed or can imagine. And it is happening to one of us. The recovery is going to be lengthy and tumultuous at best. My heart goes out to Mark and his family and I truly hope that he will overcome whatever is in the way.*

That evening I say an early good night to Adrian and climb into bed. I don't want to read anything; I don't want to write in my journal. Sleep is my only refuge. My pillow is wet as I drop into a deep slumber of nothingness.

Chapter 7

ALYSSA FINDS MARK'S RING

Adrian and I are greeted by Alyssa when we arrive in Mark's room. Being in her presence feels like a ray of sunshine, warming us instantly. We exchange the usual pleasantries and I ask about Mark's vitals. His temperature's still elevated but it's come down a bit to 101.3.

I share what Dr. Williams told us about Mark's upcoming amputations. I mention that Mark's a fighter. It's as if it really will be true if I keep saying it publicly. It's so hard not knowing what's going on inside him when he's lying unconscious day after day.

"I can see that about him," she declares. "I was here the day Mark was admitted."

I didn't know that. No wonder she seems more personal with Adrian and me than the other nurses do. She actually met Mark while he was conscious.

"When he arrived, he asked Dr. Hale, the supervising doctor, how long he would be in the hospital. Dr. Hale told him his recovery would take two months."

Adrian and I are riveted. We've heard so little about Mark when he was still conscious in the ER. We've yet to meet any of the doctors or interns who received Mark that day. I'm realizing that Dr. Reese was the receiving doctor who called me from ER. Dr. Hale was the supervising doctor.

"Do you know what Mark said?" Alyssa says, smiling. "He said, 'But that's too long!' and he tried to sit up from the gurney he was lying on."

"My goodness. That sounds like Mark." I turn to Adrian. "Doesn't that sound just like your dad, Adrian?"

Adrian nods. "He was always so busy."

"He was the Energizer bunny," I add. "God knows how he managed it all—his job in Reno running sales and marketing for a start-up, commuting between Tahoe and home. International travel. Keeping up his flying. Advising entrepreneurs. Mentoring high school students."

I thought of our last weekend together before his accident. We enjoyed exploring Reno's downtown at a leisurely pace and having a drink at one of the newly opened hipster lounges. We drove to Virginia City, going window shopping and taking in the sights of this old gold mining town perched among dry, straw-colored hills. It was a quaint historic place full of little souvenir shops, bars, ice cream parlors, an art gallery, and a huge candy emporium. The town was such a tourist trap, but looking back now, I know that where we were mattered less than the quality of time we spent together. It was one of our more quiet, relaxed weekends. I remember listening to songs by Patty Griffin and Bad Company on my playlist as we drove along the winding roads wrapped around those golden hills. We didn't talk much, just enjoying the music, content to be together.

I'm now so grateful we had that weekend to ourselves. It was like that Stanford GSBer had written—"*you never know when your life is going to change in an instant*."

Alyssa's voice interrupts my thoughts.

"Oh!" Alyssa exclaims, looking at me. "I reminded myself this morning that I had to tell you something important."

I wonder what news she has. It must be something about Mark's condition. Maybe she spoke with one of the doctors today.

"We had to take Mark's wedding band off when he arrived in the ER," she reminds me. "I've been trying to track it down for you. I found out Security had his ring."

I appreciate Alyssa paying attention to personal details like this. Of course, I do want Mark's ring. "Okay. Where do I go?" I ask.

She starts walking to the cabinet. My sense of urgency suddenly kicks in. I want his ring because it's a reminder of the love between us. Our thirty-first wedding anniversary is on July 2, just a few weeks away. It sounds so cliché, but Mark's my soulmate. I remembered us holding each other in bed one night, as we did so many times before. My head was resting on his shoulder while I said to him, "Honey, it's amazing—but I'm realizing that we're now closer to each other than any other human being. Because we've shared so much of our lives together." It occurs to me now that I've lived more years with Mark than with my dad, who died when I was twenty-three.

Alyssa slips into my hand a thick, clear plastic pouch with a glint of gold.

"Thank you, Alyssa." I take the ring out of the bag and hold it in my hand. It's big and heavy. It feels so good to hold this loving reminder of what Mark and I mean to each other. We were never much into material things, but our simple gold wedding bands do mean our love for each other has endured and is still thriving after thirty-one years.

"When Mark and I were first engaged, he said to me, 'Now Jenny, you're a good feminist. You went to Wellesley. Surely you don't want an engagement ring from me, do you?' I remember thinking in that moment, *Well, hmm. I don't know*. You see, I hadn't really thought much about getting married up to that point in my life. I was only twenty-four. So few of my friends had tied the knot by then."

I look at Adrian, who has heard this story so many times before. I throw him a "Please humor me" look. He shrugs his shoulders, knowing I have to tell the story.

I explain that Mark had told me that he thought that, being a good feminist, I wouldn't want an engagement ring for the simple reason that the tradition dated from medieval times and the ring was a sign you were a man's property. He thought that wedding bands were okay because we exchange them.

"But in reality, Alyssa, I didn't really care about that kind of stuff, rings and such."

"How long did you date before he proposed?" Alyssa asks.

"He proposed after four months."

"Whoa—that's fast!"

"We had lunch for the first time in late February. We didn't really see each other again for three weeks because Hurricane Gloria blew through Long Island, where we lived. Mark dealt with a power outage at his house and neighborhood for a couple weeks after the storm. Our next date in March was an evening in New York City. Dinner and a jazz club."

I'll never forget that night. Mark drove his very quirky 1974 BMW 2002 with a heater that started working only after he had driven it for fifteen minutes. His nickname for the car was "Otto the Auto." It would start out so cold in the car because it was a New York winter. When the heat would kick in, it would rapidly switch to the other extreme, blasting hot air in your face. But I barely noticed because he and I never stopped talking late into the night, driving back from the city.

I look at Adrian. "Your dad proposed to me on my birthday in the car after a nice dinner out. June 25."

"How romantic!" Alyssa has a dreamy look in her eyes.

"That was fast, Mom," Adrian says.

"It sure was. It's why I needed five months to think about the idea of marriage and before I said yes. Let's see—he proposed in late June and I finally said yes in November."

"It took you five months to say yes?" Alyssa looks perplexed.

"Yup. Look—I hadn't thought about getting married at that point in my life. I was completely focused on my career. Now don't get me wrong. I loved Mark. No question. I just needed time to get used to the idea of getting married. That's all."

"I was your age, Adrian. Engaged by twenty-four."

"Don't look at me like that, Mom. You're scaring me," Adrian says good-humoredly. He knows I'm teasing him. He and his San Francisco girlfriend broke up when he moved to Zurich last year. Adrian told me he's in no rush to get married anytime soon.

"After a few months Mark resigned himself to thinking I would turn him down."

"Five months *is* a long time to keep a guy hanging," Alyssa murmurs.

"I used to call Suzie, my Wellesley friend, every week to debate the pros and cons of marriage. She asked me one night when we were on the phone for the umpteenth time deliberating over the decision. Suzie point-blank asked me, 'Do you love him?' I said yes. And she said, 'Then just marry him and stop calling me about this 'cause I'm sick and tired of talking about it!'"

I explain that the next day after work I went to Sears to buy Mark an engagement ring, picking the tackiest one I could find—a men's silver pinkie ring with blue crystals. I drove to his house the next morning, surprising him by bursting into his kitchen and announcing, "Yes, I'll marry you! Let's buck tradition, honey! It's equal if we exchange engagement rings, right?" I pulled out the box and presented him with the blue crystal pinkie ring. "Here's my engagement ring for you. Where's mine?"

I can't remember exactly what Mark said, but he did stare at me as if I were crazy. A few weeks later he told me that he didn't quite believe that I really meant yes. He thought I would change my mind so he couldn't quite trust what I said and was waiting to see if my answer would stick. It did.

"Mark and I were married in Madison, Wisconsin, and a year later, when we moved to California, he finally gave me an engagement ring."

Alyssa's face lit up. "Can I see it?"

"Our first Christmas together as a married couple, he gave me a handmade ring made of holiday wrapping paper. He made it himself. It had a red heart with a green band. It was nestled in silver icicle decorations in a blue velvet box."

"How incredibly sweet!" Alyssa exclaims, her eyes misty.

"May I say that it was the best gift I have ever received from Mark? Especially since he was not artistic. It took a lot of work for him to create that ring."

I gaze at Mark, silent, a big white figure in bed. All I can think of in this moment is how much I love this man lying in a coma in front of me. My life is to be here with him every single day until he recovers. For someone who is as independent as I am, I suddenly can't bear the thought of being apart from Mark.

Chapter 8

SPIRALING

Dr. Williams stops by today while Adrian and I are in Mark's room. Mark's scheduled for amputation surgery tomorrow. He mentions that he and Dr. Jameson will perform the surgery. He confirms that they'll amputate mid-thigh because they need functioning blood flow and enough muscle below the amputation site to create a muscle flap. That's what his lower thigh will be for. If Mark can tolerate it, Dr. Williams will also amputate the first digit on his thumb and all the fingers on his left hand tomorrow. There's a time urgency so that his dead limbs don't get infected and spread to the rest of his body.

I'm feeling sick thinking about what he'll lose on his left hand.

"We'll need to go in another time to amputate Mark's right ring and pinkie finger," Dr. Williams says quietly.

I remember him explaining this at our traumatic meeting with him a few days ago.

"To what digit will you need to amputate?" I ask, holding out that it might be partial amputations like the left hand.

"I'm afraid we can't save those fingers. We'll have to remove them entirely. I've been monitoring them, hoping they could be viable, but they're still really dark."

I'm hoping they won't need to amputate anything more of his fingers. Having some finger digits and whole fingers left will ensure that Mark has some reasonable quality of life to grip and hold things.

Until this very moment there was an invisible boundary that kept me from fully understanding that Mark would lose parts of his body. But now my mind just can't cross over that line. It's unbearable to think of him disabled, knowing how much he loves to ski. He is a double black diamond skier, and the sheer beauty of watching him fly down the edge of a mountain in a powerfully graceful dance always took my breath away.

I'm forced now to understand what's going to happen next.

"How long will it take for Mark to recover from his amputations?" I ask.

"In a normal body, amputations heal in six weeks. For Mark, as a burn patient, it will take a few months. Three, maybe four months," Dr. Williams explains.

That's such a long time. I shudder at the thought of him being a step more vulnerable than he is already.

"Okay, I'll see you both and Mark tomorrow then," Dr. Williams says, nodding to Adrian and me before stepping out of Mark's room.

I sit back down in my chair. The room is quiet. There's a hello text from Jeff, Mark's high school friend who lives in Phoenix. When I break the news to him about Mark's finger amputations, he texts back:

> *"That's not good news. But knowing Mark, I can picture him on those skis for handicapped people zooming down the mountain having a blast!"*

I text back, *"That would be so him, right?"* It's one of the things I've always loved about Mark—his formidable "can do" attitude. It gives me just a tiny bit of hope.

Alyssa enters the room, having stepped out to get something for Mark while Adrian and I spoke with Dr. Williams.

"Alyssa, what is Mark's temp? Is it still running high? Did we get the lab tests back yet?" My questions rush out in a jumble. My anxiety is spilling out.

She glances at one of the monitors, "Right now his temperature's 103.2." She has a look of concentration. "It's higher than we want it to be."

Alyssa picks up a report and reads it quickly. "The lab results show that Mark has an infection in the lungs. The night shift nurses changed out his antibiotics to ones that are more targeted for the type of lung infection he has."

"Oh, good. But is his temperature too high for him to go into surgery tomorrow?"

"Dr. Williams told us to notify him if Mark's temperature increases to 104."

Wow—that's not much higher than where he is already. My anxiety grows. I can't even look at Adrian in my need to manage the worry that's growing inside me. I hope they don't find more they have to amputate when they go in to work on his right hand.

"It'd be Dr. Williams's decision whether Mark can go into surgery," Alyssa adds.

I post an update on Lotsa Helping Hands, letting everyone know about the amputations tomorrow. I ask them to pray that Mark has no complications and will have a good recovery. I share my anxiety about what they'll need to amputate on his right hand.

I end my update with this:

> *I remind myself there's no fear in love. We're entrusting Mark to God and all the love in the universe.*
>
> *His doctors and nurses are incredible. I gave his nurses hugs today—they're doing the hard and detailed work to keep Mark alive every hour, every day, every night. They are so good at what they do, and they care about him. Alyssa, Matt, Lindsey, KC, Jeanne, Darby, Emily, and so many others.*

The next morning the nurses call me early to let me know that they're taking Mark into the OR earlier than planned. I always like to be there when they take Mark in for surgery, so we rush through our morning routine to get to the hospital in time.

Adrian and I quietly watch as the nurses unhook Mark from his monitors. He's an immobile body of white bandages. The last machine is the respiratory machine. They put him on a manual pump ventilator that makes a rhythmic and noisy burping sound.

The staff maneuver his large bed out of the room, holding up his manual ventilator as they head toward the OR. I try to ignore the sound as I accompany him and the attendants, stopping short at the OR door to tell him one last time how much I love him. "We love you, Mark! Everyone's praying for you, darling!" I call out. I messily wipe tears from my face with my hands, scarcely realizing the churn of emotions inside me over what is about to happen to Mark.

When I return, Mark's room is depressingly empty and quiet. Adrian and I decide to get some fresh air and head to a nearby café. It's not stiflingly hot just yet, so we sit outside at a small table on a patio out back, knowing that in another hour the heat will drive us inside. It's a rare and welcome opportunity to be outdoors. I realize how much I miss being outside. I'll never again take it for granted.

What happened to Mark and me was the kind of thing we always thought we would read about happening to other people, not us. We had lived a charmed life for so long, even though we had lost both our parents over the years. Our life wasn't perfect but we had a happy marriage, Wesley and Adrian were content and well-adjusted kids, and we enjoyed and deeply appreciated our circle of family and friends. After many years spent balancing intense careers and raising the boys, we were about to retire to Tahoe to hike, ski, travel, and spend more time with the people we cared about. Mark and I were healthy and we were positive-thinking people. We didn't worry about much. We weren't the type of couple who constantly checked in with each other when traveling to make sure the other had arrived somewhere safely.

I thought about whether I regretted not doing that more now after the unthinkable had happened to Mark. What if Mark and I had been in more constant communication about his comings and goings between Scottsdale and Carson City the day leading up to the crash? *No, it wouldn't have changed anything.* Just like that, the thought passes through momentarily and poof—it dissipates as quickly as the thought had shown up.

Adrian is sitting next to me, reading on his phone and drinking his tea. Suddenly, he gently nudges me and points to a delivery truck that's parked near us.

An athletic-looking delivery man in his forties is unloading boxes from the back of the truck. He has a gleaming silver prosthetic leg on one side. He looks so capable with his high-tech leg, moving with ease around the truck, loading up the pallet and wheeling it into the café. Back and forth, back and forth.

I'm fascinated, watching him move. Adrian and I both stare, silent until he finishes the job, climbs back in the truck, and he and the driver head off, rumbling out of the parking lot.

"Maybe that's what Dad will look like, huh?" I say to Adrian, who nods. Maybe it's a sign that Mark will be able to use prosthetics. I don't know for certain, but it gives me a glimmer of hope.

Sure enough, we last an hour outside before the heat overwhelms us like a thick blanket and we retreat inside. Alyssa calls to let us know that Mark's out of surgery and that they need extra time to get him settled because of his amputations. I tell her that we'll leave for the hospital soon and will be in the waiting room when they are ready to update us.

Adrian and I are sitting in the crowded waiting room when Dr. Jameson enters the room and sits down next to us.

"So—the good news is the amputations went smoothly," he says confidently.

"What a relief!" I reply, putting a hand over my heart.

"We didn't get to his hands today. Look—I'm truly sorry that we couldn't save Mark's legs, but it was necessary in order to reduce his metabolic challenges."

Adrian and I nod, silent. *What more is there to say? It's done.*

"We'll work on his finger amputations next week. Let's give Mark a rest. He's been through an awful lot today." Dr. Jameson pauses thoughtfully. "I had the nurses put him on a good dose of morphine after he got out of surgery. We want him to be comfortable."

Adrian and I thank the doctor and head back to the condo, where I post an online update about what Dr. Jameson shared with us. I don't tell anyone about the prognosis that Mark's not likely to ever walk again. Instead, I ask everyone to pray for Mark's recovery and healing and thank them for their love and support.

I'm all too conscious that tomorrow we'll have to face seeing Mark in his new condition. I push aside a feeling of dread. Sleep is all I want. I have to listen to my nighttime ocean meditation a few more cycles tonight in order to drift off into what I hope will be a dreamless oblivion.

Chapter 9

MORE SURGERY

I sleep fitfully, waking up in the middle of the night worrying about how Mark's body is handling the amputations. *Does he know what's happened? I don't think so, but I can't be sure. Thank God he's in a coma.*

When Adrian and I arrive at the Burn Center, I'm afraid to go into Mark's room. I stand in the doorway and cautiously peer in. Mark is covered in a thick white blanket from the waist down so I can't see what's missing. I know I'll have to face it eventually but I'm grateful I don't have to deal with it just yet. I'm going to need time to internalize that a third of Mark's body is gone.

"How's Mark doing today?" I ask Alyssa as I walk into his room, trying to sound upbeat, Adrian right behind me.

"His temperature spiked to 104 degrees, which is due to the stress of yesterday's surgery, but we're closely monitoring it and giving him ibuprofen. Unfortunately, he's back on dialysis."

Yes, how could I not notice the big machine next to Mark? The only view Adrian and I have of my husband today is from the foot of his bed.

It's upsetting to know his kidneys can't operate on their own. He was doing so well without the machine for the last week and a half.

It's a quiet afternoon in Mark's room. I ask Adrian to play the meditation playlist I created for Mark. I hope it can support his healing. Adrian found some music at a frequency that's supposed to be deeply relaxing, so I ask him to play that music first. I close my eyes, taking a deep breath as I listen to the light piano melody and soft background chords. I gradually give into a feeling of being surrounded by the gentle waves of the ocean. I visualize Mark enveloped in a soft cloud that's healing him. I have no idea where this visual comes from, but I just stay with it until the music ends, hoping that he can feel it in some unconscious way.

When we return to Mark's room after grabbing dinner, we are greeted by the night nurses, KC and Kate.

"How's Mark doing?" I ask.

"The good news is that Mark's temperature has come down to 100.7 degrees," KC announces.

Well, that's a relief. I let out a big breath of air. The tension, like a knotted ball inside me, releases itself and we go home that evening feeling lighter than we have in days.

The next afternoon when we're back in Mark's room, Matt and Ginger are taking care of him. Ginger lets us know that Mark's temperature has come further down. Maybe they can take him off kidney dialysis by tomorrow. We'll see. I just hope Mark's amputations will heal well over the next few months. He may not be out of the woods yet, but I've learned with the unpredictable ride we're on that for now, when his temperature's down, we need to relax a bit and appreciate the moment.

After we greet Mark as we do daily, Adrian settles down in his chair while I fiddle with the music player. I'm grateful that the nurses follow my instructions to play Mark's playlists even when we're not in the room, knowing that when he needs calm, they play classical or meditation music, switching to his rock playlist when he's doing well. The Allman Brothers are playing on the music player. There are days I need my own music to endure our marathon visits. Today's one of them, so I click on my personal playlist. It includes some songs Mark likes, but mostly it has music that I enjoy. Music has always moved me in ways that I have no words for. I instinctively know that I need it now to help me process what's going on at a purely emotional level. Lately I'll listen to a song and cry. I don't understand why, but I know that my heart is breaking in some way as I watch what's happening to Mark. Most days my rational mind takes over to help me soldier through the marathon. I realize it's my training as a leader in an organization. It's a familiar and comfortable place for me to operate from. But at times, hearing a song will catch me in an unexpected way and I'll drop into a sudden wave of emotion that pulls me under its current so completely—so fully that I can't even articulate afterward what just happened, my eyes swollen and my voice hoarse from sobbing.

Dr. Jameson stops by.

"I want to let you two know that we're scheduling Mark for the OR on Monday. We need to remove burned skin from his back. The burns look quite deep."

Visualizing raw, burned skin on Mark's back makes my own skin tingle.

"We'll cover his back with allografts and xenografts."

Dr. Jameson had explained to us when he first started his three-week stint that they would be putting allografts and xenografts on Mark's raw body. "We want to amputate Mark's left fingertips and his right ring and pinkie finger. I'll assess what's viable with the rest of his right hand, of course."

"How often do you have to change out his grafts?"

"Every five to seven days. I've sent out for a lab culture to see how Mark's doing with his lung infection. Oh, and some good news. Ninety-four skin grafts were grown from Mark's skin cells and will be arriving from Boston on July 11. Each graft is the size of two postage stamps."

"How exciting!" I exclaim. "So—we can begin covering Mark up with his own skin."

"That's what's best. We'll have to experiment this first go-around and see how Mark's body takes to them."

Dr. Jameson wishes us a good night and goes home.

Later that evening, after dinner, Adrian and I are back at our condo, relaxing on the couch.

"Mom, did you know we're up to five hundred people who are members of our Lotsa Helping Hands community?"

Adrian's a community administrator and has been helping me approve each person who requests to join.

"Really?" I'm shocked. I had lost track of how many people we had been approving over the last few weeks. "Who are they?"

"You should take a look online."

I pull up our community site and scroll through screen after screen of names. Reading what feels like an endless list of names that I recognize,

I realize that Mark and I have accumulated a lot of friends and acquaintances over the years. I think back to my daily posts, sometimes multiple updates in the same day. It's astounding to me how many people are following my updates.

I'm touched that they read my daily posts and send their well wishes and prayers frequently. Every morning there are new messages waiting for me. They're all encouraging, loving, and supportive from close friends and family as well as acquaintances Mark and I didn't know well. I hadn't known just how kind people could be until now.

I'm beginning to internalize just how long our journey will be, that it's a daily fight to keep Mark alive. We get a few days when he's stable, and then Mark's back to fighting for his life again. It's the roller coaster his doctors told us to expect.

I post an update on Lotsa Helping Hands, again asking everyone to keep Mark in their thoughts and prayers for a good recovery from his amputations.

The next morning I wake up to a flood of messages of prayer and well wishes that pour in from the community. I'm perched on the dining room chair, first cup of coffee in hand, hungrily reading the many posts that show up. There are notes from Mark's family friends from Wisconsin, his extended family in Texas, California friends, Stanford classmates, University of Wisconsin classmates, my Wellesley friends, and the many friends Mark and I had made personally and at work.

My dear friend Stacy sends me a note.

> *The Greeks have a word, Mystikos, which is the mystery of the universe. The Mystikos holds everything, the good, the bad and everything in between. It doesn't answer why this happened to Mark nor why such suffering must be endured. When I pray in this space, the Mystikos comes over me and I can urgently petition that Mark is cradled in the arms of the powerful love of Mystikos and that you and your family are given the strength to endure, one day at a time.*

It's words like these from loving friends that help me stay strong.

There's some kind of virtuous circle between our online community and me. My posts are now daily and sometimes a few times a day. In response, I receive posts of support and encouragement every day. I used to value my privacy, but for some reason I've begun to pour my heart out in my posts, my hopes and fears. Anger. Anxiety. They spill out of me when I type. I ask for prayers and positive thoughts. I've come to depend on the many people who offer their kind thoughts, comments, and prayers. They compliment me for the strength with which I've carried forward day by day. I find myself ignoring those compliments. *What else would I do?* It's never been an option for me not to be strong. I *have* to be. For Mark. Shoot, maybe it's for me. I can't bear the consequences if I'm not strong. The abyss of what that would bring scares me more.

Chapter 10

HEALING

Mark's finger amputation surgery, which was scheduled for today, is now delayed. I'm learning that an OR day is like the airport. The later the surgery is in the course of the day, the more likely it will be delayed or bumped into the next day. The doctors don't always know how long a surgery will take until they get into the OR and assess a patient's condition.

Mark's surgery being delayed to tomorrow is out of my control. I'm upset for a minute or two and then I let it go. I have to trust God and the universe that Mark will be okay. Sitting in Mark's room with the news, I take a deep breath and look out the window for a minute. Pausing this way reminds me that Dr. Williams made it clear several times now that it's a medical miracle that Mark had come this far. I try hard to keep this in mind when there are setbacks.

That evening in Mark's room we learn that Mark's temperature has spiked to 106 degrees. *Will it come down in time for him to go to the OR tomorrow?* It's wait and see. I'm suddenly exhausted and want to go home. I ask Adrian to drive. It's a relief to have him take over. That night in bed, before I turn the lights off, I visualize releasing my worry to the universe. I imagine it like a toxic air current flowing out of my hands as I sweep my arms upward in the air. Anyone watching me now would think I'm crazy. But in the privacy of my bed, I don't care. In my present world where nothing is normal anymore, who's to judge what's normal or abnormal? That night I sleep soundly without waking up once.

The next morning the nurse who answers my phone call explains that they're skipping Mark's morning dressing change since they're expecting him to go into surgery. They don't know when yet and suggest that we come to the hospital. She reports that Mark's temperature has come down significantly in the night to 101. Adrian and I breathe a sigh of relief. It means he can go into the OR with no problem for his needed finger amputations.

When we arrive in Mark's room, the OR team is already prepping him for surgery. I tell Mark how much we love him as they wheel him toward the surgery center.

Adrian and I camp out in the waiting room, and after a while, Dr. Jameson enters and tells us they had to postpone the finger amputations because debriding the burned skin on his back was the priority and they ran out of time to get to the fingers.

Another delay. Again. I take a deep breath. *Let it go. Let it go, Jenny.*

After Dr. Jameson leaves, Adrian and I kill time in the waiting room, knowing it will take the nurses an hour to settle Mark back in his room post-surgery.

I abruptly tell Adrian I'm going for a walk. There's nothing to see in the hospital, but I have to get up and get moving.

Shortly after I return, Adrian and I enter Mark's room and notice that the nurses have removed a layer of bandages on his face. His eyes are closed still, but the stitches are gone. Mark's face and lips are starting to heal. It feels so good to see his face. Adrian and I marvel at how smooth his skin looks. His wrinkles are gone! He looks younger than his brother, his sisters, and me. We're all younger than Mark. How incredible that something as natural as honey can so powerfully heal skin. Jillian, the nurse, explains that for more surface burns, medical-grade honey can do wonders. *If only it could be so for the rest of Mark's body.*

Mark always had a ruddy complexion, and now his face is a picture of health and vitality. Some part of Mark has been returned to us. Nothing can shake the cheerful mood that carries Adrian and me forward into the afternoon.

Jillian shares with us that Mark's vitals look good. His temperature, heart rate, and blood pressure are normal. It's finally a day to celebrate. His vitals are good and his face looks great. It lifts my spirits back up. Adrian's too.

I pick up Wesley, our twenty-six-year-old son, at Sky Harbor Airport this morning. It's so good to see him. He's built like Mark, tall and sturdy. When Wesley gives me a long hug, I'm completely enveloped by his big shoulders and arms. It's the same feeling I have when Mark hugs me, a feeling that all is well in the world in this moment. Our little family feels complete now that Wesley and Adrian are both here. I feel happy for the first time since I've come to Phoenix. After all that we've been through with Mark, maybe I appreciate more deeply the bond of love and flesh and blood that the boys, Mark, and I have together.

We grab a quick lunch and go straight to the Burn Center.

Wesley is here for a few days to stay through the Fourth of July holiday, which is also Mark's birthday. Mark's brother, Steven; his wife, Kim; and his daughter, Megan, will join us from Michigan. I'm looking forward to showing Wesley how wonderful his dad's face looks. But I know it will be hard for him to see the loss of Mark's legs. I remind myself, *Just take it a day at a time, Jenny.*

When we arrive in Mark's room, Wesley puts his backpack down on an empty chair and walks over to Mark's bed to be close to him. He pauses and looks at his dad, taking in everything. His face, his bandages. How the blanket drops off below his thighs. I cheerfully tell him how great his dad's face looks with his honey treatment. Wesley hovers closer to examine Mark's face.

"Yeah, Dad's face does look really good."

"Have you noticed his wrinkles are all gone?"

Wesley nods. "Oh, yeah. His face is so smooth-looking."

It's quiet in the room. Adrian's reading something on his phone. For him it's just another day in Mark's room. I'm amazed at Adrian's tenacity in coming to the hospital with me every single day without complaint. He's been so helpful, driving us home during the evenings when I'm too tired to trust myself on the road.

Jillian steps into the room to hand me several cards that have arrived for Mark and me. We receive a continual stream of cards from family and friends almost daily.

"Talk to him, Wesley. Dad may be in a coma, but a friend mentioned that people in a coma can sense the energy of those in the room even if they're not conscious of what they're saying."

"Okay." Wesley sidles in among the monitors to get closer to Mark. "Hi, Dad."

Watching Wesley's hesitation around his dad reminds me of years ago in New York when my own father was in the hospital after his leg was broken in a hit-and-run accident. He was in the hospital for a month, which seemed like an eternity to the seven-year-old that I was. Dad told me later that when my mom first brought my sister, Teresa, and me to visit him at the hospital, I held back from hugging him, uncertain and shy. It hurt him to see me hold back, knowing that his absence affected me.

I need to help Wesley. "Hey, Wes—tell Dad what's been happening at home."

"Well," he says, looking at Mark. "I've been trying to save money by eating at home more."

Wesley's on a budget since he finished his contract job and is now looking for another one.

"I went to that Indian restaurant you like, Dad. Mantra. Oh, their butter chicken is so good!"

It's quiet. The ever-present swooshing of Mark's respiratory machine fills the background.

"So Dad's still in a coma, huh?" Wesley looks at me. I can tell making conversation with his dad, who's unconscious and can't respond, is hard for him.

I nod.

"How long will he be in a coma?"

"We don't know." I wish I had more to tell him, but I don't.

I look at the green-and-yellow Packers flag on the wall. Wesley and Mark share a love of watching football.

"Hey, Wes—tell Dad about the Packers. What's the preseason talk?"

"Oh, yes!" Wesley perks up. He mentions how Aaron Rodgers is becoming one of the older quarterbacks in the NFL. Wesley happily rattles off stats for the Packers and how he thinks they'll do against the stronger NFL teams this upcoming season.

When he comes to a lull, I pull out the cards I just received.

"Honey, why don't you read these cards to your dad?"

Wesley announces out loud who each card is from and reads them to Mark. He furrows his brow in concentration, clearly taking it all very seriously. Wesley's no longer the teenager Mark lectured about lost homework. He's an adult son reading to his near-fatally injured dad. The roles are reversed but in an extreme circumstance.

One card is from a family friend of Mark's from his hometown in Wisconsin. Another is from friends at a start-up where he used to work. There's so much love and encouragement in the words they write. The start-up friends tell me that I'm one of the strongest people they know. A Wellesley friend writes that my strength and love for Mark are inspiring and heartwarming. I brush them aside because all I care about is anything that can help Mark survive and live. It's my only focus.

Chapter 11

LOSSES

"We're going to work on finger amputations today," Dr. Williams says. "Our approach is to amputate only what's necessary on the chance that Mark's hand could surprise us. It's always possible to remove more later."

"That makes sense," I say with a nod. I'm glad that the doctors can hope for the best and are not assuming only worst-case scenarios.

"Okay, so to summarize, we'll amputate the first two digits of the fingers on his left hand. We'll have to go in to know how much to amputate on his thumb."

"I hope he can keep enough of his thumb that he can hold things."

"Yes, that's what I'm thinking too." Dr. Williams has a thoughtful look. "We'll go in and see what we can save."

"Okay, sounds good," I reply.

Dr. Williams excuses himself to check on another patient. I suddenly feel nauseated. *Did I really just say that it sounds good? There's nothing good about this. So this is what's happened. I receive bad news and I adjust. I receive more bad news and I adjust again.*

I close my eyes and take a deep breath. I take another couple of deep breaths. I try to relax, dropping my shoulders, feeling the tension dissolve a bit. I can feel the blood pumping in my ears. It's a loud drumbeat. Then, ever so gradually, a blanket of calm softly settles into the jagged crevices of my psyche. When I finally open my eyes, there's a bright light streaming in from the window by Mark's bed. Wrapped in white lying in his bed, Mark's lit up in a warm, golden glow.

Impatiently I wipe away tears with one of my hands. *My beloved husband is in the hands of God and the universe. All I can do is pray.* I've never prayed so much in my life.

Mark goes into the OR around 2:30 p.m. I'm glad to have the boys with me. I'm not alone as we wait. It's endless. I wait for surgery to be over. I wait for the next surgery. I wait for him to get scheduled for surgery. I've lost track of how many surgeries Mark's had. I wait for the dressing change. I wait for skin grafts to arrive. I wait to get an update from the doctors. Ultimately I'm waiting for Mark to come out of his coma.

The waiting room is crowded with people. A large extended family takes up most of the chairs. They're friendly and one of the grandmotherly-looking women offers the boys and me some potato chips. She explains that her granddaughter fell in a large pot of stew at a campground and suffered some pretty bad burns. They're from the Navajo Nation in the northeastern part of Arizona. Other relatives—an uncle, a grandfather—chime in while I chat with grandma. It's a good distraction while we wait.

A few hours later, Dr. Williams returns to the waiting room. Wesley, Adrian, and I huddle around him for the update.

"We amputated his left index finger. Although the ends of his other fingers and thumb are dark—this means they're seriously damaged—we decided not to amputate anything else."

I take a deep breath.

"We want to see how his fingers evolve on their own."

Good.

"For his right hand, we amputated all the fingers. There are some that have a bit of a nub above his hand and others that are completely gone."

My heart starts beating faster. *Oh, no.* A split second before I know my distress shows on my face, Adrian's already gently placed his hand on my arm and is watching me.

"We did not amputate his thumb."

I blink. *What?* Okay, that's good, right? *Of course, it is.* I let out a sigh of relief.

"We wanted to keep his thumb intact even though it has serious damage. Again, let's see how that thumb evolves. It may self-amputate, which means the dead part can fall off on its own."

"I hope we can save enough of his thumb so he can use some of his right hand rather than not at all," I say, seeing Mark sitting in a car, his thumb grasping the steering wheel. *Please, dear God—save his thumb.*

Dr. Williams nods. "Yes, let's just see what happens."

My mind starts racing to the idea of hand prosthetics. I make a note to research that and ask Adrian to consult his biomed friends at ETH.

"We debrided more burned skin from Mark's front lower chest."

Debriding more? It's never-ending.

"There was some pus on the ends of both thighs, so we cleaned them up and put antibiotic ointment on them to prevent infection."

"How are his vitals?" Adrian asks. He's been with me every day on this crazy up-and-down ride, so he knows now how important this question is.

Dr. Williams turns to look at him carefully. "His vitals are stable. Everything looks good."

Adrian's face visibly relaxes.

After the doctor leaves, I feel shaky with relief as I sit down.

With Mark's finger amputations behind us, it means when his brother and his family show up in a few days, we can celebrate his birthday, assuming he remains in stable condition. I hope. I've learned we can't assume anything. We just have to take it a day at a time.

I'm sad to see Adrian leave for Zurich the next day. He's going back to help his ETH team prepare for that European driverless car competition. He has a long flight ahead of him. I take his backpack out of the trunk while he hauls his suitcase to the curb. Putting on my cheerful mom face, I say, "Go help ETH win that competition, okay? Your dad and I are so proud of you. You know your dad will want to know all the details when…" Adrian watches me intently, gently touching my hand. He's already anticipating what's coming.

I choke up, shaking suddenly as I stumble through the rest of my words. "…When…he wakes up." I hug him because I'm starting to weep and I don't want him to see me falling apart. But instead, I'm sliding down a dark chasm.

"It's been so hard not being able to talk with Dad."

He knows what I'm feeling. He hugs me back and we hold each other for a while.

"I'm so sorry, Adrian." I pull back from him to wipe my eyes.

Adrian pulls back and looks me in the eye. "For what, Mom? *Of course*, you're sad. We're *all* sad about Dad."

I feel terrible. I'm supposed to be the mom taking care of my boys and here I am falling apart in front of my kid.

"We've been through a lot together, haven't we, Adrian?"

"Yes, we have." Adrian solemnly nods, his eyes gentle.

"Okay, I hope you and the team build the best self-driving car in the competition. I love you, sweetie."

"I love you, Mom." He hugs me one last time before he has to go.

I watch him walking confidently with his bag and suitcase through the airport entrance. My heart feels full, watching my smart, handsome son leave, knowing that Mark and I did something right in our life in raising him and his brother. I never thought this moment would come when I would depend on my sons. There have been some obstacles in the last month that have felt insurmountable, and it's been a relief to have Adrian to lean on. He has an uncanny way of knowing just before I'm about to cry, get upset, or freak out. It's a gift that's been a joy for me to discover about him.

Chapter 12

MARK'S BIRTHDAY

Mark's brother Steven; his wife, Kim; and his daughter, Megan, fly in from Michigan the day before to celebrate Mark's birthday on the Fourth of July. Until this year it was always fun to enjoy the fanfare of sharing his birthday with our nation, complete with fireworks, barbecues, parades, and a holiday. Lucky for Mark, he loves all the food that goes with the Fourth of July—smoked brisket, coleslaw, and pecan pie. He is the only person I know who likes to make his own birthday meal, because he relishes preparing food exactly the way he likes it.

When his brother and his family arrive, they carry with them a very large poster tube and decorations for Mark's room. Their family is tall, including Kim, who must be almost six feet. The space expands with their presence—Steven, his lanky build and cheerful face, and Megan, attentive and smiling but holding back a bit in her usual shy way. Kim's checking out the room, looking at the photos of Mark on the wall by the supply cabinet.

Steven asks if there are any new updates since yesterday. I let them know all's quiet for now and no, there's nothing new to report on.

"Let's get this banner up on the wall," Steven says as he gestures to the black tube. "Kim did such a nice job of getting this color photo banner created at Costco, just in time for our trip."

I play along with their enthusiasm and the commotion of putting up the decorations. *How wonderful! Thank you so much for making the effort. Oh, wow—sorry Costco had to reformat it twice.* I know Steven and Kim mean well—they went through a lot of work to get this huge banner printed.

While it feels nice for all of us who are conscious in the room, it only underscores the fact that Mark can't see a thing and can't participate in his own birthday. I want to scream, *For God's sake, he's in a coma!* The banners are not for him—they're for us. It makes me feel even more sad. Without saying a word, I step back and let Steven, Kim, and Megan take over Mark's room.

Silently I watch them finish taping up the banner. Mark's plane crash and his condition have been hard on Steven. They were close, as Steven is just a couple years younger than Mark. They used to talk almost weekly. I know it means a lot to him to do all this for his brother.

On the Fourth of July, the next day, Wesley and I arrive in Mark's room after his dressing change. The nurses are lenient today about allowing all of us to be in the room to celebrate Mark's birthday. Wesley and I put up a small shiny red, white, and blue Fourth of July decoration that Rene had mailed to us.

Jeff, Mark's local high school buddy, and his friend Traci show up with trays of cheese, cold cuts, and crackers for the Burn Center staff as a thank-you.

Jeff has visited Mark enough times to know how much the nurses did for him. He and I carry the trays to the staff break room, where many of the nurses and technicians thank us for the food. It feels good to do something for the people who do so much for Mark and me.

Our Phoenix family friends, Sue and Neal, also join us. Sue brings a stack of more cards from family and friends, as she does every week or two. I've told our online community to send mail to Sue and Neal's address.

Steven and Jeff spend the afternoon sharing stories about growing up in a small Wisconsin town, a landscape of red barns, open prairies, green bluffs, and gently winding rivers.

I hope that Mark can feel the love and laughter that surrounds him on his birthday. What a relief it is to let others take center stage. I have nothing to do for the first time since I've come to the Burn Center. I can relax. I leisurely write a post describing this place of purgatory where I spend my hours, days, and weeks—a benevolent netherworld where the nurses and doctors are kind and competent. It's a place in which Mark is in physical purgatory, floating in a coma, a murky sea of unconsciousness. Only God knows how he'll describe his experience when he wakes up.

Watching Wesley laugh loudly and join in the many lively conversations with his Uncle Steven's family and our friends, it occurs to me how lonely he must have felt being home alone. Because I've been in survival mode and completely consumed with Mark's condition, I hadn't given a thought to what Wesley must be going through until this very moment.

I desperately want these few days to make up for his being alone at home worrying about his dad. Mark's family has had a greater and more consistent presence with the boys than mine. I appreciate that for a few days, Wesley can experience being surrounded by family and the sense of belonging it can bring.

After a day full of Wisconsin stories, I want to interject at least one California tale. After all, I point out to everyone that Mark has now lived in California for many more years than in Wisconsin. As much as Mark was grounded in the rich and fertile soil of his farm upbringing, his curiosity and need for adventure destined him for a future far beyond the small town he grew up in. I tell the story about one Fourth of July when Wesley and Adrian were "cute munchkins," as Adrian now refers to themselves from that time. They *were* cute, but isn't that every mother's bias? We were at Lake Tahoe enjoying holiday fireworks by the lake. At the end of the fireworks show, there were special fireworks that lit up the sky with the initials MB. "Look!" the boys chirped to Mark. "Special birthday fireworks just for you, Dad!" The next day we discovered that the MB was for Michael Bolton, the famous pop singer who owned an estate along the lake. Our family joke for years afterward was how Dad was enough of a VIP to be treated to personal Lake Tahoe fireworks on his birthday.

Nobody's hungry for dinner after snacking all day. By seven o'clock we decide to call it a day. After everyone leaves and it's just Wesley and me in the room, I stop by Mark's bedside.

"Sweetie, I hope you can feel our energy in the room. It's Wesley and me. We love you so much." I look at his face, which almost looks peaceful. His mouth looks relaxed tonight. The rest of his body is unchanged and mummy-like, wrapped in a formfitting white cocoon.

"Here's to hoping that next year on your birthday we'll get to celebrate it with you fully awake. We'll have everything you love—smoked brisket and ribs, coleslaw the way you like it with vinegary red cabbage, potato salad with extra mustard, and your beloved pecan pie, Betty Crocker style."

"That's right. I'll bake you an apple pie too if you want, Dad," Wesley chimes in. That's another one of Mark's favorites. "And Dad, Adrian and I will even clean up without you having to be Captain Nag-a-lot."

I chuckle and feel grateful that Mark had a good day—a good day, as in no grim talks with the doctors and no crises over Mark's vitals. Before we leave, I say a quick and silent prayer for Mark's amputations to heal.

The next morning I call to check in as I always do. KC, who's wrapping up the night shift, answers the phone. She reassures me in her animated voice that Mark had a stable night. She tells me that she didn't want to rile him up with any talk of politics. We have a joke that if Mark's blood pressure is too low, she has my permission to mention some names of politicians that Mark detests. She adds that, during the dressing change, Mark's different amputation sites looked clean, with no obvious signs of infection.

That's good news. I hope we can pass another peaceful day while we have family visiting. It was wonderful that Mark was crisis-free on his birthday yesterday. Caught up with family visiting and his birthday celebration, I suddenly realized that I'd forgotten about our wedding anniversary on July 2. Thirty-one years with the hope that one day soon Mark will wake up and I'll have him back.

After Mark's dressing change, Wesley and I head for the hospital. I'm thrilled to find a parking spot close to the pavilion walkway stretching from the pediatrics and ER entrances.

The friendly police officer on duty at the reception desk recognizes us immediately and buzzes us through.

It's been humbling to be at a county hospital every day. I've met people from all walks of life here: prisoners in their orange jumpsuits, a large extended family from a Navajo Nation reservation, and nurses like Alyssa, who went into their profession because they had a family member suffer a severe burn.

We're really all the same, aren't we? We love, we laugh, we grieve. I've been confronted in a more real way with how our bodies will fail us someday. Outside the Burn Center, the world may view us differently, whether we're a student, a house cleaner, or an executive. But in this nondescript waiting room, we're all the same. Each of us has a loved one suffering from one of the worst traumas a human being can experience. *We keep vigil for a son, a brother, a daughter, a husband. It's a bond that makes us fully human in a way only trauma and tragedy can.*

That evening we have dinner with Neal and Sue at an Italian restaurant. While Steven, Neal, and Sue chatter on about their college days, I'm in my own world. I'm busy thinking about the race to skin grafts. How this is the longest I've ever gone not talking to Mark. It's been now what, five weeks? The last time we were apart the longest was two weeks, when Mark had a hectic ten-city business trip to China. Back then we talked on the phone every few days—unlike now, when Mark is mute. I wonder what's floating in his brain. What dreams is he dreaming? Will it feel surreal when he wakes up, unsure of where the line is between reality and his subconscious visions?

The following day, Steven, Kim, and Megan leave to return to Michigan. It was comforting and reassuring to keep their company, reminding me of the people and place that shaped who Mark is at his core—honest, forthright, and grounded in the here and now. It had been a relief having them be the center of action. It's now a relief to have my peace and quiet back.

Chapter 13

BACK ON THE ROLLERCOASTER

After everyone leaves it's strangely quiet in Mark's room. We're alone now with the nurses. Wesley moderates a Discord discussion group and has his head down, catching up. I can hear the familiar rhythmic, steady hum of Mark's machines. The ever serene and calm Lindsey is back on day shift with Mark. She patiently explains that Mark's in some pain because she noticed his respiratory numbers are inching up. He was doing really well the last two days but now he's agitated. There's a grimace on Mark's face. My chest feels heavy. It's so hard to witness Mark's pain. I watch Lindsey giving him hydromorphone, which is a stronger pain med, so he can be more comfortable.

The color photo banner looms large over the window next to Mark's bed. He's still frowning. Knowing that it will take time for the pain meds to kick in, I desperately need to distract myself. I open one of the packages that Sue brought by yesterday. The white-and-light-blue Amazon plastic package reveals *The 5-Ingredient Italian Cookbook* from our Serbian friends, Branko and Stanka. They know how happy our family was every time we returned from our Italian vacations—tanned, relaxed, and well-fed—and how much Mark loves to cook. In the enclosed card they suggest that I read recipes to him with the idea that he can cook when he gets out of the hospital. They mention what an inspiration Mark's cooking has been to their son, Misha, Adrian's best friend in middle school who's now an assistant appetizer chef at a Michelin-starred restaurant in San Francisco. I'm sniffling, blinking back tears.

The idea of reading recipes to Mark reminds me of something a high school friend told me after he first heard the news about Mark. He said that when he was in a medically induced coma for months, the way he processed what he heard in his room came out in his dreams. When he woke up, he had difficulty knowing what was a dream and what was reality. If I read recipes to Mark every day, maybe when he wakes up he'll think he cooked an enormous Italian feast. I chuckle at the thought of chatting with Mark about this when he wakes up.

Dr. Williams stops by. He explains that Mark's amputation sites will take months to fully heal. In a healthy patient it takes six weeks. Mark's skin grafts will arrive from Boston next Thursday. They plan to start skin grafting in Mark's upper extremities first but warn us that it will be a painstakingly slow process. Sometimes skin grafts don't take right away, so they'll have to try several times.

It occurs to me that without his calves, feet, and some fingers, there'll be less of him to skin graft. It doesn't take away the lingering sadness I feel that Mark's lost important parts of himself. I don't look forward to the day when he wakes up and sees what he's missing—and what happened to the plane. I close my eyes and take a slow, deep breath as if I can exhale the pain I feel deep inside me. *Hsing tung*—it's a Chinese word for sorrow. It literally means "my heart hurts."

The rest of the day passes uneventfully. Wesley takes over for Adrian in keeping the playlist going so that there's always music. Otherwise, it's mostly quiet with us looking up from our phones and chatting with the nurses as they come in and out of the room. I spend time talking with Wesley about how his job search is going. It's sobering to suddenly realize that I'm a single parent now. Mark would have a lot to say to Wesley about his job search, so I make an effort to represent what I think his dad would coach him on. It's a new feeling.

When Wesley and I leave for dinner, Lindsey reminds us that today is the last day of her rotation and that someone else will be cycling in tomorrow.

That evening after dinner, Mark's face looks back to normal—whatever normal is when someone's in a coma. His grimace is gone. That's all I care about. KC and Kate, our favorite night nurses, are working together.

Kate reassures us that Mark appears to be comfortable. I relax my shoulders as I sit down, feeling immediate relief.

KC tells us hilarious stories about growing up in Malaysia. She's petite, with a bubbly personality and permanent grin on her face. Kate's husband is from Hawaii, so she tells stories about family vacations with her in-laws on Oahu.

"We go to Hawaii every summer to see Dale's parents. Our kids go totally native, spending their days barefoot at the beach, in their grandparents' backyard, playing with the neighbors' kids. On the day we fly into Hawaii, they take their shoes off the minute they get out of the car at their grandparents' and don't put them back on until we're ready to get on the flight going home."

I chuckle. "When my sister and her family moved from Honolulu to Wichita, Kansas, their little daughter, Daphne, kept taking her shoes and socks off in her car seat. She wasn't used to wearing real shoes during a Wichita winter."

Kate grins, nodding her head. "Yes! That'd be my kids too."

"Daphne takes her shoes and socks off. My sister puts them back on. Daphne takes them off again. My poor sister!" Kate and I laugh.

All this talk of Malaysia and Hawaii makes me realize that I have something in common with KC and Kate. I lived in Malaysia as a kid for a couple of years, and many years later, after my dad died, my mom, sister, and her family lived in Hawaii for a while. They're also both tropical places, in contrast to Phoenix. Hawaii, especially, evokes pleasant memories of gentle summer rain showers, warm trade winds, and lush, green landscapes. Life is easy there compared to the desert. Here you can die of heat stroke or suffer severe burns from simply walking barefoot on scorching hot pavement. Outside our hospital window, nature is full of rocks and dirt, where nothing grows except cacti and straggly desert shrubs. Inside, in our darkened room, Kate chatters on, her face aglow near the sea of lights blinking on the monitors around Mark. She's talking about family beach time at Waimanalo Bay, their glee in discovering sea turtles, and how fast the kids are asleep in the car driving home, after a full day of sun and sand, their lips stained blue from eating too much shaved ice. The last time I stayed at my mom's house on the Big Island, it rained every night. Cozy inside, I would read, listening to the steady drumming on the roof and watching warm, fat drops of water fall on the banana trees in Mom's front yard, their big leaves shiny and slick. And in her backyard, orange and purple bird-of-paradise flowers and lantana bushes soaked in the gentle rainfall. It's a welcome escape from my narrow daily existence in this sterile hospital room, where everything is beige, gray, and brown, and where the only sounds I hear are the steady hum of monitors.

The next day after Mark's dressing change, Tara, the nurse on duty, greets me.

"So—good news, Jenny. Look at Mark's face."

She's taken Mark's face bandages off. His face looks so big, his jaw enormous without his beard. I can't stop staring at him. His face has a healthy pink glow. I think of the rosy cheeks that Wesley had as a little guy toddling around our house. It's extraordinary because Mark just turned sixty.

"His face is healing so nicely." Tara is also admiring Mark's face. "The medical honey sloughs off burned skin and allows new skin to grow. It'll be a little tender."

"How is it that honey works so well on Mark's face?"

"His face wasn't as badly burned as the rest of his body. It can also heal without skin grafts because there are so many blood vessels in the face compared to the rest of a person's body."

I'm still riveted. Steven and Mark both have laugh lines that fan from the outer corner of their eyes. But they're gone now on Mark's face. Everything looks so smooth.

Tara examines Mark's nose. "His nose structure looks good. Noses don't have much for blood vessels because they're made up of cartilage."

Mark's nose looks as normal as I remembered it before the plane crash.

"It's good that he didn't have much damage to his nose because it'd be difficult to restore it."

Tara also mentions that Mark's vitals look good. *Thank God.* She explains that during morning rounds, Dr. Williams noted that Mark needs more surgery to replace the xenografts and allografts on various parts of his body. They also need to prepare him for skin grafting.

"Wes!"

"Mom!"

"Your dad now looks younger than your Uncle Steven. He looks younger than *me*."

"Now, let's not get carried away. You are still younger than Dad and look it."

"Why, thank you, sir." I strike a mock Betty Boop pose, fluttering my eyelashes as best I can.

"Well, you're in a good mood."

"Yes, I am," I say with a smile. "Look at your dad's face. He looks amazing." I only hope the rest of him is healing too. It's hard to know what's happening underneath the layers of bandages he's wrapped in. The sudden flash of what's underneath is too terrible to bear. My throat constricts. I quickly switch off the picture in my mind. *Calm down, Jenny. Just turn the movie off.* I take a deep breath and stare intently at Mark's face. Nothing's going to spoil the exuberance I feel in this moment.

Seeing his new face reminds me of the Mark I knew when I first met him in New York. He was twenty-eight and I was twenty-four. We both worked at a small, entrepreneurial tech company on Long Island that recruited new college grads like us. It was the last place I expected to meet a guy who grew up on a dairy farm in Wisconsin. He was tall and rugged with gigantic Popeye calves and intelligent green eyes behind his round gold-rimmed glasses. A casual glance at him across a bar would suggest he was a more interesting version of William Hurt.

For someone who had grown up in a small midwestern town, Mark had an insatiable curiosity. His friends called him "the answer man." He was one of the smartest people I had ever met. In those years he was going through his angry young man phase, always the guy sitting in the back corner who the CEO probably dreaded, with his overtly challenging and provocative questions during all-hands meetings. Mark's irreverence, passion, and drive made me feel alive. He had a singular talent for fully savoring the moment. He was a good counterbalance to my tendency in my early years to obsessively plan for the future.

He would pick up a bucket of fried oysters and bottles of beer and invite me to dinner at a small beach near Nissequogue on a Wednesday after work. Mark had a line on all the best seafood shacks around town. Sitting elbow to elbow with him on a blanket, I would bite through the golden cornmeal crust and taste the creamy, salty pocket inside. We washed our oysters down with a cold beer, chatting nonstop while we enjoyed the glow of the orange-fading-to-pink Long Island summer sunset. Or he would call me on a Saturday for an impromptu laundromat lunch date, sharing a pizza next door while we waited for our laundry to dry. He was so good at creating fun in all the small things in life.

Mark had traveled and camped his way through Wyoming and Colorado on his motorcycle. He had slurped ramen at a Tokyo noodle stall as loudly as any polite Japanese mama-san would and had stayed out until closing time at every smoky bar in Greenwich Village.

As he got to know me, he liked me because he recognized a groundedness like the fixed center of a pendulum. The pendulum swung pretty far when my dad died suddenly in his sleep. He marveled that while I was devastated, I didn't fall apart. He thought I was smart and thoughtful, capable of a steady, true love—unlike his last girlfriend, who blew through his life like an emotional hurricane, leaving debris, wreckage, and sole custody of a forlorn orange tabby cat that she insisted on adopting but then abandoned, leaving it in Mark's care.

I needed to expand beyond the worldly background I came from. Mark was already rapidly flourishing outside the small-town life he grew up in. We were a good match, meeting in the middle of a trajectory headed in the same direction.

One evening we held each other while lying on the floor of my living room, my dark hair like ribbons cascading on his shoulder. He was talking quietly about his experience living in Tokyo. I reached out to touch his hair. It was slightly wavy, softer and finer than mine. The words he shared and his silky hair told me that he was a sensitive person underneath his rugged exterior. It was a combination I loved. I knew then that he was the one for me.

A technician walks into the room, interrupting my reverie. He talks to Tara about unhooking Mark from the kidney dialysis machine. I snap to attention.

Tara explains that Mark's doing well enough producing his own urine that he doesn't need the machine. That's good news.

When the technician wheels the machine out of Mark's room, a couple of unfamiliar hospital staff members walk in. They ask Wesley and me to leave for an hour because they need to change Mark's catheter and other tubing to keep things clean. Tara suggests that we move to the waiting room and she'll call us when they're done.

When we return to Mark's quarters, I notice that his temperature has risen two points. I ask Tara about it.

"That's normal when we take a patient off the dialysis machine," she explains. "The machine artificially lowers their temperature by around two points."

During the rest of the afternoon Mark's vitals start shifting around. One minute his blood pressure is fine; the next minute it suddenly decreases. Mark's respiratory rate is fine, then drops. His heart rate suddenly jumps twenty points and then falls back to normal. Tara gives him two packs of blood and adjusts Mark's meds to find different ways to stabilize him.

With his temperature spiking, the doctors order blood and bronchial cultures to assess if he has an infection. In their regular suctioning of his lungs, they noticed he has mucus in his left one. Tara explains that they'll have preliminary culture results within twelve hours.

Maybe he has pneumonia? Don't old people die of pneumonia? Mark's not that old but he's so vulnerable. I keep quiet with my questions because it's too scary to think about what it could mean.

We're back on the rollercoaster. We had been slowly ascending and making progress. These latest fluctuations feel as if we're on the edge of a small descent or maybe even a steeper one. Tara informs us that Dr. Williams wants Mark to go into surgery tomorrow for debridement and to continue replacing some of his grafts.

As Wesley and I leave for dinner, I'm preoccupied, hoping that Mark's condition stabilizes in time for the OR tomorrow.

With Mark's fluctuating vitals yesterday, I wake up early the next morning to catch the night shift nurses and ask how Mark did overnight. KC gets on the phone to tell me that Mark's vitals have been stable all night.

"We've had Mark on three general antibiotics until the lab results tell us exactly what type of infection he has. Once the doctors let us know, they'll put him on more targeted antibiotics."

I hope they can start skin grafting soon. The longer he's exposed without his own skin covering, the more susceptible he is to infection. The nurses confirmed that while xenografts and allografts help, they don't protect in the same way your own skin does.

Dear God, please get Mark's infection under control so we don't miss his skin-grafting surgery.

Someone, I can't remember who, told me that skin grafts have a limited shelf life. If you don't use them, you lose them. I feel a small tremor ripple through my body at the thought of them expiring.

Tara calls to let me know that Mark's scheduled for the OR at 2:00 p.m. Wesley's flight home is later today so he should be able to see Mark before he goes into surgery. Michelle, Mark's youngest sister, will be coming from New York tomorrow to visit for a few days.

When Tara calls again to let me know they're done with Mark's dressing change, Wesley rolls his suitcase to the foyer and we head for the hospital.

Tara and Alicia, the other day nurse, are bustling around getting Mark ready for the OR. But at 2:20 p.m., we're still waiting. In the meantime, Mark feels hot when I lightly touch his big forehead. His cheeks are flushed. His temperature reading shows 105.4 degrees. Tara explains that Mark's agitated because she's watching the respiratory machine and notices that he's breathing faster.

She doesn't want to give him Tylenol or ibuprofen because it will risk dangerously lowering his blood pressure during surgery. Instead, she gives him hydromorphone and puts him on higher pressure support to help him breathe more normally.

Will they actually take him into surgery with his temperature so high? I close my eyes, asking God to bring Mark's temperature down. When I used to drive the boys around when they were young, we would come to a stop at a red light and Wesley and Adrian would chant, "Turn green, turn green, turn green…." They would burst out in giggles and go back to repeating their chant. Inevitably the light would turn green, and they would triumphantly declare, "It worked, Mom!" I feel as if I'm chanting in the same way, only now it's for Mark's temperature to come down. *Come down, come down, come down….*

Because of the delay with Mark's surgery, Wesley has to leave now. It pains me to ask him to take an Uber. I always like to pick up and drop the boys off at the airport. Now that they're adults, as their mom, it's one of the few things I can still do for them. Even though there's not much for me to do in Mark's room, the last couple of days have taught me that things can change suddenly. I have to be here just in case.

I hug Wesley for a long time before reluctantly releasing him. I thank him for coming to celebrate his dad's birthday with us.

"Of course. I had to come to see you and Dad. And we will make that pecan pie for him next year."

"Yes. Yes, we will. And an apple pie too." I hang onto his solid, big arm, so much like Mark's. I appreciate his upbeat attitude, undoubtedly buoyed by the fun conversations with family and friends from the last couple days.

"I love you, Mom."

"Aww. I love you too." Everything's blurry. *What's happened to me?* Since I've come to Phoenix, my tears are always just below the surface.

I ask him to let me know when he's arrived home safely. Our little family never asked each other to check in when traveling because we never worried. I do now.

After Wesley leaves, Tara reports that Mark's surgery will be delayed till tomorrow because they're backed up in the OR today. A new patient arrived in the ER today by helicopter and requires emergency surgery.

I know it's out of everyone's control, but I'm so frustrated by the delay. I suddenly wish Wesley were still here. And gosh darn it, Adrian's in Zurich. There's no one to complain to, no one to commiserate with, no one to whom I can just say, *I get it that the patient from the helicopter has to go first, but why can't they fit Mark in today too?*

It suddenly occurs to me, however, that waiting until tomorrow gives time for Mark's body to lower its temperature and to be better ready for surgery tomorrow. I feel a little better.

I ask our online community to pray that Mark's temperature comes down.

That evening I realize that Wesley didn't text me that he arrived safely. I berate myself that I hadn't noticed earlier. He should have been home three hours ago. I text him now. He immediately replies, "*Yes, I did,*" with a thumbs-up emoji. It's going to take some time for our family to get used to this new practice.

Part 3

SURVIVAL

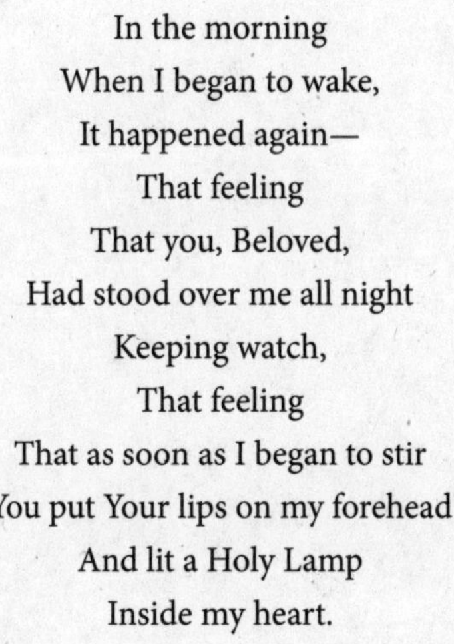

In the morning
When I began to wake,
It happened again—
That feeling
That you, Beloved,
Had stood over me all night
Keeping watch,
That feeling
That as soon as I began to stir
You put Your lips on my forehead
And lit a Holy Lamp
Inside my heart.

—Hafiz,
"Keeping Watch"

Chapter 14

CRISIS

When I arrive the next day, Tara lets me know that Mark's temperature has returned to normal. He's at 100.7 degrees. The attending doctor confirms from lab results that Mark has run-of-the-mill pneumonia but that his lungs look clear. They've started him on pneumonia-targeted antibiotics. Our ride on the rollercoaster has leveled out. I think. At least the pneumonia's treatable.

"Oh, and good news!" Tara says with a wide smile.

I look at her expectantly.

"Mark's skin grafts are scheduled to arrive from the Boston lab this Thursday."

"So they'll need to debride and get Mark ready for those grafts, right?"

"Yes."

"How many are due to arrive? I forgot."

"Ninety-four. They'll ship them out in a big refrigerated unit."

It astounds me that all of this can grow in a lab from a quarter-inch sliver of Mark's skin.

"Any word yet when Mark's scheduled for the OR today?"

Tara shakes her head.

The news about the skin grafts arriving makes me feel that we're about to begin an important race, a race to cover his body with his own skin, a race to fight infection, a race to pull him and me out of this whirlpool of a no man's land, where I'm never quite sure whether we're making progress from day to day.

I post on Lotsa Helping Hands—

Thank you again for your prayers because so far Mark continues to come out of his bad dips. Your love & support help keep me strong for him.

I pick up *The 5-Ingredient Italian Cookbook* and browse through the many recipes, trying to decide which one to read to Mark. *Spaghetti carbonara.* He would like that. It reminds me of our last visit to Rome. I wonder if they have a recipe for grilled portabella mushrooms like the delicious, smoky ones we enjoyed at a small street café in the old Trastevere neighborhood. It was a place full of narrow cobblestone streets by the Tiber River, teeming with small restaurants, tiny shops, and bars. Every new street you turned onto created the promise of discovering something delightful to see and taste. Fresh grilled mushrooms were just one of our many spontaneous discoveries together.

I can't find a portabella mushroom recipe or anything that grabs me today. *But wait—here's a recipe for lentil soup.* It's something Mark loves and has made from scratch. He always kept our pantry stocked with small woven sacks full of these little round, smooth lentils, a subtle kaleidoscope of pale green, beige, and brown.

"Mark, I'm going to read to you *minestra di lenticche*!" I proclaim loudly in Italian. It's a simple recipe, the way most Italian dishes are. It doesn't take me long to read it.

When I finish I'm tempted to read another one, but I want to pace myself so that we don't end up repeatedly reading the same recipes to Mark too soon. I think we're going to be at the Burn Center for a while. It feels deeply satisfying to curate and read one recipe at a time, to savor and relish it, the fresh ingredients, and to imagine the taste and the enjoyment of being with Mark, our family, and friends. He loved to tinker with new recipes when he cooked. By far, Mark was more creative than me in that way. I had to follow a recipe for a long time before I would venture to improvise.

Mark and I were so happy together before his plane crash. It sounds so cliché. Yet it was really that simple. Just as we explored Trastevere, we lived with the belief and promise of discovering wonderful life adventures around every corner—from feeling the cold snow on our faces skiing down the Sierra Nevada mountains near Lake Tahoe to buoyantly floating on our backs in the salty Mediterranean. Or at home, enjoying a conversation and simple meal on our deck in the golden dusk of a northern California summer. We talked of living in our favorite countries, three months in Japan and three months in Italy. I wanted to see the snow monkeys in Hokkaido. Mark wanted to hike the Dolomites.

While Mark started out with a natural curiosity and enthusiasm for life, over the years we created a secure foundation of love between us that gave us the confidence to step out in the world to live life to the fullest and to enjoy it all. Our lives weren't all rosy. We had experienced the loss of our parents earlier than most; we suffered from minor health ailments, and our careers weren't always easy. But we were about to retire, and we looked forward to the freedom our new life would bring.

And now, on the eve of our springing free, half of "us" is traumatically wounded. *How does someone who enjoyed such intense physicality lose so many parts of himself? How will he feel about himself when he wakes up? How will I feel? How will we feel about ourselves as a couple?* I have no clue. Life no longer makes sense.

We're going to get back to what we wanted, my beloved Mark. I promise. With a loud scrape, I pull up my chair closer to his bed and look intently at his face, willing him to hear my thoughts. His eyes are closed, and as always, he's silent and encased in his mummy body.

No matter how handicapped, you'll be my darling. I'll be by your side, helping us get back to living life as much as we can. I scrunch my nose to hold back the tide of oncoming tears. My eyes sting. *I only hope I can keep such a promise.*

I'm a mess, sniffling loudly, when Dr. Williams stops by, standing at the doorway. I grab some Kleenex, get up, and walk over to greet him. I'm sure he's used to seeing patients' families at their worst. He greets me back in his usual amiable, calm way.

"Given Mark's pneumonia, it's too risky for us to take Mark into surgery," he says in a gentle voice. "I've canceled his surgery for the day."

I feel as though someone has kicked me in the stomach, a sudden sharp pain. Seconds feel like very long minutes while what he says sinks in.

"So does that mean it could be days before he's ready to go into surgery?" I imagine pneumonia is serious stuff and Mark could need time to recover.

"We'll monitor and see how Mark's doing tomorrow."

While I understand why, it's so frustrating. *Can we press the fast-forward button and go straight to Mark's skin graft surgery?* If we could start putting his own skin on him, it would feel as though he were in recovery rather than being in this constant survival state.

"If we wait too long, will the skin grafts no longer be viable?" I ask, acutely aware of the use it or lose it possibility.

"We have a bit of time," he says while nodding with a faint smile.

I notice he doesn't tell me the expiration date. I would rather not know more precise facts. It would only add to my anxiety.

"It may take a few tries because the grafts don't always take the first few times."

Dr. Williams is trying to manage my expectations. It's okay. I understand why he has to do that as a doctor, but I'm determined to believe that the best-case scenario will prevail, that some of the grafts will "take" this first time around.

That evening I'm alone at the condo for the first time in a little over a week since Steven and his family left. And now Wesley. I heat up some leftover pasta for dinner and sauté some broccoli with olive oil, garlic, and a bit of salt. It's nice that dinner can be so simple. When I finish my meal, I tidy up the guest room, getting it ready for Michelle's visit. I read about Anita Moorjani, a woman with fourth-stage lymphoma who died on the operating table, only to come back to life and recover to full health. She's miraculously still healthy and in remission thirteen years later. Anita describes her near-death experience (NDE) of meeting her deceased father, who greets her with unconditional love, telling her to live fearlessly and to be true to herself. She realizes how much she's lived her life in fear of cancer and how far she's strayed from who she really is. Her story reminds me that miracles are possible. By nine-thirty I'm struggling to stay awake, so I turn in early. Tomorrow's another day. I've done all I can, which is not much because so much of today was out of our control.

It's another insufferably hot day when I arrive at the hospital, one of those July days in Phoenix when the streets shimmer from the heat as if the black asphalt is melting. Today's forecast high is 102 degrees. I dread getting out of my car because I can't find a parking spot close enough to the entrance and I hate the thought of walking through the immense parking lot under the sun's intensity. Today I remember to bring my umbrella, which I open immediately as I step out of my car. I always feel silly carrying an umbrella but I don't care. It's become my routine.

It's so good to see Michelle when I arrive in Mark's room. She took an Uber directly to the hospital after her flight from New York. Amazingly, they prioritized getting Mark into the OR this afternoon. We didn't see Dr. Williams, so I wasn't able to ask why he thought Mark was ready. Tara mentions that Dr. Hale is performing the surgery today. Dr. Williams has finished his three-week rotation with Mark, and Dr. Hale started today. I know him the least well of the three doctors even though he was the doctor who treated Mark when he was first admitted. In those early weeks it was Dr. Williams, as head of the Burn Center, who met with Steven and me.

Tara updates us, saying that Mark's labored breathing has eased up and he's breathing more normally. I'm relieved. It must be why the doctors are ready to take him into surgery.

Michelle and I are in the room when the surgery staff prepares Mark and takes him to the OR. They unhook him from the crowd of machines, put him on a manual ventilator, and roll him down the hall to the operating room. We're told that surgery should take around three hours. Dr. Williams will tell us after surgery what their skin graft approach will be.

While Michelle sits in the waiting room, I'm able to take a break to go run errands and get some personal things done. Bill payments need to be mailed. I run through my shopping list. A letter opener, file folders, and file stand from Staples. With Sue delivering my mail every week, I need to organize space in the condo for paying my bills. Then a CVS stop to pick up a supply of ibuprofen, toothpaste, a big bottle of lotion, and hair conditioner. My initial travel supplies ran out a while ago and I'm now realizing that I need to restock with larger sizes of everything. I think I'll be here for a while.

I'm at FedEx mailing something when Michelle texts me that the doctor came out of surgery and is looking for me. I look at my watch. It's been only two hours. *That was fast. Everything must've gone well.*

I text her to tell Dr. Hale I'm on my way to the hospital and will be there in twenty minutes.

When I arrive in the waiting room, I wave to Michelle and go straight to the intercom by the Burn Center entrance to let Larry know I've arrived and need to speak with Dr. Hale.

A doctor in blue scrubs enters the waiting room. He's shorter and more wiry than Dr. Williams and Dr. Jameson.

We make eye contact, and he recognizes me. Dr. Hale introduces himself to Michelle and me.

"How did everything go?" I ask.

"We did some debriding and replaced some of Mark's xenografts and allografts."

That was the plan. I feel impatient, waiting for Dr. Hale to explain where they prepped Mark for skin grafts.

"I'm afraid I have some bad news."

I have no idea what he could mean. *Is Mark not ready for grafts?*

"When we assessed Mark for grafts, we found evidence of a fungal infection on his arms."

"A fungal infection?"

"We've sent it out for lab testing and are waiting for the labs to corroborate."

"What's the treatment for a fungal infection?" When I think of fungal infections, athlete's foot is what comes to mind. You treat it with a little tube of cream.

"Fungal infections are very invasive, and the issue is that it can spread to Mark's internal organs."

Wow—it's much more serious than I realized. Michelle furrows her brow.

"The only method we have for treating a fungal infection is topical, but that won't help Mark if the infection spreads internally. Unfortunately, it's a medical limitation in that there's nothing to treat it internally."

"What are the chances that it'll spread internally?" I ask, a dull ache spreading in my temples. I'm rubbing my forehead slowly.

"It's pretty high. We're closely monitoring Mark for the next twenty-four hours. I need you to know that one viable option would be to amputate both his arms to above his elbows to prevent the spread of infection."

What? I let out a small gasp.

"It's not certain, but Mark could die in the next two to three days."

"How is that possible?" The blood in my head starts throbbing in my ears.

"If it spreads to his organs, his heart could stop, for example."

"Oh my God!" I put my hands over my face.

Michelle starts crying.

"You'll want to call your family and have them come in," Dr. Hale says in a gentle voice.

"When?"

"As soon as possible."

What? How did this happen?

"We treated his arms and much of his body with antifungal ointment. But I'm not sure it will contain the infection."

Michelle and I are quiet. There's nothing to say. We need to call our families.

"I'm really sorry," Dr. Hale says quietly. "We'll monitor Mark tonight and see if we need to take him into surgery tomorrow to assess again. If so, Dr. Lahari, who I don't think you've met, will be part of the surgical team."

"Okay," I whisper.

"Do you have any questions I can answer for you?"

I shake my head. "Do you, Michelle?"

"There are no other ways to treat it?" she asks with mournful eyes.

"Other than the ointment, I'm afraid not. Other infections can be treated internally. Fungal is one of the few exceptions."

We have nothing else to ask. Dr. Hale says again that they'll be monitoring Mark closely.

When he leaves, I collapse into a chair.

"Michelle, can you contact Steven, Rene, and Dee?" Dee is a cousin of Mark's that he's close to.

Michelle nods, her eyes red, her face blotchy.

"I'll contact Adrian, Wesley, my sister, Teresa, and Suzie." Adrian isn't due back from Zurich for another few weeks. I had anticipated that he would return to Phoenix for a wonderful update on his dad's first skin graft surgery. Instead, I have to message him that his dad might have his arms amputated and could die. I dread having to tell the boys anything but there's no time to digest the news before calling him and the rest of our families. Dr. Hale made it clear how urgent it was.

Michelle and I leave for the condo, where we'll contact everyone.

The rest of the day is a blur. All I care about is that Michelle has reached everyone in Mark's family. I message Adrian to call me when he wakes up. I don't have the heart to wake him up in the middle of the night. It's better for him to react to this terrible news after a decent night's sleep. I call Wesley, my sister Teresa, and my friend Suzie. Everyone except Adrian is working on travel plans.

I feel horrible springing a surprise like this when Wesley answers his phone with a cheerful "Hi, Mom."

"I have some bad news, Wes."

"Oh, no." His voice is flat with concern. I explain everything that Dr. Hale told Michelle and me, almost word for word. *Highly invasive fungal infection. It could spread. No way to treat it internally. Yes, it can spread internally, which could be fatal. They may have to amputate his arms if the infection spreads there.*

It's hard being unable to see the reaction on Wesley's face. *Is he covering his face with his hand? Is he frowning? Is he looking distressed?*

I can't linger on my call with Wesley because I still need to call Suzie and Teresa.

Wesley promises to catch the first flight he can find tomorrow morning.

Suzie has a lot of questions but very quickly lets me know she'll find a flight ASAP. Teresa as well. Bob will take over caring for their kids while she travels to Phoenix. Next I message Adrian to see if he's up yet and *"Can I call him now?"*

He's groggy when he picks up. It must be pretty early in Zurich. There's a long pause after I explain everything. I can tell he's trying to process what I'm saying while he's still waking up. He doesn't have many questions and, like Wesley, promises to look for a flight right away.

When there's nothing left to do, I post a long update on Lotsa Helping Hands. I tell everyone that Mark's not doing well and that their prayers are urgently needed.

> *Hi all, while his doctors are doing absolutely everything they can, I feel this is out of their control. It's really up to God and the universe to decide if Mark's going to make it or not.*
>
> *All you prayer warriors, please pray for that miracle because we sure need it now.*

I'm touched that a friend who's not religious has organized a round-the-clock prayer group for Mark among our Lotsa Helping Hands community. She firmly believes in the scientific benefits of prayer. She posts, "*We must do this for Mark.*"

I hear back from Wesley with his flight information for tomorrow.

Later in the day, one of the nurses calls to let me know that Mark is scheduled for surgery first thing tomorrow morning at eight o'clock. Dr. Hale wants to continue to assess if the fungal infection has spread further on his body.

Over our takeout dinner from Whole Foods, my mind is blank. There's a buzzing in my head like an electric current. I'm antsy.

"I can't believe this is happening."

Michelle nods and sighs heavily. "Where do you think the fungal infection came from?"

"I don't know. Mark always had sensitive skin. I guess we should ask Dr. Hale."

That night when I get ready for bed, I'm worried that I won't be able to sleep tonight. Sure enough, I wake up at around 3:45 a.m.

Mark has a fungal infection.

I power up my phone and Google *fungal infection, burn patients*. I read *large wound area, impaired immune defense, candida, aspergillus, incidence rates of 6.3 percent to 15 percent, important emerging causes of late onset morbidity*. The more articles I read the more anxious I get, both about Mark and about not being able to get back to sleep. It's a vicious cycle.

I switch to my ocean waves sleep meditation app. I desperately need help going back to sleep or I'll be a mess tomorrow. I can't afford to be in a daze. Eventually I nod off to the rhythmic sounds of the ocean inhaling and exhaling itself on the sand swooshing in and out. I'm up again at five, wide awake. There's no point lying in bed tossing and turning. I get up and start making coffee.

Chapter 15

THE FAMILY ARRIVES

Michelle and I skip our showers and drive to the Burn Center early in the morning to catch Mark before they take him to the OR. Once they've wheeled him into surgery, we drive back to the condo to eat breakfast. I work out at the fitness center as I do every day. Getting on the elliptical machine is the only time since I've come to Phoenix when life feels normal. Just thirty minutes. It's all the time I need to turn my mind off. I've come to count on it every day. When I get back to the condo, Michelle's showered and sitting in the living room, checking her Instagram where she posts her paintings.

"What do you think, Michelle? Should we eat lunch here or at the hospital?"

"Do you know when Mark will come out of surgery?" She's frowning.

"I don't know."

Michelle's face looks worn out. I notice the furrow lines on her forehead. When did those lines become permanent? Were they there before, or only since Mark had his plane crash? I'm not sure anymore, but seeing the effect on her makes me feel heavy inside.

Uncertain how long Mark will be in the OR, Michelle and I decide we'll eat lunch at the hospital so we don't miss Dr. Hale or Dr. Lahari whenever they finish with Mark.

After lunch, a determined-looking woman doctor emerges from the Burn Center entrance and walks purposefully toward us.

I glance quickly at my watch. It's been four-and-a-half hours.

"You must be Jenny, Mark's wife?"

I nod.

"I'm Dr. Lahari. I operated on your husband with Dr. Hale. Dr. Hale had to go straight to another surgery."

"How did it go?" I ask right away.

"We excised quite a bit of dead tissue from Mark's arms from what we saw yesterday."

"How did Mark get this fungal infection?" I ask.

"It's really less a question of how Mark got the infection and more a reflection that his immune system is weak. Normally we have fungus on our skin all over our body."

"Is there anything else you can do for the infection?"

"Dr. Hale may have already mentioned that we put antifungal medication on him topically. In a healthy patient it's a challenge to resolve a fungal infection. In Mark's case, the best-case scenario is that the medication will slow down the spread of the infection."

It only slows it down. It won't stop it. Really?

"It's likely the fungal infection was already in Mark's system for a while before it showed up on his arms."

That doesn't tell me anything useful. I look at Michelle, who's sitting next to me with a pinched face. This is all so difficult for her too. She and Mark are close because, of all their siblings, Mark understood and supported her the most in her move to pursue her art interests in New York.

"The good news is that Mark's lungs are surprisingly healthy and functioning well."

"Oh. In spite of his lung infection?" I had almost forgotten about his pneumonia. That felt like such a long time ago.

Dr. Lahari nods.

"So what's next?"

"We'll continue to closely monitor Mark. Dr. Hale is who you should speak with as Mark's primary doctor in the next three weeks."

After Dr. Lahari leaves, I sink back in my chair and look at Michelle. She looks back at me. We have no words between us in the moment. We're both digesting everything.

"So it means Mark may not get over the fungal infection, right?" Michelle asks.

I nod. I suddenly feel tired and cover my face with my hands. It feels good to gently massage my face.

When I drop my hands and open my eyes, I blink. Dr. Williams is standing in front of us.

"I contacted our palliative care team to schedule a meeting with you tomorrow to identify the range of possible scenarios for Mark," he says in a kindly way. He sits down next to us. "It's to help you and your family prepare for each possibility should it happen."

"What exactly is the role of a palliative care team?" I have no idea what Dr. Williams is referring to.

"They're a team that helps ensure that Mark is comfortable in whatever medical scenario he's in. They're also here to help support the family practically and emotionally in the decisions you may have to make about Mark's care and how to create the quality of life you want for Mark."

"Okay. That sounds good." Someone else is speaking and not me. Things are moving so fast.

"Dr. Hale and I, along with the medical team caring for Mark, want to meet with you and your family tomorrow to discuss Mark's condition."

I nod. "Okay. I'll let our family know."

"I'll try to schedule it for one-thirty tomorrow afternoon since I know your family needs time to travel in. We'll confirm the location for the meeting tomorrow."

I nod. I'll have to check with Michelle to make sure everyone can get here in time.

When Dr. Williams leaves, I ask Michelle when everyone will be showing up. I notice that I have already received a text from the palliative care team wanting to know if they can meet with our family tomorrow morning.

Adrian had called me with a lot of questions yesterday during one of his stopovers. He must have been ruminating and thought up questions during his flights.

"Is this really bad for Dad?"

I feel queasy. "Yeah, it's not good. They have limited options for treating a fungal infection." We both don't say what we're thinking.

The worst thing about all this is having to tell the boys bad news again. As a mother, I want to protect them. They've had happy, stable childhoods and I hate that life has interjected tragedy into their young adult lives.

Michelle interrupts my thoughts to let me know that everyone should be getting in this afternoon with Teresa, my sister, and Adrian arriving very late tonight.

"I'm going to try to stay overnight with Mark in his room," I tell her.

"I can take an Uber back to the condo so you have the car," she replies.

"That'd be great. I just need to be with Mark tonight."

Michelle nods.

Mark's sister Rene and his brother, Steven, show up in the late afternoon. Rene and Steven have a lot of questions when they arrive in the waiting room. I let Michelle explain everything because I'm exhausted. Suzie arrives and sweeps into the waiting room and gives me a big hug.

"I'm so sorry," she says simply. *There's nothing more to say*. It's so good to see her.

"Is there anything I can do to help right now?"

I shake my head, mute. I tell her I'm going to spend the night with Mark.

She lingers a minute longer, looking at me with gentle concern, then gets up to say hi to Rene, Steven, and Michelle.

I ask our online community to pray for Mark in a targeted way, to pray that the antifungal medicine cuts him enough of a break so that his immune system can kick back into gear. I explain that we still need to talk with Dr. Hale about the next steps but that my guess is they'll monitor Mark until tomorrow morning, when most likely they'll assess him again in the OR.

I don't feel like going out to dinner with everyone, but I decide I should attempt to eat some food to sustain myself through what could be a long night of sleeping in Mark's room. The group decides to go to The Macintosh, an American restaurant near our condo. Suzie graciously offers to pick up Adrian and Teresa from the airport that evening.

The mood at dinner is somber. We're not sure how it will go tomorrow, not only in the meetings we have but more importantly, what will happen to Mark.

We return to the Burn Center, where they will allow only three people in Mark's room at a time. The official policy is two visitors at a time but because they know Mark's family is from out of town, they're kind enough to bend the rules. Teresa, my sister, arrives from LA.

"I'm so, so sorry, Jenny," she says, hugging me, her dark eyes soft. "This is so awful. Bob and I are praying around the clock for Mark. Is he suffering?"

"I really don't know. I haven't seen him since he got out of surgery."

Teresa doesn't say anything. She looks at me with pity. It's weird but I can't remember the last time someone looked at me that way.

Each trio doesn't stay long. Mark, coming out of surgery, needs his rest. When everyone's had a chance to see Mark, they coordinate rides back to their respective hotels.

I hear back from the palliative care team that they can meet with us at eleven tomorrow morning. Good—it'll be right before our meeting with the doctors.

I welcome the quiet in Mark's room after everyone leaves. Chloe, one of the younger travel nurses from Arkansas, is there with Emily, also a younger nurse on staff, with wavy, dark hair. Chloe is friendly and talkative; Emily is kind, but more reserved.

They are very attentive to Mark, which I appreciate. Chloe's brother is joining the Marines, and we chat about that for a while. It's a good distraction.

Sometime around nine o'clock I'm talked out. Chloe and Emily are at their workstations just outside the room. Mark and I have the room to ourselves. I pull up a chair close to Mark and look at him. I stare at his face, which is looking healthy and healed. The back of his head is still swathed in white bandages and his entire body too. Below the waist you can now see where the blanket drops off below his thighs. I only now realize it may have been a shock for everyone to see Mark in his amputated state.

I wonder if he'll ever wake up.

"Mark, it's between you and God now." I'm swept up in a sudden conviction about this even though he was never sure God existed. "You and God need to discuss what happens next."

Can he hear me? I desperately hope so.

"The doctors are doing all that they can—but at the end of the day, it's between you and God."

Emily steps in to check Mark's blood pressure reading. She writes it down and steps back out.

I resume my urgent chat with Mark.

"Mark, do you want to live? If you do, please talk to God. *Please*. You need to fight this thing. The boys and I love you."

I close my eyes. *Dear God, please talk with Mark. It's between the two of you.*

There's nothing more to say. Fatigue sets in and Chloe helps me drag in from the hallway a couple of larger cushioned chairs, placed together for me to stretch out and sleep.

They dim the lights and bring me a pillow and blanket. I close my eyes and try to drift off. The hum of the machines surrounding Mark is a familiar and welcome sound. But his condition requires that the room be kept warm, and I toss and turn for an hour. The room's a sauna. This isn't going to work. I never could sleep in an overly heated room. At home Mark kept our bedroom windows open in summer, fall, winter, spring. By 10:30 p.m., I give up. I'll be in a stupor tomorrow if I don't return to the condo and get a decent night's sleep. I have to be "on" for the meetings tomorrow.

I tell Chloe and Emily that I need to go home to sleep and thank them for helping me with my makeshift bed. Before I leave, I linger briefly by Mark's bedside. In the glow of the monitors surrounding him, I say softly to him, "Sweetie, I hope you know how much I love you. Don't forget what we talked about."

I stare at him. Mark looks almost angelic tonight. The night light by his bed is a soft glow shining on his newly healed face. The rest of him is shrouded in white.

"Good night, my love." I want to kiss his face but I'm afraid I might pass on bacteria to him by touching his cheeks with my lips. I hold back and instead imagine kissing his face before I leave for the night.

Chapter 16

THE BIG MEETING

The next morning, I'm up early. I had no problem falling asleep, but I had a restless night. I kept waking up, my mind racing. All I could think about was *Mark's got a serious fungal infection*. I was trapped in a mental cul-de-sac. When I'm fully awake at five-thirty, I don't try to fight it. I climb out of bed. It's still dark out. I call the Burn Center to check in. Tara greets me in her usual perky, smart way and tells me that Mark's hemoglobin is a bit low so they're going to give him some blood. Mark's continuing to receive three antibiotics to treat his pneumonia. According to Chloe and Emily's handoff to Tara that morning, he was reasonably stable through the night. *Good*. I feel an immediate wave of relief.

Adrian's up and making coffee. He never drinks coffee unless he needs it to stay awake. I give him a good-morning hug, holding on just a second longer. We're a family of huggers, all guys, including our tuxedo cat, Mario, and me, the only woman. I smell the faint citrus smell of Adrian's hair gel. He looks tired. It was a long journey from Zurich to Phoenix. I imagine the contrast of leaving a city of charming Gothic-spired clock towers along Lake Zurich with the Alps in the background, to arrive within twenty-four hours in a city of mirrored high-rises and barren, rocky mountains.

Wesley has showered already and is scrolling through his iPad, always on call as a moderator for his Discord group. He's sighing loudly and grumbling to himself about intervening over inappropriate posts this morning, but I ignore him. I don't need any additional stress given what's coming today.

The two palliative care counselors, Lisa and Janice, arrive at the center and our family is ushered into a conference room. Sitting around the table, I count eight family members. It feels good to have strength in numbers and to have our family show up to support Mark. Lisa begins by explaining to us what palliative care is. She tells us that they're here to be a resource to our family to ensure Mark is comfortable and has the best quality of life he can have.

"There may be a series of decisions you'll need to make," Lisa says, pointedly looking at me. "We're here to help support you."

"We always coordinate with the doctors and medical team," Janice adds quietly. "We'll be in constant communication with Dr. Williams, so Lisa and I will stay updated on Mark's condition."

Steven and Rene both have questions. I'm lost in my own thoughts and not fully paying attention to the discussion. I catch the tail end of their conversation about potential arm amputations. *Are there resources other than the Burn Center doctors for prosthetics?* Rene is asking. Janice is responding but I lose track of the different organizations expert in prosthetics that she mentions.

I hope they don't have to amputate Mark's arms. The idea frightens me. *What quality of life would that be for him?* It would be terrible. I feel a surge of anger when I think of the plane. It's the reason we're here at the Burn Center. I want so badly to scream. I want someone to tell me, *You're right, Jenny. It's unfair and cruel how this happened to Mark.* Someone—I can't see who because everything's blurry—pushes a box of Kleenexes on the table over to me. I feel a hand lightly touching my back. It must be Adrian, who's sitting next to me.

The meeting is short. There are no decisions to make. Yet. This is just an informational meeting.

Lisa and Janice end the meeting by mentioning that they'll be reaching out to us regularly.

At lunch I can barely taste my food, and while I wait for everyone to finish eating, I Google *palliative care.* A lot of results pop up. *Serious illness. Personalized care beyond curative treatments. Address physical, mental, spiritual, and social needs. Whole-person care. Quality of life. Hospice.*

Hospice.

My mind stops as if it's hit a wall. I know what hospice is. My mother's oncologist referred us to hospice in the last two months of her life.

She had stage four ovarian cancer and was wonderfully attended to at home by an oncology hospice nurse before she died. The cancer killed her within nine months, from diagnosis to when it spread to her liver.

After lunch, we head to the sixth floor of the main hospital building for our meeting. It's the first time I've gone beyond the ER and the Burn Center.

At the meeting, Dr. Williams takes the lead. He summarizes what we know already, that the fungal infection is highly invasive, with limited treatment options.

"There are three potential scenarios for Mark. The first one is that Mark takes a turn for the better. Of course, this is what we hope for. The second scenario is that the fungal infection spreads. If that happens, we may need to amputate his arms above the elbows."

I feel lightheaded.

"If we have to amputate, it could mean a downward spiral," Dr. Hale adds.

"Should that be the case, our focus would be to make Mark as comfortable as possible before the inevitable happens," Dr. Williams explains in a gentle voice.

"What's the third scenario?" Steven asks.

"A vital organ like Mark's heart fails suddenly and he dies."

I can hear Teresa, next to me, take a sharp intake of breath.

"What causes that?" Steven asks.

"The fungal infection can spread internally and affect the organs," Dr. Williams replies.

"I see," Steven responds, nodding with a frown.

"As I mentioned earlier, there is no medication to address the infection internally," Dr. Williams mentions. "We're limited in what we can do on the treatment side."

Dr. Williams looks at me. "We need to know—do you want us to save Mark's life whatever happens to him?"

What does that mean? I don't understand the *whatever happens to him* part.

"For example, if the infection spreads to Mark's arms and we need to amputate above his elbows, do you believe he will feel that his life is worth living?"

A quick succession of thoughts race through my mind. Losing his arms would be horrible for Mark. He would be so limited. But he would want to see the boys, to be a dad and to continue being a part of their lives. He wouldn't want to miss out on that.

"Yes." I feel all eyes on me.

"Mark would want to live in spite of further restrictions. Please do everything you can to save his life." I feel certain of this. "Yes, he would want to live."

Dr. Williams and Dr. Hale both nod.

"We'll have to see how the infection takes its course," Dr. Hale says. "Whether Mark improves or declines."

"How long will it take before we know?" I ask. "How long should our family stay?"

"The next few days. Through the weekend," Dr. Williams answers.

It's Thursday.

"Mark's done extremely well for a burn patient his age and given the extent of his burns," Dr. Williams states. "I'm afraid this fungal infection is a huge setback."

"We'll go into the OR again today to assess how Mark's doing. We'll continue to excise anything that looks infected," Dr. Hale says.

It's quiet in the room. No one says anything. We're all privately processing all that's been said.

"I know Mark was supposed to receive skin grafts. So is that wasted now?" I ask.

"Let's wait and see," Dr. Williams replies, his eyes sympathetic. "The issue with skin grafts is that when Mark's sick with the fungal infection, his blood pressure decreases. This happens because the blood leaves different parts of his body to increase support to his vital organs. The loss of blood flow creates a condition that makes it difficult to support skin grafts."

"We *are* in the eye of the storm," Dr. Hale says.

If I didn't fully appreciate the gravity of what Dr. Williams is trying to convey to us before, I get it now. Dr. Hale has made that very clear. There's so much at stake for Mark. It's life or death.

Back at the Burn Center, Adrian, Wesley, and I greet Mark when we arrive in his room. Tara's bustling about. We watch her bring in fresh pint bags of blood to give to Mark. They're in thick plastic bags that make a heavy, slapping sound when she drops them onto the stainless-steel table by the supply cabinet.

Mark's face looks paler than his naturally ruddy complexion, and when I mention this to Tara, she says it's because his blood pressure is low.

It distresses me to know we're seeing evidence of what Dr. Williams said earlier, that his blood supply has dispersed throughout his body to protect his vital organs in response to the fungal infection.

"Boys, I want you to know I've told your dad it's between him and God now. Does he want to live? It's up to him. It's out of our hands, the doctors included."

Wesley and Adrian both nod. I have no idea if they believe in God. They grew up going to church. When they turned eighteen, Mark and I told them it was their choice if they wanted to continue attending.

Wesley crosses the room and gives me a big hug. As always, being wrapped up in his big arms and chest gives me such comfort, as if I'm hugging Mark. Rock solid. My entire body melts into his and I relax for a brief moment.

Sometimes a hug like that is all you can offer when nothing's going well and words aren't enough.

I post an update on Lotsa Helping Hands and end it with these words:

> *We are praying for Mark's life and the doctors are closely monitoring his condition these next couple days. Everyone, we are incredibly grateful for your prayers and sending positive healing energy to Mark. He is in the eye of the storm and we are fervently praying for him to make it through safely.*

Chapter 17

VOICES

I'm up at six in the morning to check on how Mark's doing because I'm on edge after our meeting with the doctors yesterday, wondering how fast the fungal infection could spread. I wait until 7:30 a.m. to call Tara, giving her a bit of time to settle into her shift after the handoff from the night nurses. There's a window of time to find out the day's plan—after the day shift nurses start but before they begin Mark's dressing change.

I shiver at the picture in my mind of what I've heard goes on during the procedure. As the nurses have described it, they have to heat up the room because burn patients have poor temperature regulation when so much of their skin is gone. Because they take off his bandages, he runs the risk of cooling down too fast, so they really crank up all the heat lamps that surround him. Undressing, adding whatever ointment they need for infection prevention, and re-bandaging Mark with fresh dressings is painstaking work. It can take up to three hours, they told me. They always give Mark increased sedatives to keep him comfortable and unable to feel the pain of being moved around and unwrapped, then wrapped again. The nurses are dripping wet with sweat when they're done and have to change into a fresh set of scrubs. They do two dressing changes every twenty-four hours—one during night shift, one during day shift. It's critical to keeping infections at bay.

When I call the Burn Center, Larry puts me through to Tara right away.

"Good news, Jenny. Mark's come off his medication for arrhythmia." I can hear the smile in her voice.

"He had arrhythmia?" I didn't know. I knew he had low blood pressure. I had been writing in my journal. Pen in hand, I'm clicking the ballpoint on and off, on and off.

"Yeah. They also reduced Mark's blood pressure meds last night."

According to the doctors, blood pressure meds divert blood flow that needs to circulate to protect Mark's organs from fungal infection.

"Mark's temperature's normal at 99.5 degrees," Tara adds.

It's a bright spot, however small. It's like the Whac-A-Mole game at the arcade. Just when one symptom stabilizes, another shows up.

Although we can't visit Mark until noon, after his dressing change is completed, our extended family decides to meet up in the waiting room by mid-morning. I scan the room, now mostly filled with our family: Steven, Mark's brother, and his wife, Kim, who traveled from Michigan; Rene, Mark's younger sister, who had come in from her small town in Illinois; Michelle, his youngest sister, who flew in from New York. My sister, Teresa, is here from LA. Suzie, one of our best friends and the boys' godmother, came from Denver. And of course, Wesley and Adrian. I've stopped paying attention to their individual conversations with each other, caught up in my own private world where all that matters is what's happening to Mark.

I excuse myself to go to the ladies' room. While I'm washing my hands, I suddenly hear a quiet but firm voice.

"Mark will be fine."

What? Did I really just hear that? I close my eyes to quiet the thoughts in my mind so I can focus and pay attention.

"Mark will be fine."

There it is again. I know I heard it. I open my eyes and stare in the mirror at myself. The skin under my eyes looks puffy, my face tired-looking, but I feel mentally alert.

"Don't worry. Don't doubt."

It's some kind of message or reassurance. *But from who? God? The universe? My intuition?* I don't really know. But I know for certain I heard it. It was brief and emphatic.

As I dry my hands and emerge from the restroom, I'm suddenly scared. I'm not going to tell anyone. What if I'm wrong and I'm hallucinating? I linger in the hallway outside wondering what just happened. My legs feel shaky. I lean up against the wall for support. Closing my eyes, I take a deep breath. My breath feels jagged. *Be calm, Jenny. It's okay.* I breathe again, willing myself to stop any mental chatter. I've always had a monkey mind. After a few more breaths, I feel calmer. I'm ready to go back into the waiting room.

Not long after I'm back in the waiting room, Dr. Lahari shows up looking for me. Adrian and Wesley crowd around us with everyone else hovering close by to catch as much of our discussion as they can.

"So—we removed more infected tissue from Mark's arms yesterday."

"Was there a lot?"

"There was still some."

"Is there any sign that the fungal infection has spread?"

"It's hard to say. I didn't see evidence that it's spread but it can advance very quickly. Just because we didn't see it in other parts of his body doesn't mean it might not spread by tomorrow, for example."

"Will you go into the OR again to assess tomorrow?"

"Dr. Hale will decide. We'll discuss next steps for Mark later today or tomorrow morning. For now, Mark needs a day of rest and recovery."

That makes sense. I suddenly remember that he's also still fighting pneumonia even though Tara didn't mention it on the phone earlier. There's just too much. Mark also has low blood pressure from the infection and arrhythmia. My head's about to explode.

"We also attached skin grafts to Mark's front torso."

I'm surprised. "I thought he doesn't have enough focused blood supply to support that."

"We didn't want to waste the skin grafts that came in. We attached them without the substrate layer. We'll see if the skin grafts take."

I don't have any questions, nor does anyone else. I don't know what the substrate layer is, but I don't ask. I'm overwhelmed. It's enough to know that, to the best of their knowledge, the infection hasn't spread further for now. I thank Dr. Lahari before she returns to the Burn Center.

When Wesley, Adrian, and I get into the room to see Mark, I notice that his face looks better than yesterday. He's gotten some color back.

"Dad's wrinkles *really* are all gone," Wesley announces abruptly as he stands at Mark's bedside, staring at his face. I realize even though he saw the first sign of Mark's smooth face on his birthday, it's still a startling contrast to his image of his fifty-nine-year-old dad.

"Pretty amazing, huh? He looks better than all of us older people." I surprise myself with a sudden chuckle. It's a bright spot that we can hang onto. It's small, but it's something. It's crazy to think that his face has the pink glow of good health while underneath his pristine white bandages, pneumonia and a fungal infection are waging war with his body.

I ask Tara if Mark is still on antibiotics for the pneumonia. She says yes, that he's only halfway through his treatment.

The rest of the afternoon passes uneventfully while we take turns visiting Mark.

Toward the end of the day Dr. Lahari stops by the waiting room to inform us that Mark's scheduled to go into the OR again tomorrow morning at eleven-thirty. They want to continue to assess his condition and aggressively do what's needed to prevent and contain the fungal infection.

The next morning I call the Burn Center to see if one of the day shift nurses can update me on what the plan is for Mark. Tara wrapped up the last of her three-day stint yesterday, so I'm waiting to find out who's with Mark for the rest of the weekend. I recognize Lindsey's calm voice when Larry puts me through to Mark's room. I'm glad she'll be with us for the next few days.

Around eleven o'clock Dr. Lahari shows up to explain that they will assess Mark's back in surgery today. Again, excising any infected tissue is the priority. Around noontime Tara lets me know that the OR team is getting Mark ready for surgery. Rene, Steven, and I head into his room as they do the now-familiar preparation. Two technicians, a man and a woman in scrubs, are quickly unhooking all the monitors. They move around with such efficiency and focus that it's obvious they could do this in their sleep.

"Hey, Rene—let's walk with Mark to the surgery room!" Steven calls out to Rene. They have to move fast as the OR staff starts pushing Mark's bed out the door. Rene quickly nods and the two of them step out of the room to follow Mark lying in his gurney. I stand back watching from the doorway.

Suddenly I hear Rene and Steven singing loudly. *Oh, wow. What are they singing?* With a start, I realize they're singing the University of Wisconsin Badgers fight song.

Mark is a passionate UW-Madison football fan. My memory of their games brings back vivid images: the sea of red shirts and hats in the Badger stadium, ending their fight song with a deafening stomping of the bleachers and the roar of more than eighty thousand voices shouting in unison.

I hope this song will rouse the fighter in Mark, that Rene and Steven's clear voices will break through the murky coma he's in, stranded on an island buried in a thick layer of fog that obscures sight and sound. He needs to fight this terrible infection, to fight to live, to fight to come back to all of us, his family. It briefly buoys my spirit to see his brother and sister cheering him on.

And now the wait. Always waiting. Waiting for his dressing change. Waiting for the OR. Waiting for an update from the doctor. Waiting for his blood pressure to come down.

A few hours later, Dr. Lahari emerges from the Burn Center entrance. I stand up quickly and walk toward her.

"How'd everything go?" I ask. Something flutters in my chest. I'm afraid of what she'll tell me.

Dr. Lahari fixes her serious and intense gaze at me. "We removed some fungal-infected tissue from Mark's back today. It's not clear if the infection spread to his back recently or whether it's been there for a few days."

"Why's that?"

"When we removed the infected tissue from his arms, we didn't have visibility to his back at the time. The antifungal medication works through the bloodstream so we hope it will prevent the infection from spreading to the most susceptible organs—his liver, kidneys, and eyes."

Hope. It's all we have.

"Unfortunately, the medication can't address infected tissue. That's why we have to aggressively remove it wherever we find it."

"I see."

"It's a wait-and-see situation. We're monitoring Mark daily."

"When can we go in to see Mark?" I ask, conscious that so many in our family are here.

"It's unlikely you'll see him the rest of the day," she replies. "He'll need an hour for the nurses to comfortably settle him back in his room. Then he'll need four to five hours to air out the skin grafts we put on his front torso yesterday."

There's nothing more to discuss. I thank Dr. Lahari. As she walks back to the Burn Center entrance, I turn to update our family.

When Adrian, Wesley, and I return to the condo, I notice that the sky's getting dark earlier than usual. I perch myself in front of the living room balcony. Suddenly the wind picks up and a spark of jagged white light streaks across the dark sky. Wesley and Adrian gather around me looking out the French doors. There's no rain, just strong winds whipping the palm trees and bushes in our complex. Palm fronds and small dry leaves skitter on the ground and furiously swirl in the air in some kind of mad dance. Then suddenly the rain shows up, but it's a mix of rain and dust blowing in the wind. We've never seen a swirling storm like this before. It's not the gentle rain showers of Hawaii, where my mom lived. It's not the steady downpour of a northern California winter. It reminds me how what I'm going through with Mark here in Phoenix feels strange and surreal at times.

The storm continues for some time. Wesley Googles and tells us that these storms can last quite a few hours. At some point we stop watching and settle back on the couch. Heavy drops fall on my lap as my dress catches my tears. My skirt is blotchy. I can't help it. I look up, the view blurry. No one's noticed. Adrian and Wesley are heads-down on their laptop and iPad. I sniffle loudly and grab some Kleenexes, wiping my face.

So many thoughts are flying through my brain. *Why did this happen?* Asking this question is like standing on the edge of a bottomless dark pit. The rocks and dirt are coming loose under my feet—I'm about to lose my footing. If I fall, I won't be able to climb back up. *Stop. Now.* I climb back, away from the hole, and walk away. *I simply cannot and will not torture myself with this question.*

Mark, the agnostic, never needed a reason for everything. He believed in the randomness of life. I was somewhere in between. I believe there can be coincidences and I also believe there can be reasons.

The bedraggled palm trees outside the balcony make me think of Kona, where my mom lived. I remember something Mark said to me many years ago. Before Mom passed away, she had requested that she be cremated, her ashes scattered in the Pacific Ocean off the coast of her beloved Hawaii.

To honor her wishes, her second husband, Sebastian, along with Mark, five-year-old Wesley, and I jetted out on a boat off the coast of Kona with their minister. We left Adrian with a babysitter since he was too young. The boat captain stopped at a scenic spot a few miles off the coastline.

It was a beautiful, clear blue day. The sun was shining, and the breeze was warm and soft. The boat gently rocked to the rhythm of small waves. The turquoise ocean surrounded us, the air caressingly warm and not too hot yet, since it was still morning. The minister stood up and gave a brief blessing. I was supposed to take the urn and pour Mom's ashes into the ocean. In a sudden burst of emotion, I started crying, heaving so hard that I couldn't bring myself to do the job. Instead, I blindly shoved the urn into Mark's lap and asked him to do it. I don't remember much of what happened next. At some point after my mom's ashes were scattered, the captain guided our boat back to the harbor. Nobody said anything the entire trip back to shore.

Some years later, out of nowhere, Mark asked if I remembered that time we were out on the boat with my mom's ashes.

I looked up from the book I was reading. "Yeah?"

"Remember how you were crying and asked me to scatter her ashes for you?"

I put my book down. "Yes, I do."

"I poured her ashes into the ocean."

"Uh-huh." He had my full attention now. I'm not sure where he was going. It was such a long time ago.

"Well, I thought her ashes would drop and disappear downward into the ocean. Instead, they fanned out across a large space in the ocean," he gestured with his hands, demonstrating how the ashes spread out wide. "It was glistening and sparkling."

I stared at the thoughtful look in Mark's eyes. They looked greener and clearer than usual.

"It was like her spirit was returning to the ocean," he said quietly.

"Wow, Mark. Really?" I was trying to imagine it on that bright, sunny day out on the water. This story was unusual coming from Mark, the materialist.

"I suppose the sparkles may have been the bits of bone glistening in the sun," he said, his scientific training kicking in for a logical explanation. But I could tell from the faraway look in his eyes that he still wondered what happened out there in the ocean.

I think of that conversation now.

Chapter 18

MUSIC AND SYNCHRONICITIES

Wesley, Adrian, and I are back in Mark's room early Saturday morning to see him off to the OR. Again.

Tara has finished her three-day shift, and it's Lindsey who lets me know that Mark's in stable condition. *Great.* His blood pressure is holding up with medication and his kidneys are getting good support from the dialysis machine. The plan is for the doctors to continue to do more debridement of Mark's back. They want to continue their relentless efforts to remove all traces of fungal-infected tissue.

When we're back in the waiting room, I hear that internal voice again. *Mark will be fine. Don't be afraid. Don't doubt.*

I marvel at how loudly and clearly I hear the message. This time I think a bit more about it, particularly *Don't doubt*. I declare to myself that I won't doubt and that Mark *will* be fine.

As the morning stretches on, one by one various family members show up in the waiting room. Teresa, my sister, has to go home to Southern California this morning. She stops by to say a quick prayer for Mark in his room before heading to the airport. Everyone else is still here. It's been so helpful to have Adrian here with me day in and day out. He's taken a leave from classes at ETH for the rest of the semester so that he can spend time with Mark and me. Wesley needs to return home tomorrow to continue his job search. Unlike his brother, he struggles more with sitting around unable to interact with his dad, unsure of what to do because there really is nothing to do.

I call the nurses late that morning to get a status update. Lindsey picks up and tells me that Mark's out of surgery and they're settling him in. They estimate it'll be another hour before he'll be ready for visitors.

When Adrian and I get into Mark's room, we notice he's still hooked up to the kidney dialysis machine. Lindsey reports that his heart rate is good, no arrhythmia, and that they lowered his blood pressure meds.

"What did they do in surgery today?" It can't be too bad if Dr. Lahari didn't come looking for me after the OR.

"I think they removed more infected tissue from Mark's back. He had a small area on his back that started bleeding after surgery," Lindsey says.

I cringe when she says "bleeding."

"They soaked his back with Epi Wash to stop the bleeding."

"Epi? What's that?"

"Oh, sorry. Epinephrine."

"Adrian, can you turn on Dad's meditation music?"

Adrian is already a step ahead of me, fiddling with the music player. He knows meditation music is for when his dad is under stress.

I reach up above the supply cabinet and pull down the Italian cookbook. I read to Mark the recipe for scallops with garlic and capers. He used to enjoy scallops when we lived in New York, the big juicy ones, which we don't find in California.

"*Scaloppine profumate!*" I announce in my best operatic Italian voice. It's an easy recipe with a light and bright sauce made of wine, garlic, fresh lemon juice, chopped parsley, capers, and freshly ground black pepper. It evokes a rush of happy memories of our times on the Italian coast. Cinque Terre, Positano, the island of Elba. I can smell the balmy salt air of the Mediterranean, the sand and rocks baking in the hot sun. The smell, taste, and sight of those familiar places are knitted into the bond between Mark and me. We've had so many shared experiences in different corners of the world. For just a few minutes it helps me forget that Mark and I are stuck in this drab county hospital in the desert—where, unlike on the Italian coast, the summer sun is unforgiving and dangerous.

Caught up in my enthusiasm and Mark's love of food in Italy, I flip through the recipe book and find another recipe to read, this time a familiar and tasty pasta dish that I've cooked for our family before. *Orechiette con cime di rapa e salsiccia.* Little ears pasta with broccoli rabe and sausage. I chuckle at how endearing the name is in Italian. I can see the familiar earlike pasta that could pass for little slipper seashells. I used to make this dish when the boys were younger. It was a favorite of theirs. I see their eager little faces, their bright eyes shining as they sit around the table, hungry and excited to be served.

Our Italian memories carry me for a time until the rest of our family shows up to see Mark. We coordinate our usual rotation of three at a time in his room.

Before I leave Mark's room for the day, Dr. Lahari stops by to let me know they're taking Mark into surgery Monday morning to assess him again. I ask everyone on Lotsa Helping Hands to continue round-the-clock prayers for Mark. It's all I can do in this never-ending wait-and-see game. But then I remember the still, sure voice in my thoughts that I heard in the morning. It felt like a lifetime ago. *Mark will be fine. Don't worry. Don't doubt.* I walk with a surer stride down the hall when I leave.

It's Saturday. I call Mark's nurses at my usual time in the morning, after the change in shifts from night to day. Lindsey answers the phone. I see her pretty Rachel McAdams–like face with her calm, competent voice. She explains that the intern on duty needs to change Mark's lines after his dressing change. She's not sure when the intern can get to Mark and mentions that we might not see Mark until three or four o'clock today. I send a text update to the family.

I go to our little condo fitness center to use the elliptical machine. It feels good to get moving today. It's been a draining few days. Then, as I walk past the bushes and cacti landscaping on my way from the gym to our condo unit, I feel the warmth of our love, a luminous light shining the way in this dark, untethered space I find myself in. *We're going to get through this together, Mark, my love.*

Mark will be fine. Don't worry. Don't doubt.

It's that reassuring voice in my thoughts again. *How many times have I heard that? Three mornings in a row?* I don't question it anymore. Time will tell.

Later that afternoon when we get to the waiting room, it's agreed that Rene, Michelle, and I will rotate in first to see Mark. Kim had flown home earlier to go back to work. Lindsey lets us know that Mark's blood pressure has stabilized enough that they've taken him off his meds for it. He's also getting close to finishing his antibiotics for pneumonia. It's welcome news in the midst of the fungal infection.

I had brought Mark's Bach choir CD, which I now slip into the CD player. The woody organ melody, so structured and baroque, is accompanied by beautifully soaring voices that swell and fill our little hospital room. A little piece of heaven has entered our dreary space. I only hope that Mark, as unconscious as he is, can hear the beauty of music he's sung and is familiar with, even in that dark cave where he has lain for weeks. I desperately want to believe that sound can help heal Mark.

A woman with a cheerful face and short, dark curly hair shows up in the doorway of Mark's room. She's carrying a ukulele.

"Hi there!" she calls out to us. "I'm Cindy, the music therapist here at the hospital."

We greet her and introduce ourselves. *A music therapist?* The doctors and nurses never mentioned that they had them here at the hospital.

She walks into the room and upon hearing the classical baroque notes filling the room, exclaims, "Oh, my—what exquisite music!"

I point to Mark. "You're listening to the Bach choir that Mark used to sing in." My heart is warm. It feels good to talk about Mark.

"How amazing!" She's enjoying the music, strolling through the room, taking in the wall of colorful photos. Mark on his motorcycle. Mark skiing. Mark and his brother-in-law, Todd, hiking in Yosemite on his fiftieth birthday. Mark playfully waving his wooden spoon at me as I take his photo in the tiny, rustic kitchen in our cliffside Positano villa. A full and rich life on display on the wall.

Finally she turns her attention back to us. "I heard that Mark loves music and that your family does too."

I tell her, "Yes, that's right." I introduce Michelle and Rene and explain that Mark's mom was the church choir director for many years.

Cindy mentions that she would like to play some songs for Mark. She believes that music can be very healing for patients.

The urgency for her to play for Mark suddenly blows through me like a strong wind. *Yes! This could help Mark heal.* The rest of our family in the waiting room would want to be a part of this. Michelle runs out to ask everyone to come join us.

Cindy doesn't have any of the music Mark likes—the blues, Allman Brothers, Neil Young, the Black Keys—but she does offer the Beatles.

When everyone's suited up and crowded around Mark's bed, Cindy plays "Yesterday." Surrounded by such clear voices singing in unison, I stand a little taller, feeling the strength and bond among us here in support of Mark. *I'm not alone.*

What other Beatles songs would Mark like? It suddenly pops into my mind, a brilliant ray of sunshine filtering through a break in the clouds. "Blackbird." *Of course.*

Mark's nickname in high school was "Bird." I'm suddenly struck by the double meaning of the song's lyrics. The "broken wings" of Mark aka Bird and his plane.

I ask Cindy to play the song. She finds the sheet music for it and starts strumming on her ukulele while we sing along. I'd forgotten what a beautiful song this is, even sung a cappella. It has a folksier feel played on a ukulele.

I tear up believing that this can be a message for Mark to fly again after his plane crash. He's in the dark abyss of coma-land. *Fly, Mark. Fly. Darling, I love you. You have to heal yourself of this fungal infection. I hope you and God decided that you want to live. Your boys need you. I need you.* I wipe the tears on my face with my hand. Someone, I think it's Suzie, gently touches my shoulder. Someone else hands me some Kleenexes.

In the middle of the song Adrian suddenly whispers loudly to me.

"Mom."

I dry my tears and look at him attentively.

"Remember the Eddie Vedder song you told me you wished you'd played at your wedding? It's that ukulele song 'Without You.'"

My goodness—Adrian has an amazing memory. What's even more astounding is that he connected the dots at this very moment. He actually remembered how much the song meant to me. I had told him when he was in high school that I wanted to have this song played if Mark and I were to celebrate a future wedding anniversary. The song captured how much the love between Mark and me had matured and deepened over the years. No one else had shared as much of my life with me as Mark had. It was more than the math of our years together, however—it was our shared eagerness to learn through every experience life served up. And to marvel, debate, and discuss it all. On our long drives to Lake Tahoe we had talked about everything from politics, travel, our boys, jobs, friends and family, to why brisket might be better than chuck steak for a more tender pot roast. No topic was taboo. We talked nonstop into the middle of the night on our third date about his time in Japan, my international childhood, and where the best Caesar salad was to be found in the Village. Little did we know, that evening would turn into a lifetime of fascinating conversations. I couldn't imagine life without Mark by my side. I hear Eddie singing the last line in the song about how he wouldn't be the same without his beloved. I have a sudden catch in my throat, realizing this sentence has new meaning for me now as I look at Mark's face, wishing he were conscious. When Cindy finishes playing "Blackbird," I ask if she can Google and find "Without You." She finds it right away. After strumming through it one time, she's ready for us to sing along.

While we sing, I look at Adrian, reading the lyrics on his phone. How grateful I am to have my son remember something of such heartfelt importance to me! It startles me to realize that he's a man now. I notice how tall he is; his face has lengthened, his jaw is more pronounced. He's grown up in the last six weeks since we've been here together while his dad continues to lie in a coma, wrapped in white bandages, his future so uncertain.

When we finish singing, Cindy has to leave to visit another patient. She mentions that she'll pop in from time to time. She says music can be healing for patients. It confirms for me that I was right to keep the music playing continuously for Mark. Selfishly, it kept Adrian and me going as well. Without music I would go crazy staring at the blinking machines, Mark silent in bed, the white walls of his room and the continual hum of monitors. Because Mark was such a lively conversationalist and debater, the silence from him is jarring. *Where is my husband?* I stare at his face. He's somewhere in there, his big, smart brain offline for now.

That evening our large family group meets for dinner at a Thai restaurant. Tomorrow's Sunday. No surgery is planned for Mark. Many people have to leave on Monday, back to jobs and family. I explain that I'll be talking with Dr. Hale and Dr. Lahari after morning rounds on Monday and promise to update everyone.

Chapter 19
A DAY OF REST

I wake up this morning to the sound of the air conditioning spluttering loudly. It reminds me I'm in this artificial place, protected from scorching temperatures outside. I long to be someplace where I don't have to do or be responsible for anything. For just an hour, I want to dive below the surface of the sea of daily activity where it's peaceful and still. My life has become an all-too-familiar autopilot of daily discussions with doctors, nurses, and technicians about Mark's medical and health details. I'm so good at all that left-brain talk. Facts, data, analysis, scenarios. Today I need a break, a time when I can just rest and receive and not be in charge. I'm swept up by a sudden desire to attend church.

I look at my watch. It's still early but I climb out of bed quickly, eager to start my day.

When I'm ready to leave for All Saints, the nearest Episcopal church, I'm late. It's a twenty-minute drive from the condo. When I arrive, it's already hot outside, the church parking lot shimmering in the bright sun. I enter the church sanctuary just as the congregation finishes reciting the Nicene Creed. They're now singing, "*Holy, Holy, Holy, Lord God Almighty! Early in the morning our song shall rise to Thee.... Only thou art holy—there is none beside Thee, Perfect in power, in love, in purity.*"

The chorus of voices accompanied by the soaring and majestic organ chords creates a glorious harmony of notes that burns off a fog layer surrounding my heart. A sudden break in the clouds. I can see and feel what's around me with a freshness that had been dulled by the monotony of my days at the Burn Center. I'm not sure that it's joy I feel. It's more like a sudden burst of feeling free, floating lightly, without the daily burdens of my days since I've come to Phoenix.

I'm reminded that we're a part of something greater than just ourselves. I'm certain that there's a loving force in the universe that cares about us at some very primeval level—as natural as the air we breathe, the soil under our feet, the trees and mountains that rise above us.

When the sermon begins, I'm startled to realize that the rector is telling the story of the Good Samaritan. A man is attacked by robbers on the road from Jerusalem to Jericho. The priest and Levite passed the wounded man and didn't help. The Good Samaritan dressed his wounds, put him on his donkey, and took him to a nearby inn to take care of him. *Thomas Hunnicutt*. Mark wouldn't be alive today if it weren't for Thomas. The modern-day equivalent of the priest and the Levite is the crowd that stood around and filmed Mark and his burning plane on their phones. I scrunch my nose to keep my tears from showing. I don't want people to see me, a visitor, crying. When the service is over, everyone flows out of the cool, dark sanctuary into the intense sunlight.

It's quiet when I return to the Burn Center in the afternoon. Having heard about Mark's music therapy session, Jeff offered to drop off one of his guitars for Steven and Adrian today. They want to play music for Mark.

Fortunately, Mark had a good night. While he lost a lot of blood from the last surgery, Courtney, one of the nurses, explains that Mark turned the corner last night and they were able to reduce his medication support to maintain decent blood pressure. Alyssa adds that Mark's white blood cell count also looks great; it can only help in his battle against the fungal infection.

"How does Mark's fungal infection look?" I anxiously ask.

"We're not able to assess," Alyssa explains. "That's really up to the doctors."

"What about the skin grafts on his torso?"

"It's still too early to know. Dr. Hale and Dr. Lahari will need to monitor and assess when they take over the next few weeks."

I'll have to wait to talk to the doctors. I know that the nurses have opinions but they're not allowed to offer their views.

Rene and Michelle are carefully listening to my conversation with Alyssa and Courtney. I shrug my shoulders at them. *They don't know.*

I pull down the Italian cookbook from the top of the utility closet.

"*Spaghetti vongole!*" I announce to Mark—spaghetti with clams. I read the ingredients out loud to him. Fresh clams in the shell, lots of garlic, fresh parsley. Cook the pasta. We first ordered this simple dish in a small coastal town just south of Rome when the boys were just five and seven. It was a lunch stop on our drive down to the Amalfi Coast.

"Do you remember how that was the first time little five-year-old Adrian ordered spaghetti vongole and that's all he ate the entire two weeks in Positano?" I ask my silent husband. We were thrilled to have weaned him from eating only pizza.

"We had the best time, didn't we?" I smile, looking at Mark. I feel warm and soft in my chest, a kind of glow that grows warmer as I continue talking. "Our first time in Italy. Remember how we fell in love with the Italian countryside and cliffside Mediterranean towns? Do you remember that, Mark?"

He can't respond. I look at him lying in bed, bundled in white.

"Every time we were there, we slowed down to the Italian pace of life. Italians don't rush; they enjoy life. *La dolce vita*. The sweet life. We learned to enjoy the *dolce* in our life, didn't we?" I smile, the warm feeling in my chest burrowing in deeper.

I give Mark a minute to respond, knowing that he can't. But I pause anyway.

I continue my monologue, visualizing from memory the little villages of terracotta and cream-colored stucco homes perched on craggy cliffs overlooking the sparkling blue sea. Grape arbors and the scent of lemon trees everywhere we strolled.

"That first time we stayed in our cliffside villa in Positano was heaven on earth. I know you'd agree. You didn't want to leave either." I chuckle. I can smell the hot sun baking the tiles on the patio overlooking the sea, where we sat every morning enjoying our cappuccinos.

"It was the first time I learned to slow down and appreciate each day. And to notice and appreciate you more, my darling, beautiful man." I feel a prickle in my eyes.

I stop and dig blindly in my purse for a tissue. Adrian texts me from the waiting room that Jeff, Mark's high school friend, has brought his guitar for Steven and him so they can play songs for Mark. I'm excited by the idea of Adrian learning to play "Blackbird" for Mark. I remind him that his dad's nickname in high school was "Bird."

By five o'clock we decide to call it a day. Rene, Michelle, and Steven are flying home tomorrow morning. They've stayed longer than the weekend, and so far Mark's condition with the fungal infection is not worse or better. We know, however, that with a flip of a switch, Mark could go downhill fast. My friend Laila will arrive from Boston tomorrow to stay for the rest of the week. She and her husband, John, are some of our closest, longest-time friends. It will be good to see her.

I ask Alyssa and Courtney to let me know if Dr. Hale can call since he hadn't stopped by today yet. I have a sick feeling in my stomach about what the prognosis might be, brushing the thought aside.

A half hour later while we're in the car, Alyssa calls to let me know Dr. Hale stopped by and wanted me to know that Mark is scheduled for more debridement tomorrow at two o'clock. If I could be there before then, he would stop by to talk with me. I don't know how to interpret whether it's a good sign that Dr. Hale didn't seem to be in a rush to talk to me today.

There's no point in dwelling on this. I'll just wait to talk with Dr. Hale tomorrow.

Chapter 20

PRAYERS

The next morning everyone meets up for breakfast before they leave for the airport. At eight o'clock we can already feel the heat begin permeating the air.

"You'll let us know how Mark does with the surgery today, right?" Rene prompts me with a solemn expression. Today her face looks even paler than usual. The last few days have been so stressful for all of us but today's the first time I've paid attention and noticed what's happening with Mark's sisters and brother.

I nod. *Of course.*

Steven looks at his watch. It's time to catch flights. We give a round of hugs to each other, saying our goodbyes and promising to stay in touch about Mark's condition.

When Adrian and I arrive in the Burn Center waiting room, Alyssa calls me to confirm that Mark's still scheduled for surgery at two o'clock. Dr. Hale stops by.

"Dr. Hale!" I'm so glad to see him. I'm anxious to know what they'll do today with Mark.

He greets us with a serious expression.

"Today we're focused on debriding infected tissue on Mark's arms. Dr. Lahari and I noticed there could be some areas to debride the last time we were in surgery."

It's been a couple days since Mark was in the OR.

"I'm not sure how widespread the infected tissue might be on his arms." He looks intently at me. "If it's spread since our last surgery, we'll have to amputate his arms."

I can't breathe.

"What?"

Adrian reaches out and holds my arm.

"The fungal infection could be aggressive. Either we amputate to stop the spread or it could go into Mark's internal organs and become fatal," Dr. Hale says matter-of-factly.

I cover my eyes with my hands. I picture Mark without his arms. *Oh, please, dear God. No.*

"It's also possible that we *won't* need to amputate. But we won't know until we go in to assess. The infection could spread widely and quickly. It's why we have to be aggressive in removing any infected tissue. Remember that topical treatment will be limited."

I take my hand off my eyes and stare at Dr. Hale standing in front of me in his green scrubs. I'm confident he's the best we have for Mark. In fact, I know it. I trust him. But the worst-case possibility is too terrible to bear.

"If we don't need to amputate Mark's arms, we'll need to assess all his remaining fingers. Dr. Williams didn't amputate some of the fingers to see how they'd do. It's time now for us to look at them again. I just want to prepare you for the possibility that we may need to amputate all his fingers and thumbs."

I can't absorb any more. I see Dr. Hale's mouth moving and I hear what he's saying, but my mind stopped at *amputate Mark's arms*. I think of how Mark would wrap his big, solid arms around my shoulders. He had the sexiest arms, muscular with copper-golden hair.

"Okay, I need to go in and start prepping," Dr. Hale says finally. "I'll be sure to give you an update when we get done." He gives Adrian and me a kind look before departing.

I nod.

"Oh, Adrian." I turn to him. His hazel eyes are clouded. Suddenly I think, *I have to pray. I have to ask God for help.* I'm going back to the condo to ask God to intervene.

"Adrian, I need to go back to the condo. I'm going to pray for Dad."

"Okay." He looks at me with concern.

"You can come with me or stay here."

He hesitates for a moment. I can tell he's wondering if I'll be okay by myself.

"I'll be all right. I just need a private place," I say, gesturing at the crowded waiting room. Maybe there's a chapel here at the hospital, but the thought of being in this drab place doesn't feel right to me.

"I'll stay here. You go ahead and take the car."

"I'll be back in an hour and a half. I don't want to miss Dr. Hale when he finishes."

An overwhelming tide is carrying me forward. I'm in a rush. I grab my purse and start walking briskly toward the door.

"Oh, Adrian!" I call out to him from across the room.

He looks up quizzically.

"I forgot. Laila's flight arrives this afternoon and she's taking an Uber here. Probably around three-thirty."

He nods. "Of course. I'll be here. I'll explain to her what's going on if you're not back by then."

I have no memory of driving back to the condo.

When I arrive, it's dark because the shades are closed. I don't bother turning the lights on. I've gone inward, into the dark and private room in my mind.

I put my purse down in the living room and head straight for my bedroom. I get down on my knees to pray at the end of the bed. My knees hurt since the wood floors have no cushion. I grab a bath towel, fold it, place it on the floor, and kneel on that.

Dear God, please help Mark. Please spare his arms. I'm begging you. Please, oh please.

My face is wet. My entire body is shaking, fully consumed by my desperate beseeching.

Can He hear me?

"Please, please, dear God," I now say out loud. "*Please* spare Mark's arms. What kind of quality of life will he have without them?"

Dare I say it? Is life worth living if his arms are gone? Of course, Adrian, Wesley, and I would want him, whatever is left of him. But maybe he won't want to live this life.

"Without his arms he can't do any of the things he loves—cooking, baking, using the steering wheel to drive a car."

I see Mark, his graceful figure flying down the mountain on his skis. My voice cracks. "Without his arms he wouldn't have a chance at adaptive skiing."

A sharp, shooting pain ripples through my chest at the thought of him in a wheelchair, with no arms and calves, unable to ski, a shadow of who he is.

"Please don't let the fungal infection spread further, but especially his arms. Please spare his arms." I'm conscious that I repeat myself over and over again, begging God in my mind—and out loud.

I've lost track of time. My knees are killing me. I get up. They're painfully stiff and sore. Stretching them out, I climb onto the bed. I lie face down on the bed, feeling emptied out. There are no words left in me.

I should post a request for prayer on our online community. I'm so grateful for their prayer circle, friends and family united in their support of Mark. This is bigger than me. I don't get up right away. Time passes—I'm not sure how long. Finally I will myself to get up to write the post.

Chapter 21

GRATITUDE

When I arrive back in the waiting room, Laila's sitting next to Adrian, her suitcase parked next to her. She stands up and waves to me. We hug each other. She's known Mark and me forever. That was "pre-kids," when we were as young as Wesley is now and had just moved to California from New York. I'm so grateful she's here.

Laila always had a face that makes me think of sunshine when she smiles. Her turned-up nose, the half arc of her smile, her clear blue eyes. Not a cloud in the sky. But her smile now turns serious.

"I'm so sorry about what's happening, Jenny. Adrian just explained everything."

I nod.

"He told me what the doctors are saying."

"We're on pins and needles waiting to hear if the infection has spread to Mark's arms," I say. I can't bring myself to mention the possibility of amputation.

"You haven't seen Dr. Hale or Dr. Lahari, have you?" I ask Adrian.

He shakes his head. "No, I haven't."

I feel a heaviness settle into my stomach as I sink into the chair next to Laila. I'm grateful that Laila's an old friend. I can be myself around her. My eyes are swollen from crying in the car driving back from the condo. I'm sure my face is blotchy.

Dr. Hale emerges from the double doors. I feel lightheaded, getting up from my chair quickly. I try to calm myself by taking a deep breath as he approaches us across the room.

He pulls up a chair close to us and we all sit back down. I'm trying so hard not to let the pounding in my chest cause me to lose my composure.

"We did not see any fungal infection on Mark's arms."

Did not see…did I hear him correctly? Is it too much to hope that this is what I just heard?

"So it hasn't spread to his arms?" I ask, unsure if I've heard him correctly.

"Yes. We saw no signs of it."

"Thank God." I let out a big breath.

"But we did see some small spots on his left arm that look concerning but I'm not sure what it is."

Oh, no.

"I've sent samples to the lab for a biopsy."

"How long will it take to get results?" Adrian asks. *I silently thank Adrian for asking that question. It takes some of the burden off me to interrogate the doctors after each surgery.*

"It'll take a few days. Also, we did partial amputations of both of Mark's thumbs to here," Dr. Hale holds up his thumbs and shows us where they amputated. "We amputated up to the first digit here, the distal third."

I hold up one of my thumbs, bending it to see where the line was drawn. Mark still has the joint so he can bend and maybe hook objects.

Dr. Hale explains which digits were amputated on Mark's remaining fingers. I'm relieved that it's the fingertips and not entire fingers. He'll have a limited range, but he'll have some ability to use his fingers and hands.

"Mark tolerated the surgery well today. We'll need to get him back in surgery on Thursday or Friday to assess for fungal infection on his legs. Oh, and the amputation wound sites on his legs look okay."

"Are they healed?" Adrian asks.

"It's still too early to say. When I say they're okay, it means there's no sign of infection."

"You mean in addition to the fungal infection, right?" I ask.

"Yes. Remember—amputations for a regular patient take four weeks, but for a burn patient it will take up to three months."

That's a long time. I'm worried that so many other things can go wrong and compromise Mark's amputation healing.

"So for now this is good news?" I ask.

"Yes. But as I mentioned, fungal infections are slow-moving. We need to extend Mark's antifungal medication beyond the twenty-one-day schedule he's already on."

Twenty-one days. It's helpful to know the time frame the doctors are monitoring. Just as when the boys used to get ear infections, I remembered the doctor always prescribing a ten-day course of antibiotics, the standard timeline for infection recovery.

"The tricky thing about fungal infections is that Mark could show no sign of infection on his body tissue while it spreads to his internal organs," Dr. Hale explains. "Only time will tell."

I thank Dr. Hale. It's good news for now. We're all relieved. Laila's been attentively following our conversation.

It'll be at least another hour post-surgery for them to settle Mark back in his room for visitors. Adrian and I take Laila to our favorite café to wait. While we have tea and muffins, I check my emails. Some friends mention that when they received my post about Mark's fungal infection the week before, they had fasted and prayed for Mark. Other friends and family mention asking their church congregations and synagogues to pray for Mark. I'm incredibly touched. I've been overwhelmed by the generous support of friends. A few of Mark's Stanford GSB classmates have sent me everything from Target gift cards and inspirational books to a stuffed teddy bear.

I take the time to share the good news with our online community and to thank them for their love, generosity, kindness, and for rallying around Mark.

Because of the physical distance between our family and friends and me, an ongoing online conversation has very naturally evolved between us centered on my daily posts. I'm astounded at how many people have signed up to be in our private community. Adrian, as one of the administrators, continued to approve more people to join in the last few weeks.

Laila, Adrian, and I see Mark briefly before dinner but we decide to only stay a short time since Mark needs to rest and recover from his finger amputations today.

"I love you, Mark," I say to him softly, hovering by his bedside, his face lit by a dim, soft bedside light. "You made it, my darling. God knows how many people prayed for you. Even fasted. Can you believe that? I wish you could read all these beautiful posts and emails I'm receiving from our family and friends." Mark's eyes are closed, as they have been for almost two months now. I'll take whatever we can feel good about. His condition is stable. The fungal infection hasn't spread, and his arms are intact. For now.

When I go to bed that night, I feel a lightness for the first time in a long time. I'm buoyed by a feeling of appreciation and gratitude. By receiving so much love and support, it gives me the capacity to give more to Mark and the situation we find ourselves in. It would otherwise be truly unbearable. Amputations, first his legs, now his fingers and thumbs. Arrhythmia, pneumonia, kidney dialysis, and now the fungal infection. And Mark's in a coma because treatment is too painful for any human being.

I remember what I've heard. *Burn is the most traumatic human injury there is.*

Chapter 22

SPECIAL ENERGY

Laila has some work to do in the morning from her hotel room. We meet up for lunch and then head to the Burn Center.

Adrian has brought Jeff's guitar. He's been practicing playing "Blackbird," and at my prompting, he'll attempt to play it for his dad today. It would be nice for us to share this moment with Laila visiting.

When we get to Mark's room, the sun outside seems to shine more brilliantly today. The room is blindingly bright. I give Laila some private time with Mark. After all, she and her husband, John, were one of the first friends we met when we moved to California. We've enjoyed a twenty-nine-year friendship.

I encourage her to talk to Mark even though he's in a coma, explaining the story about a friend who had dreamlike memories of what he heard in his room during his coma. I hear her say hi to Mark as I walk back out the door to wait for her by the reception desk.

Adrian's sitting in the waiting room with the guitar. We're back to our rotation of two visitors at a time.

When I walk back toward Mark's room, Laila comes rushing out into the hallway.

She gets close to me and says quietly, "Wow, Jenny! There's some kind of special energy in Mark's room." She points to his room, where the door is open, and we can see him lying in bed in his usual silent mummy state.

"What do you mean?" I'm genuinely puzzled. I have no idea what Laila could be talking about.

"It's indescribable. I've never felt anything like it before."

Laila's words quickly tumble out of her, which happens when she's worked up.

"What is it, Laila?"

"I don't know. Like I said, there's some kind of energy in there that I've never felt before." Her voice is insistent.

I walk into the room. It's so bright. I walk to the window and turn the blinds down, which provides immediate shade. Laila follows me back into the room.

I survey the room. It's the same as always, both how it looks and how it feels.

"I don't feel anything different," I say to Laila. "But maybe it's because I'm here all the time."

"There *is* something different in here."

"I believe you. How interesting! I wonder what that special energy is." We both settle down in chairs at the foot of Mark's bed.

I ask Alyssa and Courtney how Mark's doing. They explain that he started to have an arrhythmia last night and that they put him on medication through an IV drip. His leg and finger amputations looked clean when they put fresh dressings on them this morning.

I ask them if it's okay for Adrian to join us as a threesome so he can play the guitar for Mark.

"Of course, Jenny," Alyssa replies right away with a wave of her hand as if I didn't need to ask.

I love the nurses here. They've become like a second family to me.

Mark's face looks agitated. Courtney calls the respiratory technician to adjust Mark's airflow to make him more comfortable.

I'm sure he must be suffering from his finger amputation surgery yesterday. I shiver at the thought of what happened in the OR. Never in a million years did I think Mark would lose parts of himself. Never.

I text Adrian to come join us in the room. A few minutes later he shows up with Jeff's guitar.

Because Mark's agitated, I put on meditation music first, followed by Mark's California Bach Society CD. The music flows and relaxes all of us. I hope that it's soothing Mark in his pain. I feel such safety and comfort within the precision of Bach's rhythmic and harmonious structure. The world is orderly again and makes sense.

We're enjoying the music when Dr. Hale stops by briefly to let us know that Mark is scheduled for surgery tomorrow morning at seven-thirty.

Alyssa checks on Mark's breathing, which has evened out after the respiratory technician worked his magic. I also hope the music has helped ease any pain that Mark is feeling.

When Bach finishes, Adrian pulls out the guitar and starts strumming to practice. He corrects a few chords as he does a quick run-through of "Blackbird."

"Okay, I'm ready, Mom."

I nod. "Here—get closer to your dad," I say, gesturing to where he's sitting, up against the wall away from Mark.

He pulls his chair near the foot of Mark's bed with a loud scrape.

Laila and I look up the song lyrics on our phones so we can sing along.

It's a delicate melody. During the chorus, I choke up, my voice is cracking, and my eyes well up. *Oh, Mark, my beautiful man. You'll never fly a plane again, but may you be free of this bed, this hospital, and this coma—to soar and be free again.*

I think of him on the mountain, adaptive skiing with his equipment. I see him driving a car with a special steering wheel. I see him smoking brisket in the smoker, standing with steel legs, Wesley by his side helping. I see him attending Adrian's graduation in Zurich. We'll figure out a way for him to travel comfortably.

Alyssa and Courtney stand at the doorway of Mark's room, watching Adrian play.

When Adrian finishes, Alyssa says, "Bravo, Adrian. That was wonderful."

"Indeed it was. Nice job, Adrian," Laila says with a warm smile.

I can't speak—my heart feels so full as I grab the Kleenex box. Laila reaches out and gives me a hug.

We're quiet the rest of the afternoon.

In the car driving to dinner that evening, Laila brings up the energy in Mark's room again.

"What do you think it is?" she asks us.

"I honestly don't feel anything, but I'm in Mark's room every day, so I might not notice," I repeat.

"Oh, I definitely feel it," Laila insists.

"I'm sure you do. Do you feel anything different in there, Adrian?"

Adrian shakes his head. "No, I don't. But I'm in there all the time too."

I'm mystified. This is so interesting coming from Laila. Laila's my atheist, materialist friend. If she can't touch it, see it, hear it, she doesn't believe it exists. And yet she's obviously encountered something powerful and invisible to the eye in Mark's room.

Laila flies back to Boston the next morning. Mark goes into surgery as Dr. Hale planned. When they're done, Dr. Hale explains that they found no obvious signs of fungal infection on his thighs. They replaced the allografts and xenografts on various parts of his body. His leg amputation sites look good. There's no sign of infection.

Adrian and I let out a sigh of relief. For now.

Dr. Hale says that they will need Mark back in surgery this coming weekend or early next week so they can assess his back and arms for fungal infection. That will require two separate surgeries. Due to the nature of the infection, the biopsy results for his upper left arm won't be ready for another one to two weeks. The earliest would be next Tuesday.

Because Mark needs a dressing change and airing out of his new xenografts and allografts, we have the afternoon off.

With unexpected free time, Adrian and I decide to go to the movies. We desperately need a break from the monotony of the hospital and our daily schedule. The film is lighthearted and gets our minds off why we're in Phoenix. The cool, air-conditioned darkness is a welcome retreat from the heat of Phoenix and our lives.

The next morning Mark is third in the queue for surgery. Dr. Hale will examine Mark before they do his dressing change to see if there's any fungal-infected tissue to excise. If not, there's no need for surgery today.

I think of the voice that told me for three days in a row that Mark would be okay. I haven't heard that voice again since. All I can do is hope and pray that the fungal infection leaves his body. I continue to ask our online community to pray for Mark before I ask Courtney to call me when Dr. Hale finishes his assessment.

An hour later my phone rings. I jump when I see the Burn Center number on my phone.

It's Courtney. "I have good news, Jenny." I hold my breath. "Dr. Hale didn't see anything concerning on his body and his vitals look stable."

"So no surgery today?"

"Nope. Dr. Hale said Mark will go into surgery next Thursday, sooner if anything suddenly changes between now and then."

Chapter 23

OUT OF THE WOODS

On Saturday Courtney mentions to Adrian and me that there was talk of Mark going into surgery next Thursday, and not sooner unless his condition changes suddenly.

Poor Mark. He's still recovering from his leg amputations and keeping the fungal infection at bay. God knows he could use some rest and recovery time. No news would be good news, for a change.

After a few quiet days with no setbacks, Dr. Hale stops by the room with an update.

"Mark's vitals look good," he tells us. "No arrhythmia, no blood pressure issues. Everything's good—heart rate and temperature. He's still on kidney dialysis, but that's to be expected given his condition."

"What about his leg and finger amputation sites?" I ask.

"They look good. They're clean with no signs of infection." Dr. Hale looks pleased.

My chest rises and falls with relief.

"I have one pleasant surprise to share," Dr. Hale says.

A pleasant surprise? Really? That'd be a first. I look at him expectantly.

"When I examined Mark during his dressing change today, the skin grafts on his front torso haven't fallen off like we expected. Frankly, I was surprised." Dr. Hale arches his brows. "I thought they wouldn't survive when we laid Mark on his front side in the OR. We had to do so in order to excise infected tissue from his back a few days ago."

In the fungal infection crisis I hadn't given those forty-eight skin grafts a single thought. I figured they wouldn't thrive at all. I was learning to manage my own expectations. I never mentioned them to Laila, Kathy, and her husband, Page.

"Do they have a chance of taking?" Adrian asks. *Good question.*

Dr. Jameson's description of them a few weeks ago made me imagine them as delicate and film-like, the size of postage stamps. I now picture forty-eight of them spread across Mark's chest and stomach.

"It's too soon to know. It'll take around five days," Dr. Hale replies.

I mentally count the days. It should be around the time the biopsy results for Mark's left arm will come back. Adrian's faster than me. He mouths silently to me *Friday*. I nod.

"Assuming that Mark continues to be stable, when can you resume the skin-grafting process?" I remember that when Mark has blood pressure challenges, they prescribe medication that negatively affects the ability of his skin grafts to thrive. It draws blood flow away from the surface of his body to support the internal organs.

We're back in the race to cover Mark with his own skin.

"Dr. Williams, Dr. Jameson, and I, along with the entire medical team, will meet this week to review Mark's situation to determine what the strategy and next course of action will be for him. We'll keep you updated."

"What about the biopsy on his left arm?" *How could I forget that after the near-amputation of Mark's arms only a few days ago?*

"We'll receive results back from the lab next week."

Next week will be important. That's when we'll get the biopsy reports and see if Mark's skin graft took.

I really like Dr. Hale. He's candid and thoughtful in a low-key way. He's been with us through the toughest time so far. I trust him.

He adds, "I'll also be coming off my rotation with Mark this week. Dr. Jameson will be in charge starting next week. He'll be in touch with you about next Thursday's surgery. Of course, we'll still talk about anything that comes up the rest of this week."

"Thank you for all you've done for Mark," I say.

"You're welcome," he says with a bit of a smile. "You'll be in good hands with Dr. Jameson."

He excuses himself when Adrian and I say we have no further questions.

After the doctor leaves, I turn back to him. "I'm so relieved, Adrian."

He nods. "That makes two of us, Mom."

"I want so badly to get going on your dad's skin grafts. To get his whole body covered."

Adrian nods vigorously. I settle back in my chair at the foot of Mark's bed and say a silent prayer, staring out the window into the bright sunlight.

Thank you, God, and all the love in the universe for protecting Mark.

I don't dare assume Mark's out of the woods with the fungal infection. I'm just grateful that for now, all is well. I've come to appreciate every moment that is stable and good for Mark. Because we never know what tomorrow will bring.

Monday afternoon brings Adrian and me back into the bustle of a full weekday staff. Dr. Jameson stops by to confirm that Mark will go into surgery this Thursday.

"What's your current assessment of Mark's fungal infection?"

"It'll be another six weeks before we'll really know. The nurses and I will still be monitoring it closely. We'll continue to keep him on antifungal medication."

After Dr. Jameson leaves, I open the calendar on my phone and count down six weeks. Six weeks puts us into the first week of September. I mark it on my calendar as a date to watch for. It gives me a timeline to know when we can rest easy that we're past the fungal scare.

On Wednesday Lindsey updates us that Mark's temperature inched up last night to 101.6. His white blood cell count is one to two points above the max of the normal range.

Here we go again. A sick feeling creeps into my stomach.

"We don't know if it's the start of another infection," Lindsey is quick to explain, seeing my anxiety. "It could also be just normal fluctuations that all burn patients have. Without the protection of their own skin, burn patients have trouble regulating their body temperatures."

"Is Mark still on for surgery tomorrow? Has Dr. Jameson said anything?"

"As far as we know, he's still scheduled." I'm glad to have Lindsey back on Mark's shift. She's so calm.

Later in the afternoon Dr. Jameson shows up with an update from the medical review yesterday. He explains that yes, they're moving forward with the full skin-grafting phase.

"We decided in our review yesterday to continually grow skin grafts in the Boston lab. When each batch is ready, they'll automatically send them to us."

"That's such good news." I'm elated. The timing is tricky, though. The grafts have to be used fairly quickly after they arrive. Mark can't be in the middle of a raging infection or on blood pressure meds, or the grafts won't take hold.

That evening after dinner, Dr. Jameson stops by again to inform us that Mark's skin grafts on his front torso have successfully taken. Adrian and I go home buoyed by the good news. We tell jokes and laugh for the first time in a long time. It's July 24. Mark's been at the Burn Center for eight weeks now.

It's Thursday—surgery day for Mark. Adrian and I are with him in the morning before he goes into the OR again. Lindsey tells us that Mark's temperature rose in the night to 102 degrees. He was in a lot of pain so Jaime, his night nurse, gave him some pain meds, which helped. *Poor Mark.*

I close my eyes and talk to Mark's body. *Please, please, please. Don't climb any higher than 102 degrees.* I keep repeating this in my mind like a mantra, willing his body to hear me.

I turn to Adrian, who's perched on the edge of his chair reading on his phone.

"Hey, Adrian."

He looks up.

"I just realized that Dad's been mostly stable now for six days straight."

"It's good, isn't it?" he says, nodding. "I hope it continues."

"We have to hurry and get your dad covered with his own skin. I'm just so worried we'll get interrupted by another infection or high blood pressure."

"Yeah, I know, Mom," he says, his brow slightly furrowed. I know he feels some anxiety, but like Mark, he always appears calm.

A few hours later Dr. Jameson finds us in the waiting room. He looks pleased.

"Everything went well. We replaced the allografts on Mark's thighs and both arms.

"His back is still exposed but we can only do either his front or back during surgery. The allografts will fall off if we try to change major body positions."

That makes sense. I hope they don't wait too long to work on Mark's back.

"We plan to prepare Mark for skin grafting next Wednesday. We'll set up a test patch for autografts."

"What are autografts?" Adrian asks.

"They're the preparation layer that we'll grow on your dad's body to put skin grafts on top of. We want to test a patch first to make sure the autograft will take before we do more widespread preparation."

It feels good to be discussing this step. It's progress. I hope this means the fungal infection is soon behind us.

"You should celebrate the good news. If your dad gets any more bacterial infections, it'll be a reset but it's recoverable. That's not true of fungal infections."

"Does that mean Mark's out of the woods on the fungal infection?"

"Dr. Williams will talk with you about that either today or tomorrow. Just sit tight."

I type up a quick update for our online community. At the end I add—

> *"Dearest God and all the love in the universe, thank you for another miracle—the gift of life for Mark."*

After surgery, Mark has a quiet night. When Adrian and I get into his room after the morning dressing change, Dr. Williams drops in. It's comforting to see his kind face.

"I was in surgery yesterday with Dr. Jameson," he says pleasantly. "Mark's amputation wounds look good. His thighs, his fingers—they're all clean and free of infection."

"Yes, Dr. Jameson gave us an update yesterday."

"The biopsy results on Mark's left arm came back negative for any signs of infection."

"Oh, thank goodness." It's the good news I had been afraid to hope for after our arm amputation scare last week. I look at Adrian, who looks pleased. "Woo-hoo!" I raise both my arms in the air, thrilled.

"We still need to monitor that arm. It's been nine days since Dr. Hale first noticed spots there, and it can take up to two weeks for fungal tissue to grow."

What he says doesn't detract from my joyous moment. I've learned to appreciate any positive news, knowing that it can all change suddenly.

"I'm surprised that Mark made it through his fungal infection," Dr. Williams says quietly. "It was a dark moment a few weeks ago."

I nod, silent because I'm about to burst. It's huge to know that the head of the Burn Center seems to think the storm clouds have passed.

"The priority now is to get Mark covered with his own skin. This Monday we plan to take some of his unburned skin cells to graft onto his front torso to cover the gaps where the skin grafts from the lab didn't take."

I didn't know that they could transfer unburned skin cells directly, but then again, it was likely the doctors didn't mention it much because there wasn't much of Mark that wasn't burned.

"So did some of the grafts take?"

"Yes, they are tiny buds of skin that are growing. In about four weeks they should join together to become an entire section of new skin."

"That's amazing." It's miraculous how this works.

"In this next phase we'll use a mix of local skin grafts from Mark's body, skin grafts from the Boston lab, and skin cells sprayed on a mesh cover that we'll put on his body."

After Dr. Williams excuses himself, I marvel to Adrian at the technology.

"That's so cool, isn't it? That they can spray skin cells on a person?"

"It is," he says, nodding. He's amazed too. We both start Googling on our phones to learn more.

"Mark!" I call out. "You made it! I'm so glad you're alive." I can't hold back my tears anymore. I'm crying with relief. Adrian reaches over to hold my arm.

I think of what I heard three days in a row. *He'll be fine. Don't worry. Don't doubt.* I was so afraid to believe that quiet, strong voice in my thoughts. But now I'm in wonder at how I seem to possess a quiet, strong inner voice that seems to *know* things.

I'm suddenly gripped with a desire to find a poem about Mark's beloved Sierras to read to him. I search Google for such a poem but quickly discover there aren't many and what there are sound old-timey, stiff, and formal. I quiet my mind and start writing a poem on my iPad. Memories of Lake Tahoe and the Sierras rush into my mind like a scene out of a movie I'm watching. I'm sitting by the lake on a bench with Mark, savoring our coffee and staring out at the snowcapped mountains rising above the clear, blue lake like a sheet of glass.

After an hour of tapping out words, I read to Mark what I've written:

The cool morning gives way to a brilliant blue sky
The lake, sun-dappled and clear as turquoise-shaded glass
Over round, smooth dark rocks
Big and small hidden in the depth
While bleached-white rocky mounds rise out above the water

Your majesty, the ponderosa pines reflected, their long shadows on the lake
Surrounded by snowcapped mountains, the Sierras
The footpaths of pioneers who made it to the coast through the desolate salt flats of Utah
One dusty step at a time, both horse and human
New beginnings, this wide, open, arid space
Called the West

Before the mid-afternoon winds pick up, it's still here on the waters of Tahoe
I love the bigness, the openness, its wild and scrappy beauty
The snowcapped mountains

This dry landscape balanced with water and green in just the right places
Brings clarity of mind, hope in my heart and infinite possibilities
I am home

Part 4

HOPE AND HEALING

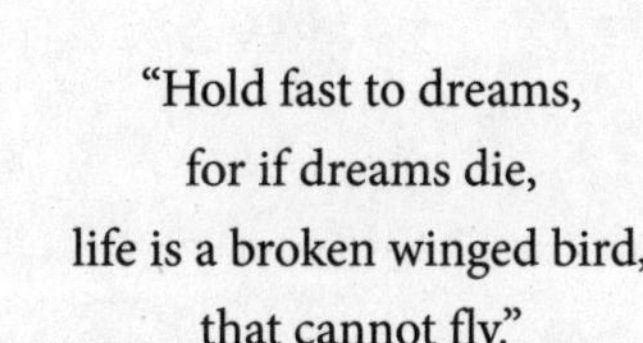

"Hold fast to dreams,
for if dreams die,
life is a broken winged bird,
that cannot fly."

—LANGSTON HUGHES,
"Dreams"

Chapter 24

THE POWER OF HOPE

Over the next few days, Mark's temperature continues increasing from 102 degrees. His blood pressure drops, and the nurses give him a couple of meds to increase it.

The doctors take blood cultures to assess for bacterial and fungal infections. Thankfully Mark's lungs are clear, so we know he doesn't have pneumonia.

My anxiety is high because the blood pressure meds, both for high and low blood pressure, always draw blood flow away from supporting Mark's skin grafts.

Through the end of July Mark continues having fluctuating vitals. His blood pressure suddenly drops to below normal at ninety-five degrees and they delay surgery. The nurses have to continually monitor the medication dosages. They surround him with heat lamps to warm him up. Mark's room becomes a sweat lodge. It becomes difficult for me to stay in it for long.

Sadly, all the lab-grown skin grafts on his torso fail and fall off. They didn't take after all. We're back to square one. My disappointment wells up like a heavy wave that knocks me off balance for a moment. This bit of fragile progress was symbolic of the shift from crisis to recovery for Mark. I have to let it go.

The nurses tell me that Dr. Jameson has already ordered more skin grafts and that now we're just waiting for them. *Just keep moving forward*, I tell myself. I know if I allow my mind to dwell on the past for even a moment, the tide will carry me out to sea. I'll be lost in a place that will be hard to return from.

By the first couple of days of August, Mark's vitals swing back to normal. Alyssa tells us they've reduced Mark's insulin dose because his body is less stressed than before. It's very good news. They start reducing Mark's sedation levels but he's grumpy when they move him around in his bed.

One afternoon he surprises us all by suddenly opening his eyes and scowling at Alyssa and Matt before he closes them again. It scares me to see how much pain Mark can suddenly express.

"We need to get Mark a more comfortable bed," Alyssa announces. "They have these mattresses with sand-like particles and temperature controls. It'll help him feel more comfortable because his back is so raw."

I wince, immediately seeing Mark's raw and burned back in my mind. He's long-waisted so he must be suffering even more. My back feels as if it's on fire.

Alyssa tells me she'll put the order in for a new bed today. I'm thankful that she's thought of a way to make Mark more comfortable.

I close my eyes and picture Mark lying on a soft mattress that will better cushion his back. I take a deep breath. My back cools down and feels back to normal.

Adrian leaves for Zurich to help the team with last-minute preparations for the European student autonomous driving competition. It's in Germany this year.

My friend Suzie flies in from Denver to see Mark and to keep me company while Adrian's away. I'm going to miss Adrian. He's been the partner by my side day in and day out. We've been through intense highs and lows together.

Suzie stays in Adrian's room at the condo, taking his place, accompanying me to the Burn Center every day, and for the rest of early- to mid-August, Mark's vitals remain stable. I continue reading various recipes from the Italian cookbook. I make my way through *pesce spada alla Siciliana*—Sicilian swordfish. Olives, cherry tomatoes, and pine nuts sauteed in a generous amount of garlic and olive oil. I think of the olive tree groves on the island of Elba, where Mark, Adrian, and I spent a week a few years ago. We hiked in the mornings through neglected, overgrown vineyards on terraced hills, lazily whiling away our afternoons at the beach.

After almost two-and-a-half months at the Burn Center, I'm getting to know the nurses here. I like and admire them. They have to be incredibly competent to work in the ICU, with the emotional resilience to do the dressing changes on badly burned patients. I know I couldn't stomach seeing raw muscles and the human body underneath the skin layer.

Many of them chose the burn unit because they like developing long-term relationships with the families. Yet ironically, as they point out, they don't hear directly from the patients because they're all in induced comas. The only way they know anything personal about their patients is through getting to know the families. A few of the nurses tell me that's why they love seeing Adrian and me every day, along with the rest of our family. Who Mark is comes shining through in my stories and all the photos of him in the room.

With Mark in stable condition, I put on a mixed rotation of rock and pop music in his room. I settle into my chair and catch up on emails and online community posts.

Joan, the wife of one of Mark's Canadian cousins, writes a post addressed to me in our online community:

> *I was doing my daily devotional reading when I came across a story about how a wet sponge can absorb more water than a dry sponge. It seems counterintuitive, yet the wet sponge taught me something important about love. When we have a little love in us, we can soak up more. Mother Theresa said, "We cannot all do great things. But we can do small things with great love."*
>
> *Jenny, you remind me of that wet sponge. I bet no one has ever called you a wet sponge! Just as the sponge has water in it, you have love in you. The love in you is helping you cope with the biggest challenge of your life. That love touches Mark, the medical staff, the other burn survivors, their loved ones, and those of us who are blessed to hear how you and Mark are doing. Your*

> *love spills out in your words online. Often I am moved to tears by what you write.*
>
> *There is no doubt that you and Mark are soulmates. In my time as a minister for the United Church of Canada, I've counseled many couples. I saw couples who didn't like each other, let alone love each other. Thank you for your love, Jenny. It spills out over so many, many people.*

I have to reread Joan's post a few times to fully absorb what she writes. From my daily existence with Mark in the four gray, drab walls of his hospital room, I had never imagined the effect my daily posts are having on the hundreds of friends and family reading them—until I read this from Joan.

Dr. Jameson stops by to chat. Amazingly, Mark's vitals continue to remain stable.

"Ladies, the real work for your family is when Mark wakes up," he announces. "He still has a long road in the ICU, but he's also got a lot of rehab post-ICU."

That gets my attention. I've been so consumed with the here and now.

"What's he going to need after he gets out of the Burn Center?" I ask.

"Physical therapy twice a day. New skin isn't so flexible. Think of it as chewing gum. You have to stretch it out a lot the first two years or the skin gets stiff."

Twice a day? That's a lot.

"Will Mark need to be in a residential rehab center?" I ask.

"Absolutely. He'll eventually transition to being home, of course."

Our home in California is two floors with the bedrooms and bathrooms upstairs. I picture Mark at home in a wheelchair. *How is he going to get up the stairs? We'll need to build a handicapped bathroom on the first floor. But where?* My mind takes off on a visual tour of our house, room by room.

"Have you heard of Mark Haley?" Dr. Jameson breaks through my thoughts.

Suzie and I shake our heads.

"Mark Haley was a patient here earlier this year. He was in a drag racing accident in Tucson and was severely burned on 45 percent of his body. We amputated one hand and all the fingers on his other hand. He was sedated for six months. He's doing really well now and thriving. Google him. His story may be helpful for you as you think about Mark's life after he gets out of here."

I immediately find several news articles about Mark Haley and an audio interview. He didn't remember anything about the accident. He was racing his car when it swerved out of control, ran into a concrete wall, and caught on fire. He was trapped inside the car, unconscious. His accident happened in January 2018, and he woke up in the Burn Center ICU in July 2019. When he left his post-ICU rehab center to finally go home, he had them play Boston's "Don't Look Back" as his farewell theme song. I loved that. I like this guy. He's got the same *make it happen—go get your life* attitude that Mark has. It's an encouraging story.

I'm glad Mark won't remember any of the pain he's been through. *How many surgeries has he had so far?* I try to count them all. I think he's had seventeen of them in almost two-and-a-half months.

"Lindsey, how long will it take for Mark to come off his sedation?" I ask.

"Around three weeks," Lindsey replies. "It's why we're starting to ease up on his sedation dosage now—so it can be gradual."

I turn to Suzie. "It will be so nice for us to have Mark more awake."

"Yes," she replies enthusiastically. "It would be so good to be able to talk with him again."

"But he'll also feel more pain." I can't shake the image of Mark with his eyes suddenly open, his mouth scowling.

"They can always increase his pain medication," Suzie says.

That's right. Of course. I hadn't thought of that. And it's good they replaced Mark's old mattress with a fancy one filled with soft particles and temperature controls. I hope he's more comfortable lying on his back all day.

Over the next couple weeks, because Mark's doing okay, for the first time I allow myself to go out and enjoy life a little. With Suzie visiting, I'm more conscious that we should do some fun things outside our long days at the hospital. In the morning while they do Mark's dressing change, we get out for some short excursions. We go shopping in Scottsdale. We go to the Phoenix Art Museum. We're addicted to watching *The Crown* series every evening on Netflix.

The quiet, air-conditioned display rooms at the Phoenix Art Museum are a welcome respite from the relentless heat outside. I'm particularly captivated by an exhibit of hundreds of black carbon wood pieces hanging suspended from the ceiling of a school that burned down. They shimmer like iridescent dark stars exposed under a bright light. It's amazing how the artist took devastating destruction and recreated it, making it a magical, atmospheric experience. It makes me think of the regeneration of Mark's burned body, a journey we've just started.

We're now a few days away from receiving a new batch of skin grafts for Mark. His autograft prep site has taken nicely. Adrian texts to let me know that his ETH team took first place in the driving competition. Suzie and I jump out of our seats, shouting. I do a little dance. The nurses poke their heads in the doorway, wondering what the commotion is.

"Adrian's team won the self-driving car competition! Oh, wow! I'm so happy for him and the team. Mark would be so proud—so proud!"

I turn to Mark. "Mark, I hope you can hear this. The ETH team took first place in the competition in Germany." I can't wait for Mark to wake up and for Adrian to share the news.

Adrian visits friends in New York on his way home from Frankfurt. He won't be back in time for Mark's skin graft surgery, but Wesley will be here right after it.

Chapter 25

REGENERATION

Mark's blood pressure fluctuates in the coming weeks. When it's high, I experiment with playing meditation music and it goes down a few points. It's satisfying to know it's one of the only things I can do to help Mark.

Dr. Jameson says it's great that Mark's tolerating his feeding tube so well. It means he's getting the nutrition he needs in order to heal.

The physical therapists start working with Mark, placing his arms on foam splints and varying their position to stretch out his arms so the area between his shoulder and arms doesn't contract and become stiff. I begin to appreciate the meaning of physical therapy for someone like Mark, who's been bedridden and will continue to be so for some time.

A few weeks ago they had to sew Mark's right eye shut because he was opening it and they were worried the cornea would dry out. The eyelid has now healed nicely, and they release the sutures that held his eye shut. They think he'll need a skin graft on that right eyelid. Dr. Jameson reassures me that they have one of the best plastic surgeons on call to help with that.

The skin grafts come in a day early and they decide to graft where he has the healthiest tissue. They put grafts on both arms, his lower right torso, and his front left thigh. They don't need to put grafts up higher on his right torso because his own skin is regenerating by itself.

Wow, the miracle of regeneration! I'm feeling so hopeful.

The nurses explain that, for the first week after skin graft surgery, they need to air out Mark's grafts for four to five hours before they do his dressing change. That means we can't see Mark until three or four o'clock now.

There's a constant rotation of visitors. Suzie leaves, and Mark's sister Rene arrives for a week's visit. Wesley shows up for a long weekend as well.

We now wait for two weeks to see if the skin grafts take. This will be our ongoing cycle. Skin grafts come in, they graft them, they air them out for a week, and we wait to see if they take. During these cycles I constantly hope that Mark doesn't suffer from blood pressure issues that require more meds to put his skin grafts at risk.

God knows how much Mark was juggling the week of his plane crash. We were in escrow for the Lake Tahoe house we planned to buy. He had given three months' notice at work that he was retiring. He was working on finding his replacement as head of sales and marketing for a start-up in Reno. If Mark were conscious, he would be in a big rush to get out of here.

Adrian and I walk in one day to see the occupational therapist molding and putting a blue, smooth, clay-like mask on Mark's face.

"Oh, wow! What's that for?" I ask.

"It's to apply pressure on his face to minimize scarring of his new skin."

After a while Adrian and I are fascinated, silently watching Ben, the therapist, mold the mask in small strokes of his fingers. It's like watching an artist at work.

It's around this time that I finally succumb to my first migraine. I get vestibular migraines, so I find a physical therapist in Phoenix to help me resolve my dizzy symptoms. My body held it together for the last two-and-a-half months because it had to. Now that Mark's more stable and we're past the worst, my body decides it's okay to fall apart. The back of my head is in a tight vise, and I feel off balance. I can only sit still without moving my head around a lot to avoid feeling utterly nauseated. But the therapy works, and the next day I'm steadier and the dizziness starts fading.

I'm glad to feel well enough when Adrian arrives back from Zurich, triumphant. He shows us photos from the competition and catches us up on the details about the other teams they competed against.

"Your dad will be so proud to hear the news," I say, smiling at Adrian as he shows Wesley and me his photos.

That evening back in the quiet of the condo, I think of how much I long for Mark to be awake so that Adrian can share with him his exciting news. It feels like forever since I'd last spoken to Mark. I hate not being able to chat with him. Every day I observe things and I catch myself wanting to tell Mark about it, to ask him what he thinks.

Mark, I drove by this outdoor brewery, Arizona Wilderness, that serves burgers and duck fries. They have some Belgians and IPAs that I know you'd love to try. What great names…Warrior Hazy IPA, Lost Highway Black India Pale Ale.…I need to remember the name of this place so we can come back here together one day. Which beer would you order?

Oh, wow—you should hear the '70s Muzak in the hospital cafeteria tonight. It's Tom Jones! And "Muskrat Love." Is that Captain & Tennille? You would run screaming out of this hospital. It's pretty depressing to be eating my taco salad alone here in the cafeteria. It comforts me to know I'm not really alone. You're just in bed upstairs. There are no windows here. Why would they put the cafeteria in the basement? You would hate it. I hate it. Can you hurry up and get better so we can get out of here? I want so much to go home with you.

Andy called yesterday to talk to me about our financial accounts. He had some suggestions. What should I do? I wish I could discuss it with you.

Cards and letters from family and friends continue flowing in. A friend who knows that Mark's an avid reader sends novels like *Waiting for Snow in Havana*, interesting books about the history of French food, and another one on the history of salt. She wants me to read to him the way I'm reading Italian recipes—chickpea soup, focaccia with olives and pepper flakes, mussels in red wine sauce.

A writer friend of mine sends me her personal volume of Mary Oliver poems, which I read to him as well. *Tell me—what do you plan to do with your one precious life?* Life *is* precious in a way I didn't understand before.

You do not have to be good. You do not have to walk on your knees for a hundred miles through the desert repenting. You only have to let the soft animal of your body love what it loves. I've seen the soft animal of our body in Mark, the collective tenderness that is in each of us. Our full humanness. We can touch that grace within us when everything around us feels as though it's spinning out of control.

I marvel at the ability of Mark's body to regenerate itself. It makes me think of our connection to nature and the universe we live in. Bits of us are from our universe, including stardust.

Our quiet period gives way toward the end of August to a constant challenge with arrhythmia. The doctors prescribe meds to slow his heart down. I learn that arrhythmia prevents blood from efficiently reaching all parts of his body. It, too, can compromise the viability of Mark's fledgling skin grafts and continued healing of his amputation sites.

Over the course of a few days Mark's heart rate returns to normal. His skin grafts seem to be doing well. And then he suffers another short-lived bout of arrhythmia.

Dr. Jameson rolls off his three-week shift with Mark, and Dr. Williams comes back on as Mark's primary doctor.

We wait for the next batch of skin grafts to come in from Boston to get him more fully covered on the front side of his body. Mark's arrhythmia has a negative impact on his kidney functions. Because his heart isn't pumping efficiently, his blood pressure is lower and effusion in his body is lower. His kidneys aren't producing much urine. The other contributor to his kidney issue is simply the cumulative stress Mark's body has been under. Dr. Williams mentions that if urine output remains too low for long, it can lead to kidney failure. The dialysis machine is keeping his kidneys going but the nurses will closely monitor in hopes his urine output increases.

"Mark's skin grafts are looking encouraging," Dr. Williams says, delivering the good news we so desperately need. "There continues to be no sign of infection."

Thank God—we can finally put the fungal infection behind us.

"The good news is that if Mark's heart rate can get back to normal and his kidneys can produce more urine, I can officially say that Mark's status is a miracle," Dr. Williams says.

I think back to how Dr. Williams was trying to tell me that he thought Mark could die within the first two weeks of his arrival at the Burn Center. We've come such a long way.

That night at the condo I write a post to our online community thanking them for their prayers and intercessions, telling them how much they truly matter. I tell them that it's officially a miracle that Mark has made it this far. I'm beginning to understand how powerful prayer and hope can be.

Thankfully, Mark's heart rate returns to normal. His blood pressure stays in a reasonable range. His kidneys are still not great. Dani, one of the tall, willowy nurses on permanent staff, explains that when Mark is more fully healed, his kidney functions will make a comeback. The worst-case scenario for burn patients is that if their kidneys don't recover by the time they're discharged, they'll need long-term dialysis two to three times a week.

One afternoon while I'm sitting by the doctor's offices waiting for the cleaners to clean Mark's room, a girl with dark hair is skipping and hopping alongside her mother in the hallway. I watch them and recognize with a start that it's Isabella McCune, the young girl I read about in the news, who recovered from burns on 65 percent of her body from a firepit accident. Her mother is chatting with the nurses. This brave little girl told Dr. Williams she didn't want to be sedated. Taylor Swift visited her when she learned that Isabella was a fan of hers. *This little girl endured, what was it, over one hundred surgeries in nine months?*

Immediately I introduce myself to them. "Bella" is what Isabella goes by. Her mom is Lilly.

"What a bundle of energy you are, Bella!" I exclaim, watching her energetically hopping on one foot. It's amazing to see how alive she is after seeing photos of her bedridden for months.

"Yes, she is," Lilly says with a wide grin. "She's starting school soon and trying to decide what sports she wants to do."

Bella shouts out, "Mom, I want to play tackle football!"

My goodness—what a plucky girl! Fearless.

"Wow, Bella! That's awesome!" one of the nurses says. "But what about other sports, like softball or volleyball?"

"Nope. I want to play football…." Bella's voice trails off as she skips down the hallway, away from us.

I explain to Lilly what happened to Mark and that we've been here for three months now.

"I remember how I got used to the sounds of the machines in Bella's room," Lilly says. "I was sleeping in there with her for so many nights. I'd just climb into bed with her."

"Boy, do I wish *I* could do that. My husband is way too big for me to slide in next to him. It's also very hot in there. It's hard for me to sleep."

Bella's mom looks at me sympathetically and nods. "It does get so warm."

The nurses and I chat with her a bit more before Bella and Lilly have to go.

"Bella and I just wanted to stop by before her treatment upstairs." Lilly turns to me. "I wish you and your husband the best of luck," she says warmly.

I wave goodbye to Bella, who has already run ahead of her mother.

Lisa and Janice from the palliative care team let me know that, with Mark out of the woods, their involvement will be to ensure proper coordination of communication between the doctors and me. I'm internalizing just how long getting Mark fully covered with skin grafts will take. If he doesn't suffer any blood pressure issues and everything's on track, I figure that the best case is that it will be the end of November to December when we'll be done.

Cindy, the music therapist, continues to show up every couple of weeks. This time she brings an instrument that makes the same sound as ocean waves. It's soothing and transports me back to my mom's home in Hawaii. I'm sure it's relaxing for Mark, but I can't tell. I'm the one who dozes off, waking with a start to the sound of Cindy packing up her instrument to go.

Mark continues having A-fib (arrhythmia) through the last week of August and into the first few days of September. They're on call to do a cardiac esophageal diagnostic procedure as needed. They want to make sure he doesn't have a blood clot.

The next batch of skin grafts will arrive on September 12. It takes grafts thirty days to fully form and join into a section of new skin. I calculate that by September 12 we'll know if Mark's arms will be covered in new skin. I can't wait and start mentally counting down the days.

That's what this time is like—constantly waiting for skin grafts to arrive, for them to decide where to staple them, air them out for seven days, and wait a full thirty days for skin buds to blossom and become skin.

Adrian and I continue playing music for Mark. Rock, pop, and classical when he's stable. Meditation music when he has A-fib and blood pressure issues.

One afternoon I read Tina Fey's *Bossypants* autobiography to Mark. I laugh out loud, reading sections of it. I know he would be chuckling with me if he were conscious. Mark has looked relaxed most of the day. I know he may not understand or hear what I'm reading, but I'm hoping he'll feel my lighthearted energy. God knows we all need moments of levity day in and day out in this hospital.

It's late August when Alyssa reports that, after more than a couple months, Mark's becoming more conscious. I notice every once in a while, his eyes open but he's not fully awake. It's startling to witness after seeing his eyes shut for so long. She explains that because he's been on sedatives for so long, he's gradually adjusted to the dosage. It would take a higher dosage now to keep him in a coma-like state. With the steady progress of Mark's skin grafts, the doctors believe the nurses can better manage his pain. It's time to ease him out of his medically induced coma.

"We're talking to Dylan about getting a tracheotomy for Mark so he can speak," Alyssa says.

"What?" It's the first Adrian and I have heard of this possibility. "How does it work?"

"The doctors want to start weaning Mark off his respiratory equipment by installing a tracheotomy. It's a device they place in his throat that allows him to speak."

Adrian is cautiously smiling at Alyssa. He's measured in his reaction because we've had so many ups and downs. I feel a jolt of energy as I get up from my chair to pace the small room.

"It'll be a little hard to understand him at first but it'll get easier as he gets used to talking with it and you get used to hearing him speak."

"Wow. Adrian!" I stride over to where he's sitting. "Your dad will finally talk again. I can't believe it!"

Adrian breaks out in a smile, caught up in my enthusiasm. "I wonder what his first words will be?" he muses out loud.

A few days later, we arrive to see Mark with a white device planted in his throat and a clear tube coming out of it. He's not ready to be fully off his respiratory equipment. They'll monitor and take him off and put him back on, making sure he can breathe as needed.

Every few days he becomes conscious for a few seconds, his eyes slightly open but not communicating. Another evening, he's awake and can speak but has no voice with the trach in his throat. Suddenly, one evening he tries to talk. We can tell from him speaking without sound that he wants *water*. He can't drink water or he'll aspirate.

Chloe, the very kind, younger night nurse from Alabama, dips a foam toothbrush into a cup of ice water and puts it in his mouth. He wants more, but she can't give him much. It's painful to watch.

Mark continues to try speaking. It's wonderful to watch, even if we have to guess what he wants to say. He's clean-shaven and his skin is smooth. He looks childlike.

His arms are in foam splits horizontally. He mouths to Kate, the night nurse with Hawaiian in-laws, that the splints are bothering him. She and Chloe take the splints off. They want him to relax and enjoy our visit and will put them back on after we leave for the night. She gives Mark a stronger dose of pain meds to help him.

Adrian looks through the internet for some jokes to tell Mark. He picks ones he thinks his dad would enjoy.

"So, Dad, here's a good one since you grew up on a farm. What do you call a rude cow?" He looks at me expectantly.

I shrug. "What?"

"Beef jerky."

Mark smiles.

His first smile in what, three months? I feel a surge, a rush of water rapidly carrying me upward to the surface of the sea. I can breathe again, after being caught in the murky, dark underwater with Mark for so long. I want to run out of the room and grab every person I pass, shouting, "Hey, everyone! Mark's awake! Can you believe it? He smiled at us." I control myself because I can't leave him right now. I'm enjoying the moment I've waited for so long. I desperately want to hold his hand. Instead, I pull my chair up as close as I can next to him.

Kate increases Mark's sedation dosage so that he can settle down and sleep after we leave. They want to help him get on a normal wake/sleep cycle.

I lean in as closely as I can to his face and look into his clear, green eyes. "I love you, Mark." I want so much to lay my head on his shoulder, but he's still too delicate.

I close my eyes and imagine hugging him.

"We're going to let you rest now. I love you, I love you, darling." Something flickers in his eyes. He mouths to me, *I love you.*

I can't believe he's speaking to me. My chest beats wildly. I smile at Mark, wanting this long-awaited and precious moment to last. But I'm aware that the increased sedation will pull him underwater soon. It's merciful so that he won't feel as much pain.

My vision is blurry. I wipe my face with my hand. *I finally have my husband back*. Phoenix isn't home but with Mark awake, I'm home again.

I take off his glasses and put them by his bedside.

I take one last look at Mark lying in bed as he has for the last three months. He has his eyes closed. The drugs must be kicking in.

Rest, my sweetheart. Just rest. May God protect you tonight while you sleep.

For the next three days while Mark is in stable condition, Adrian and I enjoy time chatting with him. I wake up every morning, eager to get to the hospital. When we show up in his room, he usually has his eyes closed. When I announce loudly, "Hi, Mark! It's Jenny and Adrian," he opens his eyes wide.

We try to limit how much we talk to him. He gets tired easily. Usually he's sleepy when we first arrive after his dressing change, because they increase his sedation dosage so he can tolerate the way they must move him around.

No surgeries are planned while we wait for the skin grafts to arrive in mid-September.

While we have Mark back, because he's now more adjusted to his sedation levels and more conscious, it's hard on him too.

KC and Jeanne are back on nights with Mark. Like KC, Jeanne has often been on night shift with Mark. She's Filipino American and the more relaxed counterpart to the firecracker that KC is. They had asked to work Mark's shift. I'm touched. During their second evening with Mark, Adrian and I arrive in his room after dinner. He seems agitated.

"Last night poor Mark was in so much pain," KC says, crinkling her nose with a frown. KC is always animated. "Jeanne and I had to reposition his body for the dressing change in the middle of the night. It broke my heart to see him cry from the pain."

My chest is pounding. I've never seen Mark cry, not even when his dad died. "Can't you give him a higher dosage of pain meds?"

"Yes, we increased his Versed. But I'll ask the doctors if we can give him Propofol, which is what we give him during dressing changes. I'll recommend that we give it to him continuously."

"That would be good, KC. Whatever you can do to keep him comfortable."

"Yes, that's our goal. The doctors do extensive morning rounds every Tuesday. That's the day after tomorrow, at the end of our shift. I'll talk to the doctors."

The next evening Mark tries to tell us something and attempts to move his arms to point to something. We aren't sure what. His body? Something in the room? KC, Jeanne, Adrian, and I try to understand what he needs.

"Are you too warm? Take the blanket off?"

He shakes his head.

"Do you have pain somewhere, Mark?" KC asks. He shakes his head.

"Do you want some water? Are you thirsty?" He continues shaking his head, trying to move his arms.

"His heart rate is increasing," Jeanne says sharply, watching the heart monitor. *Poor Mark*. He's upset that he can't communicate with us. KC pulls me aside and quietly says, "Mark's slipping into A-fib again. I'm going to increase his Versed dosage, the sedative he's on. I'm also going to give him some morphine."

It's the humane thing to do. It's hard to feel so helpless, unable to understand what he wants. A few minutes after KC gives him morphine, Mark settles down. We can tell because he stops trying to speak and his heart rate returns to normal. But we also lose Mark to the fog of the drugs.

It's become clear to me that we're moving into a new phase. Not only in the skin graft marathon, but with Mark more conscious, we have to manage his pain. It's the tradeoff of having him back, slipping in and out of consciousness. I have a new appreciation for why the doctors kept him in a medically induced coma until recently. It's the only merciful thing to do.

Chapter 26

INSPIRATION

Through early to mid-September the nurses get permission to give Mark Dilaudid, in addition to Versed, in their continued attempts to help ease his pain. They suggest that I ask to consult specifically with a pain doctor on staff. They also tell me that Mark is trying to move his arms and legs when he's awake. I'm sure he desperately wants out of his bed.

Dr. Williams estimates Mark will be in the ICU for another three months and then one month of in-hospital rehab. We've now been here for around three months. It's a marathon of physical endurance for Mark.

They continue to vigilantly monitor for any infections that might be brewing.

I try to think of several positives. Mark's heart rate is normal, and no A-fib. There continues to be no further sign of fungal infection, thankfully. The nurses report that the skin grafts on his arms and front torso look great and are growing and healing nicely. His leg amputation sites have healthy-looking tissue. They remind me that Mark's lungs are clear. Many patients suffer internal damage from smoke inhalation, which is not something we have to worry about with Mark.

Adrian leaves to visit some college buddies in Illinois. Wesley flies in to see his dad and to keep me company.

The nurses let me know that Mark has a new infection and a blood clot. I accept the news without much thought. I've come to expect the ups and downs by now, trusting that the doctors and nurses are doing all they need to for Mark. I can't let it ruin the joy of seeing Mark more conscious and the thrill of knowing Wesley can finally interact with his dad.

He greets Mark on his first day visiting with a cheerful "Hi, Dad!" Mark opens his eyes and smiles at Wesley.

"Hey, Dad! The Packers beat the Bears."

Mark's smile widens a bit. I feel a sudden joy that swells like a wave inside me. It's a magical moment.

Wesley and I spend a couple days talking to Mark. He slips in and out of sleep but is awake enough for us to enjoy his conscious presence. Wesley, who retreated into his phone when Mark was completely unconscious, is now attentive to what's going on.

We're still on track for the continued march of skin graft surgery. I just hope and pray Mark won't be too sick to receive more skin grafts when they arrive.

A week later the skin grafts show up a few days early. Dr. Jameson tells us that although Mark's unburned donor sites are a small part of his body, they've proven to be fruitful as autografts, the layer they need to create to layer the lab-grown skin grafts over. His body accepts his autografts easily.

Dr. Williams returns on rotation with Mark for the rest of September. They put grafts to completely cover his front torso and the side of his thighs. Dr. Williams and the other doctors begin discussing their strategy for covering Mark's entire backside.

We continue to ride the ups and downs of intermittent arrhythmia. At one point they need to use paddles to get his heart rate and blood pressure back to normal to support his skin grafts. He still has the blood clot and an infection. They continue the antibiotics to treat his blood infection until they realize it's resistant to the two targeted antibiotics they have been using. They keep him on Bactrim and swap out another antibiotic. The blood infection can also put his grafts at risk. We're navigating a field of landmines, each one with the potential to explode at any moment.

Every day the physical therapists rotate different positions for Mark's arms to stretch them out. His arms are in the foam splints, held in place with soft Velcro straps. Poor Mark grimaces a lot, trying to move his arms. I step up my role in observing Mark's pain and asking the nurses to increase his pain meds. The physical therapists agree to give Mark more short breaks from the splints throughout the day and night.

While we wait to see if the grafts on his torso and thighs take, the doctors take him into the OR to put skin grafts where the cosmetic surgeon made cuts under his eye. The nurses continue to report that the grafts on Mark's arms are looking great.

We deal with a hodgepodge of days when we can't get in to see Mark until four o'clock because they're airing out his new grafts, and other days when they let me visit earlier. I spend my longer days and evenings with Mark, playing meditation and classical music. He needs to heal and rest after each surgery.

The efforts of all of us to manage Mark's pain continue. Olivia tells me that one morning his trach was loose during his dressing change and Mark said, "Ouch!" They immediately increased his Propofol.

"It was good he could let us know he's in pain so we can do something to make him more comfortable," Olivia tells me. "Did you know Mark is constantly moving his thighs?"

"Really?" I suddenly wonder if he knows that the rest of his legs have been amputated.

"I think he's doing crunches!" Alyssa jokes. We all chuckle.

"The good news, Jenny, is that the skin grafts on Mark's arms have grown together. They look awesome," Oliva says with a bright smile.

"Is there any way we can look at Mark's arms?" I want so badly to see the progress. Mark's been wrapped in bandages now for over three months. It would give me a clear sign he's in recovery.

Olivia shakes her head. "Unfortunately, it's all quite delicate. We should be ready to take his bandages off in…what do you think, Alyssa?"

"In another week," Alyssa replies with a solemn nod. "We'll ask Dr. Williams. Maybe sooner."

Adrian and I exchange smiles.

"Let me know, will you? It'd be amazing for me to send photos to our family," I say.

The next day, however, when we arrive in Mark's room, Alyssa beckons us to Mark, who's asleep from the Propofol they gave him during his dressing change.

Mark's arms are unwrapped.

"Oh, wow!" Adrian and I hurry to Mark's bedside.

The skin on his arms is pink, healthy, and new. We can see a crosshatch pattern from the mesh they put underneath the skin grafts. It's a grid pattern of slightly raised red skin.

Ben and Sally, Mark's physical therapists, show up and tell us that with Mark's arms healed, they'll be stretching Mark out more every day—his wrists, his elbows. They'll alternate his arms in the splints.

"Will that mesh pattern go away with time? Or is that permanent?" Adrian asks.

"With time the redness will fade," Ben replies.

I'm mesmerized as I stare at Mark's arms. Adrian too. With Mark conscious again, this is the next important sign of progress after a very long three months. This is big. "You know, I took care of Mark Haley. Do you know about him?" Sally asks.

"Yes, the drag race car driver. I read some articles and listened to his interview."

"He's doing really well now. He didn't remember a thing about the racing accident when he woke up. Mark might not remember anything about the plane accident either."

What will *Mark remember?* I don't dare bring it up now. I don't want to upset him.

"I've noticed that burn patients who had a full life before their accidents are the ones who thrive and lead fulfilling lives when they recover. Your Mark will be one of them."

I'm encouraged by what Sally says, and that evening I write a post to our online community:

> *I posted a while ago the article about Mark Haley, the drag race car driver. One of the physical therapists shared that Mark H is doing what he can to continue to live life to the fullest. It gives me a lot of hope for our Mark, that he'll be resourceful and find ways to resume an active life despite his disabilities.*

In the coming weeks Mark continues to express himself more. He's ornery when it comes to the frequent teeth-brushing. Becca, one of his nurses, reports that Mark stuck his tongue out at her when she tried to brush his teeth. I get to dip his toothbrush in ice water and put it in his mouth. It's wonderful to have something I can do for him. When Mark's awake, he smiles whenever Adrian and I chat with him. He smiles when friends like his high school pal Jeff and his friend Traci visit. And when Marcene and Harlow, family friends from Wisconsin come to visit, he turns his head toward them and smiles. He's still soundless because of the trach in his throat. It's there because he still needs respiratory support to breathe, but the medical staff continues to gradually reduce the support.

"When will Mark be more fully off his sedatives?" I ask.

"It's up to the doctors but usually they want to taper it off very gradually. Mark's adjusted to his sedatives a bit faster than most patients. Coming off them depends on how much progress we make with his remaining skin grafts and his physical therapy. Both are painful and we want to be able to keep him sedated until his grafts are complete."

The nurses keep finding ways to help Mark be more comfortable. They find a neck pillow for him. They talk to him and always tell him what they're doing when he's awake. I ask Ben and Sally if they can do any PT to help stretch Mark's neck. I'm sure he has the world's most awful crick now from being in bed for fifteen weeks. Ben apologetically explains that there's not much they can do because of his trach and all the IV lines.

The nurses are my family now. We talk about their families. Their challenges. What they love about their jobs and what they like less. Their jobs are intense. They keep Mark alive and comfortable every minute of the day and night. The nurses who work in the Burn Center ICU enjoy people in a way that's different from the staff at regular ICUs, where patients are in and out within a few days.

I find out that Olivia and her boyfriend, Carlos, are wrapping up their three-month assignments at the Burn Center and returning to El Paso.

"Please stay in touch, Olivia. You're the best. Thank you for everything you and Carlos have done for us." I give her a warm hug. "You've been nothing but kind to Mark and our family. And you are so good at what you do."

"Aww. I've loved getting to know you and your family. Adrian. Wesley. Mark's family," she says, her eyes shining. "Yes, we'll stay in touch. I'll find you on Facebook."

That evening I ask our Lotsa Helping Hands community to continue praying that Mark's skin grafts take, that his blood infection and blood clot heal and resolve themselves.

Adrian will leave in a week to go back to Zurich for his fall semester at ETH.

"Honey, thank you for sacrificing part of your last semester to come be with Dad and me."

Adrian nods. I know it means there's no question that he would do it again.

"It's a miracle that Dad made it through his fungal infection. I look back now and realize that Dr. Williams was telling us that they didn't think Dad would last more than a week or two. Do you remember?"

"Yeah, it wasn't looking good for Dad." He shakes his head.

"Adrian, you've been such a huge help. I can't thank you enough." I reach out and give him a hug. When we release each other, I add, "It's been great to let you drive us back to the condo some evenings when I'm tired. You've been here with me through the worst times. When Dad's legs were amputated. When they thought they'd have to amputate his arms."

"That was rough," he says, nodding with solemn eyes. "I'm so glad he kept his arms. It means he can do more. Cook, drive, type on his laptop."

"Yes, thank God. It was a close one. I thought your dad would lose his arms."

Adrian reaches out and holds my hand.

I look at him intently. "I want you to get your life back after spending all these months at the hospital with me. You need to get going on your master's."

Adrian smiles, and his eyes brighten. "I'm really looking forward to it."

"Your dad would be so proud of you. Remember how independent he wanted you and Wesley to be?"

Adrian nods.

"Well, after you guys went off to college, he wistfully said to me, 'Well, Jenny, we succeeded in raising our boys to be independent. And now I miss them.' It's funny—I think he didn't expect that."

"Yeah, that's interesting because he always told Wesley and me that he'd leave no forwarding address with us after you two retired."

"Well, he got sentimental after all. He was so proud of you when you started your ETH program."

"Are you and Dad going to be okay?"

"You know, we don't know everything about the future but we're on a good path with the skin grafts. That's all I'm focused on now."

"That's great, Mom. You'll text and let me know how Dad is doing, right?"

I nod, smiling. For the first time, I feel so much hope.

A few days later I see Adrian off at the airport. Looking at his Swissair flight information on the screen makes me feel so sad. I'm going to miss him. He's been my faithful companion these last few months. It's felt longer than that, like a year. He's twenty-five years old. Mark would want him to go back to school and get his degree. I want that for him too.

Adrian slides his suitcase out of the trunk and shuts the lid.

"I hope you enjoy your semester, honey," I say while hugging him. "I'm so sorry you got interrupted the way you did last semester."

We look at each other, knowing that there's no reason for me to apologize. I just needed to acknowledge out loud that his dad's accident was a terrible reason for him to take a break from school.

"Yeah, I will. I'm excited about some of the classes I'm taking."

"Continue to be a good mediator, will you?" I grin. "Keep those Swiss and Germans working well with the international students, okay?"

"Yeah, I will," he says with a smile. "It's not so easy, but I will."

I hug him again, holding onto him longer.

When we finally release each other, he says, "And don't forget, Mom—when you're tired, take the highway and not 24th Street. It's safer."

I nod, waving to him as he heads for the doors with his backpack and big suitcase. It's hard to see when I get behind the wheel. I wipe my eyes and take a moment to compose myself before I check Google Maps for the directions back to the condo.

During this time I discover a private outdoor patio near the main hospital entrance. On cooler days I take breaks and sit outside reading. It's September in Phoenix; the temperatures are averaging in the nineties. I'll never take for granted again the opportunity to enjoy sitting outdoors without wondering if I'll get heatstroke.

Leah from the Arizona Burn Foundation has been in touch. She's stopped by a few times over the last few months to say hello and to ask how Mark and our family are holding up. She's always kind, and I enjoy talking with her about how we're doing and getting updates on her own young family. When she hears that Mark is in the skin graft phase, she stops by to chat.

"I'm so glad to hear Mark's been having some good success with the skin grafts on his arms."

"It is such good news, isn't it? We weren't sure Mark was going to make it back in July when he had that terrible fungal infection—remember?"

"I do. I understand from Dr. Williams that they're working on grafting Mark's torso and thighs now."

"Yes, and after that, Mark's backside is next." It suddenly occurs to me that this front side is going faster than it typically would because Mark's legs are amputated above the knees. A third of him is missing. I push the thought aside and focus on my conversation with Leah.

"I've been thinking..." Leah looks at me thoughtfully. "It'd be a good time for you to meet Buddy and Cece Johnson."

"Who are they?"

"Buddy's a former patient here at the Burn Center. He survived a house fire. He was 90 percent burned and was here in the ICU for seven months."

House fire. I wonder what happened. I'm learning about all the ways people get burned. Mark Haley and drag car racing. Bella at home when someone accidentally poured gasoline in a firepit. The little Navajo girl who fell into a hot pot of stew at a campsite.

"Do you want me to introduce you to them? They come weekly to the burn survivors' support group here at the hospital. It could be helpful for them to share with you what recovery and getting back to normal life are like."

"Sure—I'd love to meet them." It feels so good to be discussing recovery and what leaving the Burn Center will be like.

"The burn survivor group meets every Wednesday. I'll contact Buddy and Cece to see if they can come visit with you after this Wednesday's support group meeting."

It's Monday. Leah texts me later in the day to let me know that Buddy and Cece will stop by to see me around four o'clock after the support group meeting wraps up.

On Wednesday an older gentleman with a beard, in a battery-powered wheelchair, shows up at the doorway of Mark's room. A petite woman with gray hair in a ponytail is standing by him.

"Well, hello there. Are you Jenny?"

This must be Buddy and Cece. Buddy has prosthetic arms and one prosthetic leg. I'll have to ask him how well his prosthetics work.

"Hi! You must be Buddy and Cece?"

They nod.

"It's so nice of Leah to introduce us. Thank you so much for coming by." I'm eager to learn about Buddy's story. "Should we go sit in the chairs by Pamela's office?" Pamela is Dr. Williams's assistant. There are a couple chairs and a side table where I usually wait when they're changing Mark's lines or cleaning his room.

It's a perfect setup. Two chairs for Cece and me, Buddy sitting at the same level as us in his wheelchair.

"We heard from Leah that Mark was in a plane accident," Buddy says. I'm so used to explaining Mark's story. I go on a sort of autopilot of facts. *His plane quit working eleven minutes after takeoff from Scottsdale Airport. Tried to emergency land on a two-lane road in Deer Valley. Swerved right to avoid three drivers on the road. Lost power and balance, right wing clipped two light poles and caught on fire. Plane hit a concrete barrier, flipped upside down and landed face down by the side of Deer Valley Road.*

By now I'm used to the horrified expressions on people's faces when I mention that his right wing clipped two light poles and caught on fire, explaining that the fuel tanks are in the wings. They gasp when I then mention that his plane hit a concrete wall and flipped upside down. *It's horrific—I know.* It still astounds me now to think that Mark called me from the ER after his traumatic ordeal. I'd be paralyzed with fear if I were in his shoes. Mark obviously had the presence of mind to try to land the plane and maneuvered to avoid flying into those drivers. No question—my beloved Mark is courageous.

"Tell me—what happened to you, Buddy? How did you get burned?"

"Well, our family was asleep. It was a house fire. I woke up to flames on the deck. I woke Cece up. I checked on the kids. Luckily, they had already run out of their rooms and gotten outside. Then the next thing I know, the floor collapsed underneath me."

"Wow! What happened next?"

"I don't remember a thing. Cece here tells me that a helicopter arrived and they flew me here."

"They put you in a medically induced coma, of course, right?" I ask.

"Yes. For four-and-a-half months. That was in 2012. I was 90 percent burned. Third-degree burns everywhere."

"So they had to amputate your arms and leg?" I ask, eager to ask him about prosthetics.

"Oh, no. I was born without arms and a leg. I was a Thalidomide baby."

Ah, yes—he would be about the right age. I remembered reading that Thalidomide babies were born in the late 1950s and early 1960s.

"I was fully functioning with my prosthetics before the fire. Right, Cece?"

Cece smiles and nods. "Buddy was a rodeo rider."

"Wow—really?" I'm trying to picture Buddy hanging onto a bucking horse with prosthetic arms. "You must have amazing balance."

"I grew up riding horses ever since I was a kid. I rode in rodeos in northern Arizona." Buddy beams with pride. "Then when I met Cece, I had worked my way up from being a landscaper to running my own business."

I'm so impressed with how hard Buddy must have worked to keep up with life before and after his burn injuries. This guy already had gumption in buckets before the fire.

"Cece had to put up with a lot after I got out of the ICU."

I glance at Cece. She's quiet and just smiles. She's letting Buddy tell his story.

"I was in such a rush to get out of this place. I was so tired of hospitals after spending seven months here."

"He was climbing the walls," Cece remarks.

"Looking back, I realize I should've stayed another month. Cece couldn't handle the home care I needed. It was me, not her, that was the problem."

Buddy's a hefty, solid guy like Mark, just older, and Cece's shorter than me.

"For example, I was too weak to get into the shower by myself. Cece wasn't strong enough to help me."

"Yeah, I'm going to be in the same boat. Mark's almost six feet two inches and he was 210 pounds before his plane accident."

"You'd better hire an in-home nurse to help Mark for the first few months," Buddy states emphatically.

"There was no way I could lift Buddy into the shower," Cece adds. "That first year at home was really tough. You're going to need round-the-clock in-home help."

I look at Buddy. "How long were you in residential rehab after the Burn Center?"

Buddy looks at Cece. "Around one-and-a-half months?"

Cece nods. "Yes, that's right."

"But," Buddy says while looking pointedly at me, "I should've stayed two-and-a-half months. Again, I just rushed through everything."

"That's Buddy." Cece chuckles.

I can tell that Buddy is tough as nails, a physically hardy and determined guy. There's a sweetness to the interplay between the two of them.

Buddy continues, "Look—everyone's recovery is different. Everyone is different in how fast they'll rehabilitate. Leah told us that Mark had his legs amputated. And some fingers. He's going to need time and rehab to adjust to that. I already didn't have arms and a leg, so I was used to that my whole life. But after my recovery I was weakened and needed to use a wheelchair more."

"I assume Mark will be in assisted rehab here in Phoenix before he's in any shape to fly home to California," I explain. I know Buddy and Cece may not know since they're locals. I say it out loud more for myself. It's the first time I've thought that far ahead.

"It'll be important for Mark to go to a rehab center that specializes in both amputee and burn recovery," Buddy says. "It may be best for him to stay at one locally because they can stay in close touch with the doctors here."

Okay, sounds like we'll be here in Phoenix longer than the three-and-a-half months Dr. Williams forecasted for Mark's stay in the Burn Center ICU. It'd be good to have continuity of care with the doctors here. Maybe we won't go home until April or May 2020?

"The head of social work at the Burn Center will help you find the right rehab place for Mark," Cece explains.

It's the first I've heard of social workers. It's helpful to know what their role is at a burn center.

Buddy's quiet. "You know, it was a tough road for a long time. But I never wished I died or dwelled on why the fire happened."

"What caused the fire?"

"They never found out the exact cause. But how I look at it, there's no use looking to the past. I've always focused only on the here and now—and the future."

"That's great." I'm hoping Mark will have the same attitude. I think he will. But he will be madder than hell until he knows what happened to his plane.

Dani stops by. "Hey, Jenny. The intern is here to change out Mark's lines. It's going to take a few hours."

That means I need to wait to return to Mark's room.

"Do you want to go to the gift shop in the lobby with us?" Cece asks. "I need to find a gift for my granddaughter."

"Sure." I'm learning a lot, and so far I'm enjoying my time with them.

We get up and start walking through the halls and out the Burn Center exit. Buddy whizzes effortlessly alongside us in his wheelchair. Mark will have one of these too. It makes me chuckle to think what a speed demon Mark will be in a battery-powered wheelchair. He does love anything fast.

Buddy goes a little faster, ahead of Cece and me.

"Buddy's something else," I say, smiling at Cece. "He reminds me of my husband, Mark. Mark also has a totally can-do attitude about everything."

Cece's eyes mist over. "That man is the love of my life. I can't imagine my life without him. When he was here at the Burn Center, he had infection after infection. Of course, he doesn't remember any of it because he was in a coma."

"Yes, I know what you mean. Mark almost died from a fungal infection."

Cece nods knowingly. "Buddy's recovery was complicated because he was an amputee before his burn injuries."

Interesting. Whether you were without limbs before or after, either way it adds complications.

"What kept you going?" I ask Cece.

"God," she said simply. "I believed that Buddy was in God's hands."

I understand what she means. I trust Mark to God and the universe of love. I trust in all the prayers of our online community. Their prayers matter.

"I believe that Mark is in God's hands too. We have so many family and friends praying for him."

"That's really good, Jenny. Prayer is powerful."

I feel such a kinship with Cece. She loves Buddy the way I love Mark. She's also a woman of faith. I'm sure she's a churchgoer—unlike me, a former church attendee—and that's okay. We both believe in God and a higher power. That's all that matters to me. Buddy's attitude and spirit remind me of Mark—forthright, direct, positive, and a fighter.

It's a pleasant diversion to check out the gift shop. I just tag along with Buddy and Cece, looking at everything on the shelves, hangers, and display kiosks. I had never taken the time to browse and wander to any other part of the hospital other than the Burn Center and the cafeteria in the basement. Cece and I admire some of the turquoise and silver jewelry.

There are some cute baby blankets and kids' toys. Somehow it feels comforting to just do something normal with the two of them. We spend the rest of our time chatting about Buddy and Cece's grandchildren.

When I climb into bed that evening, I think about how many inspiring burn survivors I've met just in the last few weeks. Bella, the Energizer bunny, hopping and skipping down the hall at the Burn Center. Reading about Mark Haley and "Don't Look Back," his Boston theme song. And now Buddy, the former rodeo rider, born without arms and a leg and how he stays focused only on the here and the now and the future.

These are all exceptional people. Mark is too. I fall asleep easily that night—and not from exhaustion. It's from an inner peace that I feel for the first time since I've come to Phoenix.

Chapter 27

FRENCH ROAST COFFEE

Toward the end of September Mark continues to be increasingly awake. I had ordered a replacement for his black-rimmed Ray-Ban glasses that were destroyed in the fire. They arrive from the Site for Sore Eyes store in Mountain View. Kenny, the owner, had learned of Mark's plane crash and sent a replacement pair for free. It was kind of him.

Mark always looked so stylish and smart in those glasses. But anyone who knows him knows he doesn't just look smart—he *is* smart. In fact, he's one of the smartest people I know. The absence of his intelligent and pragmatic presence was something I had acutely missed. I didn't have anyone to talk to about so many things, big and small. Our finances, guidance for boys about career and dating. Was dill or thyme better in potato salad? What did he think of the latest global warming data? It was a topic he loved to be contrarian about.

I post to our Lotsa Helping Hands community:

> *I was thrilled yesterday to put new eyeglasses on Mark. I got a smile out of him when I put them on.*
>
> *Today I arrived in his room to see him watching the UW Badgers Northwestern football game. The nurses had propped him up with extra pillows. A feeling of normalcy has returned for the first time, hearing the din of the game, the announcers, the crowds cheering on the TV. Wow. What a milestone!*

Our days now are filled with continued airing out of skin grafts and careful management of his blood pressure. The physical therapists take over and spend long sessions stretching his arms above his head, working on the mobility of his elbows and wrists. Male burn patients are at risk for excess mineralization in their elbows, which can cause sharp, dagger-like pain. It's weird that only men suffer from this condition, not women. The physical therapists tell me they don't know why when I ask. They run an ultrasound and find no mineralization in his left elbow, but there is a question about his right. The physical therapists will closely monitor Mark for elbow pain.

He lets the therapists know if he doesn't like something they're doing. He'll mouth to them, "Pain." Sometimes he'll resist, holding back his arms when they try to stretch him out. Ben tells me it will take six months to a year for Mark to regain muscle tone.

Pain management continues to be a priority. The palliative people make sure there's enough communication between the doctors and me. But it's understood that with Mark in a productive skin-grafting stage, they don't need to be in touch so frequently.

As Mark heals from the blood infection, the nurses find yellow spots on his lower abdomen and his temperature drops. They've never let up on the oral antifungal meds, but now they step up his topical antifungal cream and consult with the doctors. Dr. Williams examines the spots carefully, and to my relief, he's not concerned about the yellow spots at all.

Mark's feisty personality comes out in his power struggle with the nurse over his teeth-brushing every two hours. One afternoon he clamps down hard on the toothbrush and Becca can't get the toothbrush out. After lots of coaxing from her and me, along with her gentle tugging, Becca finally manages to pry it out. When she does, he sticks his tongue out at her!

"Oh, no. Did he really just stick his tongue out at you?" I call out to Becca. "He's being ornery!"

Mark sticks his tongue out again at Becca. She and I burst out laughing. It's so good to see Mark express himself after being unconscious for months.

When it's time to brush his teeth again, I try bribery.

"Sweetie, I'm going to give you some nice ice water if you let Becca brush your teeth. Okay?"

I take his toothbrush and dip it in ice water. "Okay, Mark. Can you open your mouth for me? I've got some nice cold water for you."

He readily opens his mouth, sucking on the cold toothbrush. When I'm done, he's cooperative with Becca for the brushing. She and I give each other a silent high five.

Another time, Kara, one of the younger nurses, tells me that she tried to brush his teeth but Mark refused to open his mouth. When she gave up and started moving away, he suddenly opened his mouth. When she tried to put the toothbrush back in, he promptly clamped his jaws shut. He did a bait and switch with her several times. His teeth didn't get brushed.

I laugh out loud when Kara describes this. I get it. It's one of the very few things Mark has control over.

When Mark sees me show up, he mouths *water* to me.

"Okay, I'll get you water, darling. But then you have to let Kara brush your teeth first. Okay?"

Childlike, he nods his head and blinks his green eyes.

The nurses tell me that Mark asks for me when I'm not in his room. He's more aware of when I'm there and when I'm not. They often tell him after his dressing change that I'm on my way. I now make sure I'm spending as much time as I can in his room. My days and evenings become longer. On non-surgery days, I pack a sandwich and eat an early lunch in the waiting room, waiting for his dressing change to be over. I spend the entire afternoon with Mark, head out for an early dinner, then come back to stay with him until eight or nine o'clock before I go home for the night.

I'm more relaxed and have more animated conversations with the nurses, hoping that the laughter and positive energy in the room are something Mark can feel, even when he's resting.

Each patient has two nurses, one who manages the kidney dialysis machine, the other focused on bedside. They are always busy. One afternoon the two nurses, Mollie and Kendra, both brunettes, are perched at their workstations just outside the doorway to Mark's room and are rocking to the music that's playing inside.

Suddenly, when "Bohemian Rhapsody" starts playing, Mollie and Kendra burst into song. They get up and stand in the doorway, holding their phones in the air, swaying as if they're at a concert. I laugh and join in singing with them. But when they ask me to lead a Spice Girls song, I tell them I don't know any of the words. Kendra takes the lead by singing "Stop."

We're dancing to the song, sashaying around Mark's bed. I let Kendra and Mollie do the singing. I just dance, swinging myself around and around until I'm dizzy. It's exhilarating. Mark and I love to dance. I haven't laughed this hard in a long time.

Dr. Williams tells me that an area by Mark's tailbone was severely burned. He shows me a photo they took, and the tissue is dark. He mentions that the darkened tissue area is getting smaller, taken over by healthier tissue. He explains that Mark's backside is slower to heal because he's lying on his back.

Today Mark has three physical therapists working on him: Ben, Sally, and Dierdre, the head of physical therapy. I like Dierdre a lot and we talk constantly while they stretch Mark out and move his arms around, alternating splints. They're asking Mark to lift his thighs, move them sideways, and press them into the mattress. They've given him an extra dose of pain meds before they start so he can be comfortable.

I wonder if Mark knows his legs have been amputated. I pull Dierdre aside and quietly ask, "Dierdre, do you think Mark knows about his leg amputations? Has he said anything about it to you? Especially now that you're asking him to do leg lifts."

Dierdre shakes her head. "I don't really know. I don't mention the amputations for obvious reasons. It could be upsetting for him to know."

I'm anxious about how to explain it to Mark when the right time comes.

"Let's think about what we'll say if he asks," Dierdre says. "We should be consistent because he may ask us in PT or he may ask you."

"I agree." I have no idea how to handle it other than to be straight with Mark. But I feel sick thinking about his reaction.

My days spent with Mark follow a rhythm of him going in and out of consciousness or sleeping most of the day. According to the nurses, the skin grafts on his torso and thighs look promising, and the amputation wound sites on his hands are looking healthy and pink.

Suzie arrives from Denver to spend a week with Mark and me. It's good to have her back after being alone since Adrian returned to school. Dr. Williams tells us that, assuming all goes well with the skin grafts on Mark's torso and thighs, combined with his arms, he'll be 50 percent covered with his own skin. I'm soaring inside. Suzie's thrilled too.

The challenge, Dr. Williams explains, with grafting Mark's posterior is that, because patients lie on their backs, skin grafts have a lower rate of acceptance in that area. It may take several retakes, he explains. They'll plan to start with grafts to his upper back first. He's also told the nurses he wants them to wake Mark up more.

Suzie and I decide that we need to joke around, talk more to Mark to keep him awake. When we get into his room, Ben tells us that Mark had asked to sit up in his bed.

As Suzie and I enter the room, Alyssa says to me, "This morning, right before his dressing change, Mark asked me to call you."

My chest feels instantly soft and warm.

"I asked him, 'Is it because you want to tell Jenny that you love her?' And he nodded yes."

Mark's awake, his green eyes watching us. He mouths to me, "I love you."

"I love you too, Mark." I blink back tears. I so badly want to hug him, but I still can't. I can't wait for the day when we can touch each other again. I think of how we used to sit on the couch together at home, his arm draped over my shoulder, both of us reading. I would gently caress his hand, the back side rough, his palm soft. We'll get back to that again, I tell myself.

"Oh, and physical therapy is coming today at Mark's request. If you remember, Mark wants to sit up more in bed."

Excellent. Mark's taking charge of his life here in the ICU. I love it. This is the Mark I know.

Ben, Sally, Dierdre, and another physical therapist I don't know arrive to help Mark sit up. *Wow*, I think. *They brought the entire crew*. Watching them in action, I quickly realize that helping Mark sit up is a serious ordeal. Because he's such a big guy, they call in another two physical therapists to help out.

On a count of three, they hoist Mark up in his bed, setting him up for just one minute. Mark soundlessly howls in pain. His eyes and mouth are wide open in utter agony. It's because his core and back muscles have atrophied after four months in bed. Suzie steps back because it's too hard for her to watch. It's hard for me to watch too, but I'm riveted.

When they ease him back down, Mark relaxes. But the effort has taken its toll. He looks exhausted. His face is crumpled, as if he's receding inside himself.

Dierdre says, "We'll start setting Mark up once a day. Here at the Burn Center we're fairly aggressive about physical therapy so patients can achieve some minimum level of mobility when they go to acute residential rehab."

"That's great." I guess the pain must be worth it.

"The time to do it is starting now while he's allowed to have plenty of pain medication through an IV drip. The pain meds will be more limited when he leaves the hospital."

"Do you think Mark will be able to do adaptive skiing when he's ready?" I ask.

Andrea, one of the physical therapists, says, "I'm a skier. And yes, he should be able to."

"Oh, good. Mark loves skiing." It gives me hope that it's one activity Mark can return to once he adjusts to the adaptive aspect.

The next day Mark sleeps a lot. He also complains of pain when he wakes up and Alyssa steps up his pain meds. She explains that Mark's exhausted from his attempt to sit up yesterday.

Dr. Williams stops by to let us know that they've ordered another round of skin grafts for Mark's upper back. Mark doesn't have enough donor sites on his lower abdomen and inner thigh to extract sufficient autografts to put on his back. Typically these have a higher "take" rate on the back.

I look at the calendar on my phone. It's October 1. It's hard to believe we've been here since June. I'm guessing back skin grafts will take us to the end of December and maybe into January. I need to start thinking about bringing Mark home in a few more months. I'll call Jack, our contractor, to see if it's possible to build a handicapped bathroom for Mark. I begin to obsess about where it could be located. Maybe convert our laundry room into a handicapped bathroom, move the washer and dryer into the garage.

Steven's been talking about coming for a visit in October. I text Jack to see when he can come. It would be ideal if Steven could cover for me while I do an overnight trip to California to meet with Jack.

Meanwhile, a young burn patient from down the hall has reached the point in his healing that he can leave the hospital, and he is being cheered on as he and his family head for the exit. My chest feels as if it'll burst open. The hope and the anticipation that Mark and I can finally leave this place one day are overwhelming.

I sit through long physical therapy sessions with Mark. When he's on his own, he moves his arms up and down, as well as his thighs. He's exercising on his own. The physical therapy team is great. They joke with Mark, they explain everything they're doing, and they ask if he's in pain. He's not shy about letting them know if they're doing something that hurts.

Ben says, "A burn patient's mobility is like chewing gum. While the gum is still fresh, you can stretch and create flexibility, but once the gum hardens, it becomes less flexible. It's the same with burn patients' new skin. For one to two years there's a window of time when Mark must have very rigorous physical therapy every day before his new skin matures."

As noted, Mark gradually begins taking a more active role in his own PT. After the physical therapists leave, he keeps bending his arm and flexing it toward the rest of his body, then away, over and over again. His arm's strapped to a wedge foam splint. Sometimes the wedge cushion gets stuck on the bed railing, so I have to free it for him.

"Are you doing your own PT, Mark?" He looks at me, unsmiling, and nods. He's concentrating hard.

Later when Ben returns to do a bit more therapy and sees Mark flexing his arm, he says, "Hey, Mark—we need to keep your arm straight."

Mark ignores him and keeps bending his arm.

"Honey," I call to him. "Why don't you keep your arm in the splint? Ben here tells me that in another hour he'll take it off and you can relax."

He ignores me and keeps flexing.

Mark's fingers are healing. They're swollen and big, but the nurses tell me they should reduce over time. They put skin grafts under Mark's eyes to cover the cuts they had to make. They put skin grafts on the top of his hands. His palms have healed on their own.

Ben just shakes his head. "I've never had a patient do his own physical therapy."

Dani, who's back on Mark's shift, nods in agreement. "Keep in mind that Mark is still on a cocktail of sedatives."

This is what I love about my husband. He's not passive. He's always been a take-charge person.

Dierdre stops by. "Yesterday morning during PT, Mark asked me for coffee."

I laugh because I'm not surprised. "You know, he's a twelve-cup-a-day kinda guy. He won an award at his company for drinking the most coffee by noon."

"What kind of coffee does Mark like?" Dierdre asks with a smile.

"French roast."

Dani says, "We can dip a toothbrush swab in coffee and give it to him."

I'm sure Mark misses coffee terribly. "You know, the only concern I'd have is that he'll want a whole cup," I say. "It might be too much of a tease and I know if we give him any fluids, he'll aspirate."

"Okay, just let me know if you want me to give him a brush with coffee anytime," Dani says.

We're waiting for Mark's hip fracture to heal before the doctors can begin skin grafts on his back. The nurses explain that they need to air out the new grafts on his back by lying him on his left side. Dr. Williams lets me know that they've ordered skin grafts to start applying to Mark's upper back. They're expected to arrive on October 17.

After the physical therapists leave for the day, Mark mouths silently to me, "Get out, get out…get out."

"Do you want to get out of the hospital?"

He nods his head. Poor Mark. He's now been in bed for four-and-a-half months. I wouldn't be surprised if one day the nurses tell me that Mark tried to get out of bed on his own. Apparently patients have tried.

Steven lets me know that he'll fly to Phoenix on Monday, October 21, so that I can head home to meet with our contractor about a handicapped bathroom.

Mark still has an infection. The yellow spots remain on his lower abdomen and now also on his upper chest. He's on the one antibiotic he's not resistant to. He's only on day two of a seven-day treatment. We need him to heal so they can continue to use his lower abdomen as a donor site for autografts.

One quiet Sunday when Mark is exhausted from the previous day's physical therapy, he sleeps through the Packers/Dallas Cowboys game on TV. I finally have time to thoughtfully respond to friends asking how I'm doing. They're concerned about how stressful it's been for me to be here by myself in Phoenix with Mark. I thank them for caring enough to ask. I tell them that being so open in my daily online posts about what Mark and I are going through has brought all sorts of help to our doorstep in ways I never expected. Before Mark's plane crash, I didn't know how to ask for help, to be publicly vulnerable. I come from a long line of strong women in my mom's family. For the first time, I'm learning to receive help from people other than Mark.

I explain that the silver lining of being in Phoenix, away from friends, has allowed me to focus 100 percent on Mark. I see that now. I also explain that I have a few local Phoenix friends and that I write in my journal daily, which helps me process my days. I've been on leave from work. It would have been impossible for me to work even part-time, given Mark's challenges and the need for me to be with him in his room every day. Dan, my boss and the CEO of our company, had so kindly told me not to worry about my job and just focus on Mark. He sends me really kind notes on weekends, asking how I'm doing.

I continue writing my post:

> *It's felt like a really long time that Mark and I have been in Phoenix—I miss home. I was starting to really feel down after*

almost three months when Mark was still unconscious. I came down with a bad migraine with lingering effects for several weeks.

The first three days when Mark was more awake, more responsive, and not in pain was such a lifeline for me. As he's become more conscious, it's been more emotional too. I think a lot about Mark being disabled and how our life will be affected—what will change, what will stay the same. I'm preparing myself for how emotional it will be when Mark fully wakes up and learns what's happened—both the plane accident and his body. I wouldn't be surprised if he doesn't remember what happened after he took off from Scottsdale airport.

I'm trying to regularly visualize the end state of where Mark and I will be a few years down the road, that he's thriving and we're both happy. It'll certainly be a long road to get there but I know Mark and I have so many things we still want to do in our lives—a huge bucket list!

It's been a fruitful time for my own personal growth. I'm learning to listen to my intuition more. My life before was busy and fast-paced. The silver lining is I've had the gift of more quiet time. Those moments of deep insight and knowing come to me a lot now. I think we all have it in us if we just take the time to pay attention to it.

I've also learned how powerful love can be—an incredible force that I feel now with such indescribable beauty and intensity. It's what keeps me going every day.

Wishing you a very happy Sunday!

Jenny

Chapter 28

LOVE

On Monday morning the nurses tell me that the yellow spots on Mark's lower abdomen are acinetobacter, a hospital infection typically found in ICU patients. While it's resistant to certain antibiotics, there is one targeted antibiotic they think could work. I'm just glad it's a standard hospital infection, not as risky as a recurrence of the fungal infection Mark had.

I have a doctor's appointment in Paradise Valley in the morning during Mark's dressing change. Knowing that I'd be away from home for a while, I had found a local doctor. While I'm in with Dr. Parke and we are discussing my recent medical history, my phone rings. I recognize the hospital number.

"Excuse me—do you mind if I take this? It's the hospital." She knows why I'm in Phoenix.

"Of course," she waves to me and steps out of the room. *Why are they calling me? Has something happened to Mark?* I glance at my watch. They should be doing Mark's dressing change right now.

"Hello?"

"Hi, Jenny. It's Courtney." I listen carefully to her tone. When I don't detect any tension in her voice, my shoulders relax.

"I'm with Mark. He's been asking for you."

I feel a fluttering in my chest. *Oh, Mark. He needs me.*

"I'm at a doctor's appointment. Can you tell him I'll be there right after his dressing change?" I glance at my watch. "Around twelve-thirty."

"Yeah, I told him that we have to do his dressing change and that you'll be here after we finish."

"Is he okay?"

"Yes, but he keeps asking for you even after I explain that you'll be here soon. I think he's a little anxious."

I wish I were there right now in his room.

"I'm going to put him on speakerphone."

"What a great idea, Courtney!"

"Mark, here's Jenny." I hear some rustling. "I have her on speakerphone."

"Hi, Mark!" I remember that he can't speak out loud. I just have to keep talking. "I love you so much. I miss you. I'm at the doctor's but I'll be there really soon—right after Courtney finishes your dressing change." It's weird to talk to him when he can't speak out loud and I can't see the expression on his face. I keep going. "I love you. I'm giving you a kiss right now, honey. Kiss, kiss, and more kisses to you, my love." I wish I could see his face.

Courtney gets back on the phone. "Okay, I think that was what he needed. We'll start his dressing change now." I can hear her saying to him, "Jenny loves you. She'll be here very soon."

She says to me, "Great. We'll see you in a couple of hours."

I'm so touched Courtney called me for Mark. Most nurses would simply reassure my husband that I would be there soon and proceed with his dressing change.

Later, when I'm in Mark's room, he can lift his left arm on his own, but not his right. Ben, the physical therapist, explains that his brain-to-body connection has been impacted by lack of use but reassures me it will come back.

Dr. Williams stops in to inform me that Mark's ready for the next round of skin grafts.

In the following days Mark begins sitting up for longer periods of time without pain. He speaks soundlessly through his trach. When he tries to string together a sentence, I have trouble following him. He and I develop a system for communicating. We have to work through what he's saying one word at a time. I ask him to break it down word by word. I use my fingers to indicate "first word," "second word," "third word" with him mouthing each one until I understand what he's saying before I go on to the next. It's charades with me doing the speaking out loud for both of us.

I remind him of all the fun times we've had by taking him on a tour through the photos in his room. *Look! It's Laila, Suzie, Adrian, and me in Tuscany.... Remember we spent all day in Montepulciano.... Do you remember that amazing meal with the pasta and truffles?* Or *Hey, it's you and Steven in your Cobra. Remember he came out to visit right after you bought the car? What about that time, you were pulled over on Highway 280 going 120 miles an hour in your new Ford Focus GT with Steven riding shotgun?* He nods at each picture I point to and smiles when I mention speeding on the interstate.

"Do you have any song requests, Mark?"

He shakes his head. He suddenly looks tired.

"How about if I play the Black Keys' latest album? I think you'll really like it." I don't tell him that we missed the Black Keys show in San Jose. We had tickets. It makes me sad to think of all the shows we're missing this summer.

He nods.

Throughout the day Mark manages to mouth words to me that I actually understand.

> *Drink*
> *Take glasses off* (his glasses were crooked because his head was at an angle on the bed)
> *Elbow pain*
> *Sheet off, hot*
> *When can I leave (the hospital)?*

I know how picky he is about keeping his glasses clean. Every day I take them off his face and carefully clean them.

Dylan, the respiratory therapist, stops by to take Mark's reading.

"Mark's doing a really good job breathing on his own. If we can continue to wean him onto even lower breathing support, we can put a device in his tracheotomy that allows him to speak out loud."

"Really?" I perk up. Mark would love that. So would I. The idea that he could talk out loud makes me smile to myself. I know how frustrated he gets when we don't understand what he's trying to say. "How soon do you think that could happen?"

He looks thoughtful. "It could be as early as this weekend."

"Wow—really?" I didn't expect it to be that soon.

A few days later, Ben, Sally, Dierdre, and a couple of other physical therapists show up to move Mark to "the Cadillac chair." It sounds fancier than it is. It's an adjustable gurney that allows a patient to sit up. It takes five physical therapists to painstakingly hoist Mark up from lying down to a slight angle, each time a little more upright to give him time to rest before the next adjustment. He's grimacing with pain and effort with each move.

It's hard for me to watch because I'm fully aware that the chair's upright back support puts pressure on his backside. His back is raw with no tissue, thinly covered with xenografts and allografts, not skin grafts. They place extra cushions underneath his butt and behind his back. The nurses had to move his monitors and IV lines from near his bed to the Cadillac chair. Thankfully, they gave him extra pain meds in advance.

When they first attempt to hoist him upright, his face dissolves into a silent howl, a wild animal look in his eyes. It's excruciating to watch how much pain he's in. All the preparation and careful assistance takes almost an hour. But when he finally sits up, he manages to sit for a full hour.

"Mark, you're doing great!" Dierdre says enthusiastically, smiling at him. She turns to me. "It's important for him to start sitting up regularly. It's good for his lungs and for building back muscle strength."

After an hour the physical therapists spend another hour carefully maneuvering Mark back down on his back. It takes five of them and two nurses to return him to his bed.

Dylan stops by to let me know that tomorrow he'll put a cap on Mark's trach so he can talk out loud.

I'm thrilled. It's a day of firsts. Mark talking as much as he did and sitting up for the first time. It's progress. I can't wait to hear Mark speak out loud tomorrow.

Hooray! I've been gradually getting my beloved husband back, bit by bit. First, being conscious, then wearing his smart-looking glasses to being able to silently mouth words. Now, amazingly, he'll be able to speak out loud again.

I text the good news to our family. Wesley's excited because he flies in tonight to spend the weekend with Mark and me.

Chapter 29

"I WANT A MARTINI"

The next morning when I wake up I begin counting down the hours until I can get into Mark's room after his dressing change. When Wesley and I arrive and greet Mark, he silently asks for water, and *Can you move the pillow under my arm?* He lifts his right arm to tell me which one needs the support.

It's good to feel useful. I find an extra pillow in the supply cabinet, fluff it up, and carefully place it under his right arm.

"Hi, Dad!" Wesley calls out. "I'm here for the weekend!"

Mark smiles at him. My chest feels warm.

I tell him Suzie reports that it's snowing in Denver and it's thirty degrees in Reno. Mark smiles. I smile back. *Darn it—the man loves his snow*. It's the skier in him and growing up in subzero temperatures in Wisconsin.

Tara, the tall blonde who's one of the most experienced burn nurses, and Daniel, the kindly nurse with gentle eyes, are back on rotation with Mark.

"Can we dip Mark's toothbrush in some beer so he can just taste it?" I ask Tara.

She shakes her head. "No, unfortunately we can't. It has sugar and bacteria. If he aspirates, he'll get pneumonia."

"Dierdre had mentioned coffee. Can we dip his toothbrush in coffee?"

"Yes, as long as it's black coffee. No milk and sugar."

"Perfect! Black is exactly how he likes it." Dierdre had promised to bring some French roast coffee for Mark sometime. She and Mark have become buddies. She talks to him all the time. When I arrive in the afternoon, she always shares with me something funny Mark says to her or something new she caught him doing. She and I still haven't figured out what to say if Mark asks about his amputated calves. It gnaws at me every time I see Dierdre but I'm at a loss about what we'd tell him. I can only hope he doesn't notice and doesn't ask.

Because Mark will soon be able to speak out loud, I wonder if he remembers anything that happened. I want to prepare myself for the possibility he might mention or ask what happened that terrible day.

I ask Tara.

"It's likely he may not remember," she explains. "Versed, which is one of the pain meds Mark's taking, has an amnesiac effect. It's intentional because the doctors don't want patients to remember the extreme pain they experienced."

I remember that Mark Haley didn't remember anything that happened. He had said in the article I read that the last thing he remembered was driving off from the starting line and next thing, he woke up from his coma in the ICU five months later.

"It also means that Mark may not remember what he said or did yesterday," Tara adds.

Mark's Rip Van Winkle. It'll be months, not years that have gone by since he went into his deep coma cave. I decide that if he doesn't ask or bring it up, I won't talk about what happened with the plane. I don't want to upset him when he needs to focus on his recovery.

In the early afternoon, Dylan comes in to take Mark off the machine. He carefully removes Mark's respiratory vent and observes him for a few minutes to make sure he's breathing smoothly.

"Mark is now breathing on his own," he announces.

"This is so exciting, honey."

Ben says that physical therapy will be by later today to put a cap on Mark's trach so he can speak out loud.

"Wonderful! Thank you so much." I silently clap my hands.

"Mark! Did you hear Ben? You're going to be able to speak out loud soon."

Mark smiles but looks wan. Tara reports that Mark had a little A-fib last night and didn't sleep that well.

Around five o'clock Ben and Andrea show up.

"Am I glad you're here! Mark is too!" I say brightly.

"Okay, Mark. We're going to help you speak out loud. How would you like that?" Ben asks, bustling around.

Mark looks alert but doesn't say anything.

Ben reaches over to fit the plastic cap piece at the center of Mark's trach in the middle of his throat.

"Okay, Mark. Try saying something."

He says something, but his voice is raspy and soft. I can't hear what he's saying. I look quizzically at Wesley. "Do you know what Dad just said?" He shakes his head and shrugs.

"You'll have to practice," Ben says, watching Mark. "It takes a little time to get used to the cap."

Ben leaves and I pull up a chair next to Mark.

He keeps trying to talk in single words, trying to enunciate. He sounds as if he's speaking through a tube, which he is.

"I want…to…go…"

I repeat after him to make sure I'm hearing him correctly. "You want to go…"

He stops. He's mouthing words silently.

"You want to leave the hospital? Is that what you mean, honey?" *Poor Mark.* If I were him, those would be my first words too.

He shakes his head.

"I…want…to go…on…"

I nod to acknowledge what he says.

"…an adventure."

Ah, yes. "An adventure." I nod. "I understand, my love."

He looks at me through his smart-looking glasses.

"I want to mix and mingle," he continues slowly.

He must mean he wants to socialize. Mark loves parties. He's the most social introvert I know.

"I want a martini."

I smile. This is so Mark.

"It's so great that you can talk, and we can understand you!"

"You have no idea..."

I'm taken aback by his sarcasm. With a start, I realize how frustrated he's been because he can't express himself. I feel bad that I assumed a cheerful tone instead of acknowledging how he's suffered. These are new waters I'm navigating in. I can see that I'll need to learn how to talk to Mark about his pain, his suffering, and all that he'll go through, not to sugarcoat anything.

It occurs to me that it would be great to have Mark FaceTime with his family. I call Michelle, Mark's youngest sister in New York. She picks up right away. Although she's walking in the city, she's eager to talk to Mark.

He's very interested in talking to Michelle and peers into the phone that Wesley holds in front of him. After she greets him, he gives her a big smile. It's a sweet moment. He asks her what art she's working on. She describes her painting projects and her life in New York. They talk for a few minutes, with Wesley and I chiming in to repeat what Mark says at times when Michelle doesn't understand what he's saying. His voice is deep and raspy because of the trach.

Mark's not shy to speak up about what he wants. After his call with Michelle, he says, "I'm going to sleep. I'm tired." He asks me to turn off the lights and pull down the blinds.

Wesley and I go to dinner, and when we return to Mark's dimly lit, quiet room, he's awake and ready to talk again. Wesley asks him, "Dad, how are you doing?"

He replies, "I've had better days."

Ah, back to his wry one-liners.

"I've been through a lot."

"You have," I reply, nodding.

"But I can't remember all of it."

I resist the urge to ask him what he does remember. I change the subject.

"Mark, I want you to know that hundreds of family and friends have been praying for you and sending you positive, healing thoughts."

He looks at me expectantly.

"Friends from Fennimore. Your Stanford GSB class—there are too many to name. Your Movoto friends. Peter and his wife fasted and prayed for you. Do you remember Peter from the Movoto board?"

Mark nods.

"Your UW-Madison friends. Our neighbors at home. Axel, the Mountain View High School kid you've been mentoring. Family too—Dee and Rick, Buck and Ada, Myron and Lisa, your cousins...."

"Your Nevada Nano team," Wesley chimes in. He's been opening cards for Mark and reading them out loud to him.

"That's a lot...of...people," Mark says slowly.

"You may not remember who came to visit you. Your sibs—Steven, Rene, Michelle. Teresa and Bob, Suzie a few times. Laila, Marcene and Harlow, Kathy and Page, Richard, my cousin, and Christina Allen."

He looks at me, nodding.

"I'm so happy you're alive, Mark." A sudden wave hits me. I feel a dry catch in my throat. I want so much to hug him, to hold him close.

"I *want* to be alive," he says, his green eyes brightening.

I nod, feeling my eyes filling up. Wesley hovers nearby, watching.

"I want to hug you, Mark, but..." I gesture to his bandaged body. "I'm saving all my hugs for the day they finish skin grafts on more of your body." I chuckle. "It may take me days to give you all the hugs I've wanted to in the last few months." I smile at the thought. "I'll save them up!"

The upbeat moment passes, and I feel a tremor in my legs, remembering all that we've been through.

I realize I'm shaking slightly only when Wesley reaches out behind me and holds my arm to steady me.

That evening, before the nurses take the cap off his trach and put him back on the ventilator for the night, he says in his raspy trach voice, "I'll miss talking."

It breaks my heart to hear him say that. It's hard to watch this man, who loves his freedom, be so restricted.

KC tells me that she thinks Mark is a patient who will remember more than others. Chloe, who, like KC, has taken care of Mark many times now on night shift, tells me that because Mark's adjusted to such a high dosage of sedation earlier than other patients, it could explain why he'll remember more.

It takes a lot of energy out of him to adjust to breathing on his own and talking today. He's very tired, so Wesley and I leave at eight o'clock and call it a night. We want to let Mark rest.

With Mark's need to take control of his own recovery, I vow to start explaining more to him about what's happening with his skin grafts. It will help him stay motivated to know.

Dr. Jameson lets us know that the grafts for his back will arrive next Thursday.

Wesley leaves Sunday night and I'm back in Mark's room by myself. Adrian's started back at ETH and updates me on the classes he's taking. I enjoy describing them to Mark, who nods in response. I spend my days with Mark, continuing to help him when he feels pain or discomfort. It's a daily challenge to get him to allow the nurses to brush his teeth every two hours. I find different ways to sweet-talk him into it. I explain the progress and plan for skin grafts on his back. I read to him from *Bossypants*, which makes me laugh out loud, and Mark Kurlansky's fascinating book *Salt: A World History*.

Mark's arms are fully exposed, without any bandages. His torso and thighs are loosely covered. The nurses give me a peek at the skin grafts on his torso and his thighs, which have now grown to join together. His new skin looks so pink and healthy.

I show him gifts that friends have sent. Suzie sends a couple of large, framed photos of the Dolomites, the Italian Alps where Mark and I had planned to be in early September with her and her boyfriend, to celebrate his sixtieth birthday. I canceled our trip, but Suzie and her friend Brian went ahead on the trip. I read out loud the card that Suzie sends with it:

> *Hi, Mark—The hiking in the Dolomites has been amazing. They are such beautiful mountains. When you're healed and recovered, you and Jenny will have to get back out there to hike and to come to the Dolomites in the future. P.S. Because it's the Italian part of the Alps, the food is nothing short of fabulous. You will love it.*

Suzie

Mark wants to see the photos up close, so I lean over to show him, one at a time. He's silent as he looks them over.

I don't want to say more because I don't want to make him feel bad that he's still stuck in a hospital bed.

As a distraction for him and maybe myself too, I say cheerfully, "Hey, look! My friend Mary Ellen sent you a Packers flag." I open the package and pull out a big green-and-yellow flag with a giant G on it. "Mary Ellen's my Wellesley friend who's from Green Bay. When you get out of here, Mark, we have to get together with Mary Ellen and her husband, John. They're Stanford MBAs too and you cheeseheads have to stick together." I laugh out loud.

It's NFL season, so when I tell Mark his Packers are playing the Detroit Lions, he's insistent that I message Jeff, his high school friend who lives locally, to come visit. Jeff can't come because he drives for UPS. Mark manages to stay awake for most of the game but complains that he can't see the action on the TV monitor. Lindsey explains to me that it's because they put special antibiotic drops in his eyes that make his sight blurry. I explain this to Mark.

Tomorrow, Mark is scheduled for autograft prep surgery on his upper back to get him ready to receive skin grafts soon. Dr. Jameson, who will perform the surgery, stops by to update me.

I tell them that Mark wants a martini.

Dr. Jameson says, "You know what? As soon as Mark's off his trach and can swallow fluids, I'll put in an order for a martini for him."

"What kind of gin does Mark like?" Dr. Jameson asks—someone who apparently understands martinis.

"He likes Bombay Sapphire, up, with a twist. And olives."

"Ah, he's a gentleman. We'll make sure he gets a martini the way he likes it."

"Wonderful." I know how much Mark would love that.

The next day, Mark sleeps all afternoon. He must have worn himself out, talking so much the day before. When they wheel him into the OR, he suddenly wakes up, eyes wide open, and tries to get up out of his gurney. I step in and explain to him what's going on, and he settles down.

The doctors end up doing more than I expected. They had enough skin grafts to staple sixty of them to his entire back. They put autografts on his buttocks. They now need Mark to avoid lying on his back. He's on a round-the-clock schedule of alternating three body positions every two hours—lying on his left side, his right side, and his back. His arms are in airplane splints, which he hates and resists. It's painful but it prevents skin contractures and helps to get enough air near his shoulders, where his upper back skin grafts are. Ben also puts the blue compression mask back on Mark's face to prevent his new skin from pulling down. The nurses increase sedation and pain meds.

I can't see much of Mark because he's surrounded by foam wedges, and his arms are on pillows and foam splints. Dr. Jameson tells me this is the hardest phase of skin grafting because the back is the most challenging to heal when Mark's lying on it.

I'm looking forward to Steven arriving in a few days to cover for me while I go home to California to meet with our contractor about building a handicapped bathroom. I've been in touch with our health insurance company about special medical transportation for Mark when he's ready to go home.

The next day I don't get in to see Mark until 5:00 p.m. because they needed eight hours to air out Mark's back.

Daniel lets me know that Mark's been sleepy most of the afternoon. When I arrive, he wakes up slightly. He doesn't say anything but is lifting his arms and legs, doing his own physical therapy.

"Mark's blood pressure has softened," Daniel tells me in his usual, serious voice. "We gave him Levophed a few hours ago."

"But that will reduce blood flow to support his new skin grafts," I reply. "They're so new."

Daniel nods solemnly. "Dr. Jameson told us to reduce Mark's sedation tonight by 50 percent."

I'm not sure how that will help.

Tara sees my confusion. "Sedatives tend to depress blood pressure. Dr. Jameson's hoping it'll lift Mark's blood pressure."

We've been down this road before. His blood pressure has frequently fluctuated. We just need to get through another cycle of this. As with so many times before, I post a quick note to our online community to pray that Mark's blood pressure normalizes.

I stay for a couple hours and decide I'll go to a late dinner and call it a night. I'm prepared for not seeing as much of Mark for the next week. They need to rotate his lying-down positions to air out his new skin grafts every couple hours.

He's sound asleep when I leave. He looks childlike without his glasses, his face healthy, pink, and new. I visualize in my mind kissing him on the lips. On his face. Brushing my nose gently against his. His tall, narrow nose. My soft, fleshier one. I'll miss seeing more of him.

Daniel had already dimmed the overhead ceiling lights. I switch off the small light above the head of Mark's bed.

"Good night, my love." A warm breeze swirls around me, gently pulling me into its embrace, the way the cool, calming Hawaiian trade winds felt during warm summer evenings when I used to visit my mom. My chest feels so warm and tender, radiating.

I lean over toward Mark. "Sweet dreams, Mark. May you get all the rest that you need."

When I pick up my purse and make my way out the door through the hallway, I'm surprised at how slowly my feet move. It's felt like a really long day.

Part 5

Love Is All There Is

"In the midst of winter,
I found, there was,
within me,
an invincible summer."

—Albert Camus,
The Return to Ripasa

Chapter 30

DARK NIGHT OF THE SOUL

My phone is ringing. I rouse myself from a deep sleep. The ringing is insistent. It stops after a while and then starts again. Groggy, I look at the number. 602. Phoenix. I finally pick up the phone.

"Hello?"

"Jenny, it's Emily."

Emily. Dark, curly-haired, young Emily with the earnest gaze. From the night shift.

"We've been trying to call you since three-thirty."

I glance at my watch. It's four-ten.

"I'm sorry, Emily. I must've been in a deep sleep. I didn't hear a thing until now."

"Yeah, I thought so. It's why I kept trying you. You need to come in."

Oh, no. What's happened?

"Mark's blood pressure's not holding up. He's got an infection."

I'm gripped with a sick feeling in my stomach. "Did the fungal infection come back?" I plead with God. *Please, dear Lord. Not the fungal infection* again…*Please, please protect Mark.*

"No, it's not fungal. It's his liver. His liver's not doing well."

His liver? This is the first I've heard about Mark's liver.

"Okay." My eyes are still closed in the dark of early morning. The air conditioning sputters suddenly. My room is as cold as an icebox. I shiver. "I'm coming."

It must be bad. I had always reminded the night shift nurses never to hesitate to call me in the middle of the night if there was an emergency. This is the first time they've called.

Emily greets me when I arrive in Mark's room.

"Hi, Emily. So, what's happening?" I'm out of breath from rushing down the hallway. My chest is pounding.

"Mark has sepsis. He has some type of bacterial infection. We've had him on two different blood pressure medications and albumin. His heart rate is irregular. The doctors are concerned about Mark's liver. His liver enzymes are elevated."

I have no idea what that means. *Liver enzymes?*

Emily continues. "His blood sugar's elevated."

Okay, that means Mark's body is stressed. That much I do know.

"Dr. Jameson's in charge. He's put Mark on several antibiotics starting around three this morning."

They must've tried calling me immediately after that.

People are coming in and out of Mark's room doing things to him, staff I don't recognize because it's the night shift. I sit down on a chair at the end of Mark's bed. I don't know enough yet to understand what this all means but I ask our online community to pray for Mark. They've become my go-to group whenever I receive news that doesn't sound good.

Mark's eyes are closed. I can't tell if he's in pain or not. I try to stay out of the way of the constant flow of people. I wish he were awake and could talk to me as he's been doing the last couple of weeks.

Dr. Jameson appears. I stand up and rush to his side. He looks solemn. "It's not looking good for Mark."

I put a hand on my chest to stop a sudden tremor in my body.

"His liver enzymes are elevated. We're doing everything we can to address Mark's blood pressure. It's too low and he's not getting enough blood flow to properly support his internal organs."

"His organs?"

"His liver, kidneys, intestines. His brain, lungs. We're hoping the blood pressure meds will get blood flow back to support everything. He's got an infection. I've put Mark on three different antibiotics."

I don't like how serious Dr. Jameson looks.

"We're throwing everything but the kitchen sink at him—whatever we can do to fight this infection."

"Do we know what type of infection he has? Emily told me it's not fungal."

"It's a standard hospital infection but likely resistant to antibiotics."

Something drops like a rock inside from my chest to my stomach. That familiar sick feeling deep in my stomach comes back, the way I felt when Mark suffered through his fungal infection.

"Mark's liver is in distress," Dr. Jameson says. "Sit tight. We're doing everything we can." His concise manner confirms that things are not going well.

I sit back down and write an update to our online community, pleading with them to pray that Mark's blood pressure and heart rate stabilize. That he can fight this latest infection. I end my short note with—

I haven't given up hope, but the medical facts are not good right now.

I close my eyes and breathe deeply. I try to visualize blood flowing throughout Mark's body. I picture his heart pumping regularly. *Please, dear God and all the love in the universe. Please help Mark right now. His life is in your hands.* I fight an inner torrent that wants to burst through but I can't help it. My eyes feel full. I blink back my tears.

I lose track of time. Mark's room is crowded with hospital staff. It's a blur. I'm in my own private world, trying so hard to control my growing feeling of distress. I send a group text to our families to let them know what's going on. Everyone responds back immediately with questions. Rene asks if they need to make plans to travel in. I tell her *Sure, we just don't know what's going to happen. But Mark's life is at risk.* That last sentence is all they need to know.

Teresa tells me she's catching the first flight she can get from LA. I'm grateful she's close enough to come so quickly.

I don't text the boys. I can't. Not yet. I dread the idea of telling them what's going on with their dad. *Dear God, please don't let Mark die. Please don't let Adrian lose his dad at the same age I did. I was twenty-three when my dad passed. Adrian's twenty-three. No, no, no.*

My mind stops and can't go there. I pull it back hard. I can't step off the cliff.

I look up and notice for the first time that it's now daylight. The sun's shining and the room has cleared out. I'm alone with Mark. I look at my watch. It's 10:15 a.m. Mark's rock playlist is playing. I'm annoyed. The nurses know to play meditation or classical music when Mark's not doing well. *Why didn't they change the playlist?*

Irritated, I get up from my chair and cross the room to switch the playlist.

When I reach the music player, I'm startled to realize that the song that's playing is "Sirens," by Pearl Jam. It was a favorite song of ours, although as Mark once pointed out, the lyrics were sad and beautiful all at once. Eddie Vedder sings about ambulance sirens coming for him and he turns to the woman he loves to tell her how much he loves her.

This is Mark's song. I let it play. As I listen to the words and remember the familiar lyrics that Eddie's singing, my body is tingling. *My God, Mark's saying goodbye to me.* I wait until the song ends before I switch the playlist to meditation music. I keep praying for Mark while I check my phone every time I hear a ping.

I notice Daniel, one of the kindest, gentlest day shift nurses, quietly moving about Mark's room. He's a younger, tall guy with earnest eyes. Daniel's taken care of Mark many times. I wonder what he must be feeling, knowing how dire things are for Mark, the patient in his charge. Do they learn to tuck their feelings away in a box while they go about their jobs? I'm glad he's taking care of Mark today.

Dr. Jameson walks in at around eleven o'clock.

"I'm afraid there's no hope for Mark. We'll continue to do everything we can. There's really nothing more we can do."

When he leaves the room, I sit down. I feel nothing, as if my nerve endings have been cut off. Numb. It's now up to God and the divine powers that be. *Is there room for a miracle?* I don't know, but I can't yet accept that all hope is lost just yet. Something inside me wants to keep fighting for Mark's life. I can't give up.

Teresa shows up from the airport, bringing lunch. She hugs me and looks at me. Her warm, dark eyes are worried. "Oh, Jenny—I'm so, so sorry." I hug her. We just hold each other for a few minutes. There are no words.

At around one o'clock Dr. Jameson shows up again. He looks so serious. I introduce him to Teresa.

"I want to go into surgery to examine Mark's internal organs to see if we need an intervention for any of them," he says.

"What does that mean?"

"Some organs can be supported, like his kidneys. Others can't be, like his liver. If his intestines are dead, we'll just remove them. There are ways we can support him without intestines."

I nod. I hear him but I really don't. This is all happening so fast.

"I need your permission to go into surgery to assess. This is the only thing left for us to try. You should know that there's mortality risk going into surgery, given Mark's weakened state."

I'm not sure what the benefit is.

"I think we have no choice but for me to go in to do this. If we don't try to assess and address what we can, he will definitely die. He might still die but this is our last shot."

Now I'm clear. I nod. "Yeah, go ahead." I'm nauseated imagining Dr. Jameson cutting into the healthy, pink new skin on Mark's front torso.

"Okay, we're going to operate on Mark in his room here—in the next forty-five minutes."

Teresa and I leave and wait outside Mark's room. We sit in the chairs outside Dr. Williams's and Pamela's office. I group-text the family to let them know they need to fly in as soon as possible, that it's not looking good at all and that Mark may die.

Next I text our local friends—Jeff, Neal, and Sue; also Mike, a Stanford GSB friend, and his wife, Kathy, who've been so kind during the last few months, taking me out for dinner, visiting with me.

Around 3:30 p.m., Dr. Jameson and Dr. Williams come by where Teresa and I are sitting.

"We went in and looked at everything. Mark's liver is enlarged and swollen," Dr. Jameson says. "A healthy liver is a reddish tan color. Mark's liver is dark brown."

I turn to Dr. Williams. "Can his liver recover on its own?"

"I never say never," Dr. Williams says softly. "His liver's failing."

His liver's failing. I give myself a minute to let that sink in. My mother died when her cancer spread to her liver.

Dr. Williams continues. "But at some point we're going to ask you when we can take Mark off all support."

I nod, mute.

A short time later the attending physician, whom I don't recognize, stops by.

"Mark's blood pressure has dropped to the thirties."

I look at Teresa and take a big breath. *Oh, no.* She looks at me, her luminous dark eyes reflecting back to me my own sadness.

"If Mark's heart fails, do you want him resuscitated? There's a risk of brain injury if we resuscitate."

Without hesitation, I reply, "Yes, please resuscitate."

I can't give up hope.

A woman with gray, short hair and glasses shows up in the room.

"Hi—Jenny? I'm Gwen, the chaplain here at Maricopa Hospital." She has a kind-looking face.

I introduce her to Teresa.

"I'm here to pray for Mark."

"I haven't given up hope."

"You have every right to hope for a miracle," Gwen looks at me intently. "I've heard about Mark's case from the doctors, so I know you've experienced some real miracles already."

I appreciate that she knows everything, and I don't have to explain it now. I don't have the energy.

"Let's go pray for Mark," she says, beckoning me to get closer to Mark's bed. I hold back, feeling a sharp pain in my chest, picturing him cut open in the abdomen, all that new skin ruined.

I glance at Mark. He's unconscious, his eyes closed. His body from the neck down is covered in a very thick blanket.

Gwen gathers Teresa and me around Mark and prays for him. She asks for God's merciful love and grace. She asks for a miracle. She mentions the deep love our family has for this special man, Mark. I close my eyes, fervently following along with every word she speaks. I'm holding on tightly.

The attending physician and other staff show up in the room to urgently attend to Mark. We have to leave the room.

Teresa, Gwen, and I stand outside his room, watching what they're doing. The nurses are putting paddles on Mark's chest to try to jump-start his heart.

A few minutes later the attending physician comes out to tell me that Mark has died. He suffered septic shock, and his blood pressure dropped so much that his heart failed. Daniel and Dani made repeated efforts to resuscitate Mark but they couldn't revive him.

Everything happened so fast.

I cling to Teresa, crying. I'm thinking of Adrian and Wesley. I didn't want Adrian to lose his father at the same age I lost mine. I had been so devastated. I didn't want that for Adrian.

"Teresa, I don't want to call the boys…I can't."

"You don't have to yet. There's time. Let me contact the rest of the family first. And Suzie. Okay?" Teresa touches my arm.

I know I need to let Adrian know soon because of how long it'll take him to get here from Zurich.

Instead of calling Adrian, I call Wesley first.

"Hello, Mom." He sounds cautious. I know he's wondering what my update is.

"Your dad just died," I whisper. "I'm so sorry."

I can see Wesley's face crumple. "Oh, no."

I explain the medical details. But I'm not in my body when I explain everything. It's my voice but it's a robot doing the talking for me.

"Okay, sweetie. Please come soon."

"I will. I'll let you know what flight I'm on."

Dani stops by. "I'm so sorry, Jenny." She looks at me, her eyes soft. "I just want you to know that we're going to leave Mark's body in his room until noon tomorrow. After that, they'll need to move him to the hospital mortuary."

I nod.

"I know you have family flying in. They'll be able to view Mark's body until the end of day tomorrow."

Knowing tomorrow's deadline, I have no choice but to call Adrian soon. I look at my watch. It's six-thirty.

I drag my feet. By seven o'clock I take a deep breath, step outside, and enter Adrian's number.

The phone rings and rings. I look at my watch. It's 3:00 a.m. in Zurich. I stare at the blank wall in the hallway, willing myself to stay focused. I shut the door to all the feelings that are about to burst through.

"Hello?" Adrian's voice is heavy with sleep.

"Hi, hon. It's me. Mom."

I can see him lying in bed, squinting and disoriented, abruptly woken.

"Hi, Mom."

"Sweetie, I'm so sorry to be calling you right now." I pause, but not long enough for him to say anything. "Your dad caught an infection that's resistant to antibiotics. He just died."

There—it's out. All I see is spiky, jagged light, then darkness. I grab the arm of a chair to steady myself as I slide into the seat and close my eyes.

There's a long pause. "What happened?" I can see the bewilderment in Adrian's eyes.

"It happened so fast. I was asleep. The nurses called me during the middle of the night to tell me your dad's liver wasn't doing well. He caught an infection. Dr. Jameson did everything he could for your dad, gave him all kinds of antibiotics."

Adrian's twenty-three, the same age I was when my dad died.

"His infection was resistant to the antibiotics?"

Why, dear God, is this happening to Adrian the way it did for me? I hold back a huge wave that's about to burst through the door. Stop, stop, stop. I have to hold it together.

"Yes. But Dr. Jameson also discovered that Dad's liver was failing."

Adrian is quiet. He's in shock. I was only just messaging him two days ago about how his dad was taking control of his own physical therapy.

"Can you come as soon as you can?"

"Yes, I'll find a flight now."

Poor Adrian. It's a déjà vu moment to the late-night conversation we had when he first found out about Mark's plane accident—only this time, what's happened is so much worse.

Now that I've called the boys, I collapse into a chair across from Dr. Williams's office, which is closed and dark. I can't bear to go back to the room to see Mark's body draped in a white blanket. *Just like that, he's gone.* It happened so fast. I feel slightly dizzy. I close my eyes, breathing, still trying to hold the wave back, trying to breathe. *Just breathe, Jenny.* Shallow breaths at first, then deeper breaths. I cover my eyes with my hands.

Someone gently touches my arm.

"Jenny."

I look up. It's Dani.

"I just wanted you to know that instead of noon tomorrow, we can delay moving Mark's body to around three o'clock instead. I figured it'd help since your family's not local."

I nod. I hear her words but I feel strangely disembodied. The rest of me is floating somewhere.

"I know it'll take Adrian time to get here from Switzerland. Anyone can still see his body in the morgue downstairs once we move him."

The next day is the day Steven was supposed to visit so that I could go home to meet with our contractor about building a handicapped bathroom. Instead, he finds an earlier flight, as does the rest of our family. People show up throughout the morning and afternoon.

Mark was doing so well just a couple days before. He was at the start of the home stretch with his skin grafts. The doctors had just stapled sixty skin grafts to his back.

I'm suddenly very busy. The logistics of death kick in. *Do you want Mark cremated or do you want to fly his body back to California? We never talked about it. Let's cremate, I think that's what he would want. How many copies of his death certificate will you need to order? Where do you want to hold a ceremony for him?*

As an afterthought, I realize I have to move out of my condo and get my car back to California. Michelle offers to drive my car and take Mark's ashes. It would give her comfort to go on a solitary drive through the West with what remains of her brother.

I write a post to our online community to let them know that Mark died at five o'clock the day before. I thank them for their ongoing prayers the last few months. I thank them for their love and support. I end with the following:

> *I believe Mark's in a good place and no longer suffering. He had a formidable mind and spirit but I think his body was exhausted.*
>
> *Perhaps it's a mercy that he didn't have to live as a disabled person. He was such a robust, active, and "make it happen" kind of guy. I knew he'd be deeply disappointed about having physical limitations even though I still believe he'd get past that if he could be surrounded by the people he loved.*
>
> *If I don't reply to you right now, please know that I appreciate your notes, but our family and I are grieving. I'm also dealing with a lot of logistics such as getting funeral arrangements made and getting Mark back to California.*
>
> *Thank you again for your prayers the last five months.*

Chapter 31

THE FIRST THREE MONTHS

Mark's memorial service is held at the Episcopal church that the boys and I used to attend. I ask Suzie and Kathy to cohost a celebration of life for Mark after the service in the church courtyard. Mark loved life so much—it feels right to have friends and family tell stories about who he was to them.

He didn't know if God or a higher power existed, but I knew he would like Lisa, the rector. She's smart and articulate and would hold her own with him in a discussion about intuition and ethereal matters.

The day of the memorial service is a blur. The church pews are overflowing with familiar faces. What carries me through the day is the steady outpouring of love from everyone for Mark, the boys, and me. During our time in the courtyard, Suzie and Kathy pass around a mic. People share so many funny stories and heartwarming comments about Mark. In honor of Mark's love for beer, Kathy sets up a tasting table with the homemade brew she made for Mark. He never made it home to taste it as she had expected, as with so many other plans of ours that went unrealized.

Steven, Mark's brother, says a few words first. One by one, people take the mic to tell a story about Mark, stories about his integrity at work, how he was a mentor and friend and how much fun he was. His UW-Madison college friend Dave Schwalbe tells a funny story about how one drunken night he and Mark climbed into the UW dairy barn and were busted by campus police for hanging out with the cows. Laila talks about how much she and Mark enjoyed the *Messiah* sing-along at Stanford Memorial Chapel.

Thomas Hunnicutt, Jakki, and little Avery, their daughter, fly in from Phoenix to join us. Our friends wanted to meet Thomas to thank him for his courage on that important day. He was a hero. Thomas gave us the gift of five months with Mark. Without Thomas being at the right place at the right time, Mark would have perished that day.

I place half of Mark's ashes in his niche at the memorial park in Palo Alto. I find a niche column backed by a small creek and the natural pavilion of live oak trees, glossy dark green leaves dotting an upward embrace of dark branches. There's a faintly sweet smell from the flowers on the manzanita bushes nearby. It's the perfect spot for Mark's ashes because the park reminds us of the type of hiking trails he loved so much. I hear him stepping on dry leaves, their crunchy sound and the smell of the dusty trail in the hot sun when we hiked in the hills nearby. Wesley places a Sierra Nevada Pale Ale beer bottle, knowing it's Mark's favorite, with wildflowers in front of his dad's niche.

We save the other half of Mark's ashes to scatter near Lake Tahoe when Adrian can visit again from Zurich.

After everyone has driven and flown home, Laila calls me from Boston to tell me something important.

"Jenny, I heard from Mark."

I suck my breath in. *What could she mean?* She's the materialist and yet she was the one who felt a special, unexplainable energy in Mark's room when he was unconscious, deep in a coma.

She continues, "I know this sounds crazy, but I wanted you to know."

I can hear her taking a deep breath. "Right after Mark died, I was lying in bed one evening thinking about what I wanted to say about Mark at his celebration of life. I thought about skiing on a crisp, cold day at Mount Rose and watching him zip past me at ten times my speed, his skis perfectly parallel…and I wasn't exactly skiing slowly myself." She laughs in her melodic, charming way.

I chuckle. I know what she means. Mark used to swoosh right past me in the "fast lane" and flick snow in my face.

Laila continues. "I also thought of his concert in Menlo Park when I watched him sing with his Bach choir. I was sitting in the fourth row. Or the many times Mark and I would have a beer, enjoying our time, just shooting the breeze."

I'm touched by the memory of her magical moments with Mark.

"I was thinking so hard about the words I could say that would capture Mark's love of life. Then I realized that I was struggling to grasp that he was really gone. I…I just couldn't go on and broke down crying."

I hear the tremor in her voice and the silence that follows. *She misses him too*. I rub my face with both of my hands, blinking back tears.

"Then I felt Mark's presence. He said to me, '*Laila, I'm fine*.'"

What? I'm astounded about this experience coming from Laila, our friend the materialist who didn't believe something existed unless she could see it or touch it.

"How did you know it was his presence? Did you see him?"

"I didn't see him. What I felt was this completely overwhelming presence of love. I *knew* it was him."

She pauses and says in a thoughtful, hushed voice, "I think he was just acknowledging my sadness and wanted to let me know he was okay."

I'm quiet, trying to absorb what I've just heard.

"Do you think *I'll* hear from him too?" I finally ask.

"He loves you, Jenny. I think you'll hear from him when the time is right."

I'm struck by how certain she sounds.

People continue posting messages in our online community after Mark's death. Courtney, the nurse who had put me through to Mark on speakerphone when I was at the doctor's, posted—

> *Tomorrow is Christmas Day and the Brandemuehl family is on my heart. The first time I ever took care of Mark, he was sedated and would open his eyes and smile only on occasion. Jenny told me about their wonderful love story and I told her their story is a true inspiration and because of it I set my bar even higher. There was one time I will never forget. Mark was due for his dressing change. He had his speaking valve in. Before we started, I could tell he was getting anxious and he just kept repeating one name over and over: "Jenny."*
>
> *Working in ICU for a couple of years, I have never ever had anyone call out for their spouse. It's usually random, incoher-*

ent conversing or a request for a basic need such as water or food. Mark's need was Jenny. Mark was there—through all the sedation and medication he knew he needed his Jenny. We all stopped and I went to dial Jenny on her phone. She spoke to him and gave him motivation. He stopped calling out for her and before we started a sedation medication, I saw he was relaxed and at ease just by Jenny's voice, more relaxed than any sedation we could ever administer. I told Jenny this is something straight out of the movie The Notebook.

Jenny, I am so happy to have met you. You are a humble person whom I aspire to be like one day. Your love story could move mountains. I just want to wish you a very Merry Christmas! You deserve it and much more.

Courtney lets me know that what she witnessed between Mark and me inspired her to look for the kind of romantic partner who would be capable of that kind of love. In raising the bar for herself, she started dating Daniel, a fellow Burn Center nurse. They are now engaged. Courtney messages me:

"I want you to come to our wedding. Promise me you will."

I tell her that of course I'll be there.

"Just let me know the date. Mark will be smiling from heaven or wherever he is now."

I'm touched. And then I remember that Daniel was the very kind and capable nurse who took care of Mark the day he died. *Can it really be that from death comes birth? Birth of a love between two people, inspired by our love?* I'm humbled to realize that the love Mark and I shared had a ripple effect on those around us during the most devastating time in our lives.

Back home in Mountain View, I think often of everything nurses like Courtney and Daniel did for Mark and me. They were my second family. A couple of weeks after Mark's service, I fly back to Phoenix to host a thank-you lunch for the Burn Center staff. Dr. Williams presents an award to Thomas Hunnicutt during a brief press conference outside the hospital. I say a few words to the press about how thankful I am for Thomas's courage in saving Mark's life. I also thank the people of Phoenix for the kindness they've shown me during a challenging and difficult time for Mark and our family.

Because everyone's working their shift, we have lunch laid out on a table at the Burn Center, and the staff eat and chat in the hallways. I know people think it's unheard of for someone who's lost their beloved to come back to do this for the staff. But what they don't understand is that the staff had become my second family. I was dropped into Phoenix by myself, not by choice, and away from what was familiar. Their day-in, day-out compassion and support got me through the long days and evenings I spent by Mark's side while he was in a deep coma. They were the glowing spark of humanness that lit up and kept me warm in that drab, gray hospital room every minute, every hour. It was a marathon of waiting and worrying.

Dr. Hale drops by. I feel a wave of controlled calmness in my arms and legs. My body feels both electric and still at the same time. It happens when I'm completely focused, noticing nothing else around me. It's the feeling I often had when the Burn Center doctors came to chat with me about Mark.

"I was the receiving doctor when Mark arrived at the Burn Center the day of the accident," he says.

I didn't know that. I realize now that I had spoken to a more junior doctor when Mark first called me.

"I believe Mark knew the gravity of his injuries when he came into the ER. It's why he was so insistent about reaching you on the phone."

He didn't want to die without talking to me. I only now realize that. I remember how my phone kept ringing. I hadn't recognized the number and didn't pick up the first time. Thank God I did the second time he called.

"I've always wondered if Mark knew his legs were amputated once he was more conscious," I say. "When he was doing daily physical therapy, Dierdre and I had debated whether and when we'd tell Mark about his leg amputations."

I was worried at the time, unsure of what to say if Mark asked. "We never said anything to him because he died so suddenly."

Dr. Hale looks at me with sympathetic eyes. "I think he knew."

We're both quiet while I contemplate that possibility.

I decide to tell Dr. Hale about some of the things that happened that were scientifically unexplainable. I hadn't mentioned these events to any of the doctors because I was afraid they would think I was crazy. I won't be surprised if Dr. Hale is skeptical, but I can't help it. The story spills out of me.

"The day Mark died, Mark said goodbye to me through a song right before Dr. Jameson told me Mark wasn't going to make it."

I describe to him how Pearl Jam's "Sirens" song was playing in Mark's room, our backstory about the lyrics unique to Mark and me. I'm watching Dr. Hale's face carefully. He listens attentively. Encouraged, I also describe how the "Sirens" song was playing the morning before Mark died, right before Dr. Jameson informed me that there was no hope for Mark. It was also a Sunday morning.

"I look back now and believe that Mark was saying goodbye to me with that song. He and I loved music. He always noticed lyrics, so it's not a surprise that he would communicate with me through music."

"I believe you, Jenny," Dr. Hale nods. "I've experienced all sorts of unexplainable things. Let me tell you a story."

He has my attention. I think of a couple books I've read by doctors describing unexplainable events that happened to their patients at the hospital. The message that Dr. Laurin Bellg, the ER doctor/author, mentions in her book *Near Death in the ICU* is that doctors and nurses need to be more open to their patients' near-death and other unexplainable experiences by not dismissing them. She believes that just because current science can't explain the experience doesn't mean it didn't happen.

"We had two patients admitted into the Burn Center the same day," Dr. Hale says. "They were two separate and unrelated cases."

"So they didn't know each other?"

"No, they didn't. One was a man, the other a woman. A few weeks later, on a Sunday, they both died at exactly the same time."

He doesn't say so, but I can see from the expression on his face that what happened was not typical at all in his experience.

A couple of nurses interrupt us to say hello and then Dr. Hale has to leave. I thank him again for all that he's done for Mark.

Later I stop by Dr. Williams's office to thank Pamela. She tells me a story too. Dr. Cartwright, one of the Burn Center doctors, died of cancer a few years ago. Most likely he was exposed to chemicals from burn patients who suffered industrial accidents.

"It was so sad when we lost Dr. Cartwright. He was in his fifties."

That's young. Like Mark.

"After he passed away I had a dream that Dr. Cartwright visited me," she explains. "He looked transcendent."

"What do you mean by the word *transcendent*?" I'm curious. It's such a specific word.

"He looked like a perfect version of himself."

"Dr. Cartwright said to me, '*Pamela, I'm fine*,'" she adds.

Mark said the same thing to Laila, only it wasn't in a dream and she didn't see him.

Pamela says, "When I described my dream to one of the nurses, she told me she had exactly the same dream. And when we talked with a few other people on staff, they also shared the same dream about Dr. Cartwright reassuring them, too, that he was okay."

I fall silent, wondering if it's the power of suggestion. When a person hears about the dream, he or she then has a similar dream.

"Several of us independently had the same dream about Dr. Cartwright before we knew anyone else had one." It's as if Pamela read my mind. "It seemed that Dr. Cartwright was trying to let us all know he was all right."

"How interesting!" I reply. Mark did the same thing with Laila by making his presence known. He, too, wanted Laila to know he was okay.

Later in the afternoon we have drinks and appetizers at a local restaurant, which Cynthia, one of the drivers Mark swerved to avoid on Deer Valley Road, helped organize for the other drivers, the night shift nurses, and Thomas Hunnicutt and Jakki. Leah, the director of the Burn Center Foundation, joins us.

I fly home the next day. I'm struck by the goodness in each person I spoke to. For the medical staff, it's their job—what they did for Mark. But more than a job, they also cared. They cared deeply for Mark, the patient, for me, and our family as well. It wasn't Thomas's job, but he was there at the right place and the right time, ready to run into action. Jeff, Mark's best friend from high school, pondered that if he were in the same situation that June day, would he be brave enough to run out to rescue Mark as a stranger? He was honest enough to say, "I don't know." Thomas said, "I would always run out there to help. No question."

I fly home the next day, truly glad that I could thank everyone who saved Mark's life multiple times, from the day of the crash to those marathon days at the Burn Center.

When I arrive home, a package from Dierdre is waiting for me on the front doorstep. She hadn't been able to come to the lunch when I was in Phoenix. The box reveals wind chimes with a plaque inscribed with a message:

> When I am gone,
> release me, let me go
> I have so many things to see and do,
> You mustn't tie yourself
> to me with too many tears,
> but be thankful we had
> so many good years

It's the kind of message that Mark would send me. In spite of his infirmities, Mark's personality shone through during his time at the Burn Center. His independence, his motivation to get on with life, and his love for the boys and me. *I've never had a burn patient do their own arm lifts.* It's how Dierdre knew what message to engrave for me.

Chapter 32

SIGNS

After the Phoenix thank-you lunch for the Burn Center staff, I can't bear to be home over the holidays without Mark. Christmas in Vienna and skiing in Switzerland had been on our bucket list. I'm determined to travel and do all the things that Mark and I would've wanted to do if he were alive. But when I return home in January, standing alone in the long immigration line at San Francisco Airport, my heart's heavy when I realize that Mark isn't coming back—ever. He's really gone.

I'm in shock. Mark, who was so healthy and vibrant, disappeared suddenly from my life. My brain struggles to make sense of it. The only words I can think of to describe what I feel is *utter disbelief and bewilderment.*

Every day I expect him to walk in through the front door, backpack and suitcase in hand from his Reno flight. But he doesn't show up. The house stays quiet.

Thankfully, Wesley's still living at home. He has an accounting job at a start-up. He's gone all day and home most evenings for dinner. I notice that Wesley has many of Mark's mannerisms. The way he holds his hands out in front of him when he talks to me. We can keep each other company through our time of grief. Adrian and I call each other on Messenger video every Sunday. With their dad gone, I want to be 150 percent present as a parent for each of the boys.

One Saturday night, driving to a friend's house in Belmont for dinner, I look to my right passenger seat and can't believe that Mark's not sitting right there next to me. The empty seat fills me with an emptiness in my chest. I feel completely alone for the first time in my life.

Nights are the hardest. During the day I manage to keep myself busy. At night his empty side of the bed jumps out at me. I crave his touch, his voice, his big, solid body next to mine. I want to roll over, hold his hand, and talk to him as we always did before going to sleep. I cry a lot at night.

God, can you give me my husband back? Now. I need him.

During this time COVID-19 shuts down the world. It's surreal. My shock and grief seem normal in a world where abnormal has become the norm. Everyone's in a mask in my Bay Area neighborhood and in places like China and Italy. It's also isolating. Hospital scenes of COVID-19 patients hooked up to respirators trigger me. There's no running away because no one can travel.

I join a partner grief support group. I need to be around people who understand what it's like to lose the love of your life.

Several family members and friends reach out to share some remarkable experiences. There are so many of them.

Some people saw or felt premonitory signs that something bad was happening to Mark the afternoon he died. My friend Showa had told me before Mark's accident that she had a premonition in a dream about his plane accident two nights before it happened.

Fast-forward to now. My cousin Richard in New Jersey tells me that the night before Mark died, he had a dream in which his mother, my Aunt Qing Ling, who had died a few years ago, told him that Mark would pass away the next day.

Christa, a Wisconsin family friend, was at a knitting circle gathering the day Mark died. She didn't have a Wi-Fi connection so she couldn't read any of my online updates. At 5:00 p.m. Pacific time, she told me, she had an ominous feeling and wondered if something terrible had happened to Mark. The next morning, when she returned home to decent Wi-Fi, she read my post and realized that Mark died at the same time she had that bad feeling.

Our dear friend Branko shares that he and his wife, Stanka, were in New York City the day Mark died.

"Jenny, I'm not religious, but every few days while Mark was in the Burn Center, I would just talk to him."

I'm touched. He and Stanka were the friends who mailed me the Italian cookbook to read to Mark. It was such a brilliant idea.

"That Sunday I was in our hotel room staring out the window where I was having my usual conversation with Mark. From your daily posts I knew he was not doing well. Our room was up high on the twenty-fifth floor. Suddenly a bright red heart-shaped balloon showed up, floating outside the window. I thought, *That balloon showed up so suddenly just as I was chatting with Mark. It's so cheerful-looking.* Then suddenly the balloon quickly plummeted downward. I had an intense feeling that Mark had just died. The balloon disappeared from my sight. I told Stanka that I thought Mark's condition had taken a turn for the worse. I didn't know for sure, but at the time I somehow just *knew he had died.*"

On a sunny February day I'm recovering from a vestibular migraine and washing dishes in the sink. Mark usually drove me to see my vestibular therapist but instead, I had driven myself the day before, feeling off-kilter during the ten miles it took to get to San Jose. Wesley's in his first week in a new job and I couldn't ask him to take time off to chauffeur me. I'm finally cleaning up what I had neglected around the house because I felt unwell. After indulging in my own private five-minute pity party for myself, I suddenly feel surrounded by an overwhelming presence of love. My body softens.

I hear Mark's thoughts. Some unspoken strong force pulls me in. He's communicating to me telepathically. "Jenny, I'm so sorry I'm not there to help you."

Am I hallucinating? I don't think so. I feel clear-minded. *I did hear him speak to me.* It was very simple and to the point. It's Mark's style of speaking.

I marvel at how my own encounter with Mark is so similar to Laila's description of his presence. *I felt him as an overwhelming feeling of love.*

Laila was right. *Mark loves you and you'll hear from him at the right time.* I hear from him when I'm brought low by my migraine, without him here to help me.

I tell Showa my story about hearing from Mark. She tells me that she heard from Mark one day at home in Half Moon Bay after his memorial service. She was one of the last friends Mark and I met for lunch before his accident. Mark had offered to fly Showa and me to Sonoma for a special dinner to celebrate our June birthdays.

"What did he say to you?" I ask Showa, curious now.

She replies, "Mark said to me—take care of Jenny."

Chapter 33

WHO AM I?

I retire from my company as Mark and I had planned. My days are caught up in an endless treadmill of paperwork. Taking Mark's name off financial accounts, utilities, and credit cards and opening new accounts. Nobody prepares you for how much you have to do when your partner dies.

I dream about Mark often. We're in the car driving to the dry cleaners. We're rushing to the gate to catch a flight to Tokyo to start a three-month visit, our dream to spend more time exploring Japan. He and I are finally having the financial discussion I've been wanting to have. He speaks to me in his reassuring voice.

I confuse my dreams with memories. His green eyes crinkling when he laughs. The glint of auburn gold hair on his arms and the smell of warm sunlight in the car. The soft touch of his plaid shirt when it's cold out. The sound of snow flicking in the sparkling cold, dry air when he speeds by me on his skis.

My nights are spent with Mark, only to wake up every morning to the jarring fact that he's gone. The morning sun feels too bright. The air too crisp. There are days when I tumble into a dark chasm of despair, when I can't stop crying. In the evenings, when Wesley's home from work, all he can do is hug me. Sometimes there are no words that are adequate for the sadness we both feel. Other days I stand resolutely at the edge of the cliff but manage not to fall down. Then there are days when I'm mad at the universe. *Why did I lose Mark, who was sixty years old, so close in age to my dad, who was fifty-eight when he died? What did I do to deserve losing my husband who was healthy and a lover of life? Why did his exit from this world happen in such a cruel way?* My breath catches when I think that

Mark and I won't grow old together. When I see old couples together, I feel a spasm in my chest. *That's not our future.*

One night, I wake up in the middle of the night to go to the bathroom when I hear, through the window, the wind rustling in trees in our backyard. I think of how windy it was when I went into labor with Wesley, many years ago. I woke Mark up and together we walked around the backyard counting the time between my contractions before we realized it was time to go to the hospital. It's one of the most intense experiences a couple can have together. I never felt alone. Mark was always by my side. A deep ache swells up inside me sending me back out to sea.

My partner grief support group starts out meeting in person at a church in Palo Alto. A couple weeks later, we receive an urgent email that our group's been exposed to someone diagnosed with COVID. They don't ask us to quarantine but our meetings are moved to Zoom. Little do we know, it will permanently replace our in-person meetings.

There are five of us. After a month, when nobody in our group gets COVID, Wesley confesses to me that he'd been scared to lose me to the disease. He was so frightened, he couldn't even tell me his deepest fear. It's a reflection of how little we knew about COVID in 2020. But mostly I'm heartsick that he's been robbed of the innocence he had before Mark's accident. It's a door he's walked through that he'll never be able to close.

One Sunday while he's out for a walk, Wesley messages me.

"Mom, I can't remember what Dad's voice sounds like anymore!"

My throat closes, my hands clammy when I read his text. He's panicked.

I call him.

"Are you okay, sweetie?"

"No, I'm not. Oh God." He goes quiet for a minute. "I suddenly realized I don't know what Dad's voice sounds like anymore."

"It's been a while, hasn't it?"

"Yes. He was in a coma most of his time at the Burn Center."

That adds five months to how long Mark's been gone.

"Can you send me a video with him talking? I need to remember his voice."

"Yes, yes, of course. I'll find a good one to send you."

"Okay, thanks, Mom." He sounds calmer.

I scroll through the videos on my phone and send Wesley a video of him, Adrian, and Mark chatting and walking around the Wisconsin farm where Mark grew up one summer a few years ago.

The person in our grief support group that we feel saddest for is Brian, who is the youngest among us. He's thirty-two years old and he lost Lauren, his twenty-nine-year-old, non-smoking wife, to lung cancer. We agree that life isn't fair. Those of us who have been married longer think that Brian is still young and, unlike us, can easily meet someone again. But there's the other side of the coin. He feels robbed of the bright, shiny future that he thought he and Lauren would have.

One thing we have in common is that everyone adored their partners and respected them. It makes each of us sit up a little taller when we share our stories, proud of who our beloved was. The stories about partners flow easily into our conversations. *He had an infectious sense of adventure! She was so smart and generous with her time. He had so many hats, there must've been twenty of them on racks, in his closet and the garage—fedoras, 49ers and Giants hats, straw hats from Mexico.* I share my story about the holiday wrapping paper engagement ring that Mark made me.

I tell friends and acquaintances that if they don't know what to say to a friend who lost their partner, child, or parent, to just share a favorite memory or story about the person who's died. A ray of sunshine breaks through the clouds when someone recounts a wonderful memory in our group and we all bask in its warm rays.

Our grief support facilitator tells us that typically, people in their groups begin to see a light at the end of the tunnel of their grief after three months. After three months, our group is still pretty down. She tells us that COVID and lockdowns have really affected our emotional state.

When I read about Kobe Bryant and his daughter's tragic death in their helicopter accident in Calabasas, I'm instantly nauseous. It brings back a flood of memories of what I now acknowledge was Mark's horrific plane crash. What I don't have in common with my grief group is that I'm the only one who lost my beloved after a tragic plane accident. Everyone else's partner died of an illness. They knew about the possibility of death in advance, even if it was just a couple weeks. I now know I always carried hope during those five months in Phoenix. Hope was a bright, burning light in a dark forest, leading the way. Thomas's rescue of Mark, and the fact that he didn't die within the first two weeks, created the small bud inside me that grew and could believe in miracles and the possibility that Mark would come out of his coma and come home.

I realize now that I brought everyone else along with me. The boys, our families, and the thousands of people who read my daily posts. No wonder I'm still in shock.

I shout at myself, *Life is unfair. Get over it, Jenny. Mark's not coming back.* I take my diamond ring off. *You're not married to him anymore. He's really gone.*

I wrap the ring in some tissue paper and carefully place it in our safe deposit box at the bank, texting the boys, that whoever proposes first to a fiancée, can have the ring.

Next, I Google to look for grief organizations that support people who lost a loved one to a plane accident. ACCESS shows up on Google. They support families who've lost a family member to a plane accident, whether it was on a commercial flight or a small private plane. Heidi Snow, their founder, lost her fiancé in the TWA Flight 800 explosion in 1996. She's so kind and warm when she calls me. She knows what it feels like to lose your beloved suddenly in a violent accident. Heidi connects me with Anne, who lost her husband, Matt, after his plane went down in Maine. She was at a kids' pool party with her three children when she received a call from the airport. When Anne saw the airport number on her phone, in a flash, she knew something terrible had happened to him. They wouldn't tell her anything, just kept saying she had to come to the airport ASAP. She thought—*My life is about to change.*

Looking back now, my life also changed. In an instant.

Happily remarried five years later, Anne gives me her advice.

"Enjoy your singlehood, Jenny. When you have a new partner, you'll go back to negotiating with your partner how you spend your time. Would I want Matt back in a heartbeat? Of course. But I look back now and I'm also grateful for how much I grew as a person after he died."

I listen to her but I'm skeptical because right now all I know is that it's beyond words to describe how much I miss Mark and that I don't want to be alone for the rest of my life.

"Did you know that you wanted to date and meet someone again after Matt died?" I ask.

"I wasn't sure at first. Of course I was in shock. But over time, I asked God to take away my desire if it wasn't in his or her plan for me to be with a new partner."

Clearly, she met her current husband so it worked out. I'm not ready to meet someone right now, but I wonder when I will be.

As the fall of 2020 rolls into the winter of 2021, COVID shuts everything down. I stop seeing many of my friends. I have no choice but to face the constant churn of emotions within, dropping into an inner world where I'm hyperaware of what I'm feeling all the time. I'm hooked on Beck's new *Hyperspace* album, which pulls me into a dreamy musical landscape, an ethereal contemplation of human love, loss, and the galaxy of stars. I put the album on autorepeat while I do everything. Cooking, gardening, cleaning. The music taps into a deep vein of sadness in me. It's a dark, cavernous space where I float in a dark sky of luminous stars and shimmering gas clouds that swirl around me. I read that Beck wrote the album after his recent divorce. I've connected to his personal world of loss and loneliness. I feel deeply sad and comforted at the same time.

More dreams. Mark and I are hosting a party for fifty people.

I'm standing in front of our Mountain View house. I know that Mark's gone and I'm devastated. He's holding my hand, his arm outstretched as he walks slightly ahead of me. I always thought he had the sexiest arms. I'm sobbing.

My life is the opposite of what it's been for so many years. Mark and I were doers. We made things happen. We helped others. I don't know how to ask for help. But when I'm faced with Wesley and I'm unable to figure out how to do something ourselves, I finally give in. My desire to make progress in my life eventually wins over my discomfort with asking. I ask our friend Rick to help me sell Mark's cars, including his Cobra. I ask Suzie for financial advice, an area that Mark spent more time thinking about for both of us. I ask Art, my neighbor, how to use an electric drill to replace a cabinet knob in the bathroom.

My friend David, who lost his wife, Margaret, a few years ago, told me that he opted for one-to-one grief therapy instead of joining a support group. He thought it would be too much for him to be around the sadness of others. That isn't what I experience with our group. We help each other out. We offer ideas to each other on how to get through our days beyond crying and being sad. I offer that I read somewhere how it helps to do small things that bring us joy.

One night, I write:

> Annie Dillard says, *"How we spend our days is how we spend our lives."* Instead of waiting until we're happy to enjoy the small things, we should do the small things that make us happy.

I'd love to travel, but I can't because of COVID. I'd love to spend time in Italy and visit Adrian in Zurich, but the EU is restricting Americans, Russians, and Brazilians from entering their countries. It was great skiing last season. *What else would give me joy?*

Stuck at home like everyone else, I watch a lot of Netflix and Amazon Prime. Lately, I'm enjoying Italian movies. It brings me joy to hear the expressiveness of the Italian language and memories of happier times. I watch the vintage *L'Avventura* with Monica Vitti, then Luca Guadagnino's *Call Me by Your Name*, a sensuous movie that pulls me into its aliveness. Languid summer days reading and swimming. The ever-present delicate, sweet warbling of birds and the steady trill of frogs. Unhurried family breakfasts on the patio at the villa in a lush northern Italian countryside. I love the expressive and passionate cadence of Italian. Listening to it spoken instantly softens my heart. If I can't travel to Italy, I can at least learn the language. I persuade Suzie to join me for a three-month intensive Berlitz Italian course on live video with an instructor. I fall into an easy rhythm of classes twice a week. Every week, I find and declare my new favorite Italian word. *La spazzatura! La forcetta! Certo!*

Writing gives me joy. I go back to work on my draft novel that I had written seven years ago in between jobs. In the past, I wondered how I'd fit the solitary life of a writer in with my soon-to-be-retired couplehood with Mark. My solitude during COVID now creates an endless horizon of time to write.

I liked kayaking and imagined that in Tahoe, Mark and I would row out on the lake, stop to enjoy our morning coffee with views of the mountains. In reality, he didn't like kayaking because it wasn't fast enough. Speed was his middle name. I'll now find friends to kayak with. I start searching on REI for a pair of inflatable kayaks.

With my local YMCA fitness center closed, I walk a lot. Regular contact with people and activities shapes my time in a way that creates a predictable structure and cadence to each week. It helps a lot, especially during COVID.

Journaling becomes a compulsive daily habit as I pour my heart out about the good, the bad, and the ugly in my life. Nothing is off-limits. Each blank page in my notebook represents a new day, reassuring me that I can start every morning afresh—the sorrow, the anger, the emptiness of yesterday left behind.

I peck away at my novel. In Italian class, we're not allowed to speak any English even to ask questions. The sheer concentration required to perform in class takes intense focus. I continue to meet with my weekly grief group on video. Wesley and I cook and eat dinner together most nights. I discover that Wesley's a good cook and it pleases me to know that Mark was a great role model in the kitchen.

A group of women friends start a weekly Friday cocktail group. We meet on our friend Gwen's outdoor patio, since she has a big wall-installed heat lamp and a circle of Adirondack chairs, perfect for an outdoor gathering. We take turns hosting a cocktail of our choice. Mark was the bartender in our family. I take over now by finding his cocktail shaker to make my first drink. I make a thyme-infused gin drink with a slice of blood orange. It's an instant hit and it builds my confidence. I discover that I love cocktails more than wine or beer. However small, mastering cocktails and learning Italian, gives me a feeling of accomplishment. The cocktails provide the festive backdrop for our group's lively discussions about our families and our local community and offers a safe place to talk about politics and what's happening in the world.

When I tell one of my cocktail friends how incredibly grateful I am for the group and their friendship, she says, "You were a good friend first." I hadn't thought of the currency of goodwill and love that Mark and I had created by having made room for friends and the people we mentored over the years.

It's also a time of firsts for me, however small. Each new accomplishment helps me find more of the "me" in me that I never anticipated. *I'm getting to know who I am without Mark.*

I have more dreams about Mark. We get married again. He's chasing little Adrian in the yard in a mock football game. I'm in a nice restaurant with him but we're surrounded by prisoners in orange jumpsuits, like the guys I encountered at the Phoenix hospital. I tell him I'm afraid to go to the bathroom. I end up going by myself and I'm fine.

My life was perfect before Mark's accident.

The idea of dating flits in and out of my mind a couple times at first, then constantly. Mark and I went on our first date when I was twenty-three. He proposed on my twenty-fourth birthday. I was twenty-five when we got married. I had seriously dated two men before Mark. Listening to stories from Michelle, Mark's youngest sister, and Suzie, I know that online dating is what people do now to meet each other.

One day I think I'll be ready to date again. Mark will be a hard act to follow. How will I ever find someone like him again? He was one of the smartest people I knew. An independent thinker, intuitive, accepting of others, always curious about people. You could drop him in at any party and he'd have a great time. And obviously, he enjoyed all things fast—motorcycles, cars, skiing, speedboats, planes. He possessed such a big appetite for life. It was infectious.

Dearest God, can I have him back?

It's a push-pull of moving forward, learning new things, creating new memories with moments of real joy, then I fall back into the hole again, bewildered and wondering where he's gone. His side of the bed, empty at night. His sink, where his toothbrush hasn't moved in months.

I wake up from a dream where Mark comes back from the dead. I'm incredibly happy and keep hugging him, not wanting to let go. After a day with me, he disintegrates, his body falling apart into hundreds of splinters like someone took an axe to a big tree trunk.

I'm rereading a Buddhism book by Steve Hagen that I first read seven years ago.

He describes how the universe is reborn every moment. And you are reborn with it. I remember reading somewhere that the world is dynamic—you aren't who you were yesterday, five days, five months, or five years ago. It occurs to me that I might find a soulmate again. That I might be happy again. It doesn't feel like my world right now, but I feel a glimmer of hope.

Chapter 34

THE LOVING UNIVERSE

I've been thinking about how much I still love Tahoe. Just days after Mark's plane crash, I had let go of the house he and I had planned to buy in retirement. While I can't envision myself starting over in Tahoe without him, I would still like to buy a place where I can spend time skiing, enjoying summer at the lake, and Thanksgiving, which was our family tradition with the boys. For three years before Mark's plane crash, he worked for a Reno start-up, living in our Incline Village family ski condo and commuting back to Mountain View from Friday to Monday.

I need something bigger and realize while cleaning the condo that there are also too many painful reminders of Mark.

I call Patty, our realtor, to let her know that if any of the townhouses near the lake go on sale, I would be interested. Without Mark I don't want a house and the winter maintenance that comes with it. In early May she calls to let me know that there's a very desirable unit that's come on the market, close to the condo Mark lived in and three blocks from the lake. She and one other realtor are the only ones who have access to it before it goes on the market.

I drive up to Incline Village the next day to see two properties that she thinks I would like.

After months of living within the confines of my suburban Mountain View house, it's exhilarating to speed up Highway 80 as it gradually climbs into the foothills near Auburn and into the mountains. The faster I drive, the faster I feel as though I'm running. I feel so free. Some force of energy inside my body feels as if it'll burst out. I catch my breath when I first catch a glimpse of Donner Lake, like a lustrous azure gemstone set in a valley. Stepping out of my car at a lookout point, I breathe in deeply the sweet, wet smell of the pines, rocks, and snow. Closing my eyes, I feel wind gusts encircling and tugging at my body. When I open my eyes, there's an endless horizon of deep-green trees stretching out over craggy rocks and mountains. A couple of eagles fly overhead. I'm blown away by the beauty everywhere I look.

There are more trees than humans here.

A deep sense of quiet swells inside me like a gentle wave. I feel at home.

After months of living in Mark's gray hospital room and sheltering inside from the punishing summer heat of Phoenix, then the confines of home because of COVID-19, it's no surprise the freedom I feel coming to Tahoe. But it's more than that. I notice more of my natural surroundings, as if I'm wearing new glasses and seeing the world in a way I hadn't before. I notice birds and the way the wind is swaying the branches of the pines.

The first townhouse Patty takes me to is farther from the lake than I prefer, but it has the fourth bedroom that I want for guests. When we arrive, the realtor hosting the home looks exhausted and informs me that I'm her tenth appointment of the day. The price is higher than my budget.

After we finish the tour and climb back into Patty's car, she tells me, "The market's hot right now. If you see something you like, we should move fast."

We drive to the second townhouse, which is close to the lake and next door to the condo Mark was living in. The living room has a soaring cathedral ceiling with tall windows. I feel a sense of peace looking out the windows at the gentle, green canopy of trees that surround the home. The kitchen is huge. It's a great place to cook and entertain. I instantly know that I want this townhouse.

Patty puts my offer together and contacts the seller's realtor. I wait by my phone for her update.

She calls me back a couple of hours later.

"Jenny, the realtor representing the buyer made a mistake. Before he saw your offer, he'd mistakenly listed the townhouse on all the real estate sites—Zillow, Realtor.com, and so on."

"How did it happen?"

"I'm not sure what happened, but he's already received an offer at the asking price."

"So I need to counter then."

"Yes. Let me know how much you want to counter with."

I don't take long to think. I need to move quickly. Patty helps me put together a counter.

"Fingers crossed. They're getting a lot of interest in the townhouse."

Shoot. What was a golden opportunity to get in early was now threatening to become a bidding war. I resign myself to the possibility that I may lose the townhouse to other bidders if it goes higher than I can afford.

Early the next morning my phone rings. It's Patty.

"I spoke with the owner's realtor and told him about what happened to Mark. He shared it with the owners."

I'm not sure what's coming next as it relates to my offer.

"Well, it turns out that the wife is a recreational pilot just like Mark. When she and her husband heard what happened to Mark and his plane, they said, 'We want Jenny to buy our townhouse.'"

I can't believe it. I was certain I would be in for a brutal bidding war.

"They accepted your offer and decided not to pursue any others."

I can't believe that, as simple as that, they've decided to sell the house to me. That's kindness in action. Pilots are their own special tribe. The pilots in Mark's Stanford GSB class made a personal effort to reach out to me. One GSBer even sent me a pilot's poem, which our family read aloud during Mark's memorial service.

Patty and I discuss the logistics of the inspection, the owners' timeframe, and the closing.

Suzie sees the photos of the townhouse that I send her. She messages me:

> *How wonderful, Jenny! It's time for you to create new memories in your own place in Tahoe. Btw, Mark would love the kitchen.*

Back home in Mountain View, one evening I reflect on all that's happened in recent months. However you choose to explain it, I feel cradled in the loving care of the universe, with Laila and Showa hearing from Mark, "I'm fine. I wish I was there to help you. Take care of Jenny."

Then this wonderful and peaceful Tahoe home drops right into my lap.

Mark and I were successful in life because we were take-charge people and good at taking care of others. We excelled at it. It's a completely new feeling to experience and recognize that instead, the universe is taking care of me.

It's the first time I bought a house without Mark and it went well.

When I go for a walk near the lake, I stop and look out the deep blue water, surrounded by sloping mountains.

Thank you, God and the universe. If you are there, I thank you for taking care of me.

Having bought my new home in Tahoe, I finally drop into the condo that Mark lived in on the days he worked in Reno. I can't afford both places and need to rent the condo out. That means packing up Mark's belongings, mostly his clothes. When I see his rust-colored ski pants hanging in the closet, I grab them and close my eyes. They smell woodsy and clean. He used to zigzag through the trees and meet me on a run. I see him speeding down the mountain, cutting a formidable figure, a combination of strength and grace. I'm crying; the world feels jagged all around me, my tears blotching his pants. I can't believe I'll never see him ski again. When my body stops heaving, I let go of his pants, eyes still blurry while I stumble to my new mattress, climb onto it, and lie down in a fetal position. There's no headboard yet; I'm waiting for it to be delivered. It's my new life, post-Mark. Everything's in flux. My head feels so good on the soft pillow. I sink into the deep oblivion of sleep the way I used to in my little condo in Phoenix, exhausted from my long days at Mark's bedside.

The next morning, I have to run errands in Reno. Driving on Mount Rose Highway from the city back to Incline Village is a trek Mark and I had driven countless times. I feel a prick of sadness. Flashes of our life together. The late-night drive home after an Elvis Costello show, shopping at Lowe's, then drinks at the Depot Brewery. Stopping at Raley's for groceries and a six-pack of Sierra Nevada Pale Ale for Mark. I wonder if it was a mistake to buy a place here. Maybe all it would do is remind me of Mark.

A few days later, skiing by myself, feeling the rush of pure joy dancing down the mountain and witnessing the beauty of snowcapped mountains glittering in the sun, brings me back to myself. I discover that strangers on the lift and in line talk with me because I'm alone. Single people are apparently more approachable than couples. Nobody approached me when I was with Mark. A woman compliments me on my jacket. A travel photographer tells me stories about living in Spain before he moved to Reno. A couple raves about their phone lanyards and enthusiastically shares where they bought them.

I decorate my new place for the first time without Mark to negotiate my taste. Friends are eager to visit and stay with me. They all agree that Mark would love my new home. My friends Matt and Jane come to stay, bringing my labradoodle goddog Ka'ia, a curly, soft bundle of love. We take her on mountain trails for her debut hike in snow.

I'm sleeping soundly and deeply in my new place, a first since Mark's accident. Every window I gaze at looks into a sanctuary of trees, their willowy, tall trunks surrounded by lush, delicate green leaves. I'm creating new memories in Tahoe.

One morning, I wake up from a dream about Mark again. I know that he's disabled though I don't see anything obvious like his amputated legs. He's upset that he can't keep up with hikers on a trail. I'm thinking to myself in the dream, *It matters to him that he can't physically keep up with others anymore.*

Maybe it's a mercy that Mark died. I catch my breath at the thought. Never in a million years would I wish that, but in the end, is it fair for him to live and suffer not being who he was before the accident? Especially since he was such a lover of the world?

Memories float to the surface. He's sitting on a covered deck in Tahoe during a thunderstorm, watching it rain. He's dancing at a party in his lime green tuxedo, martini in hand. He's skiing down the chutes, a straight drop down.

Driving home through the mountains, I pass Donner Lake, a blue, sparkling gem surrounded by snow. Eagles fly overhead in the valley just past the lake. I'm soaring like those majestic birds, my heart feels so full. *I'm happy but I'm a bird flying with a mortal wound because I lost my mate.*

Then I see an image of plums coming out of a woman's mouth. She's not anyone I know. *What could that mean?* I have no clue.

Two hundred miles later when I arrive home that evening, I Google plums.

> *The Japanese and Chinese thought plum blossoms symbolized perseverance and hope because they bloom in winter. Plums themselves can represent the potential for new beginnings.*

Chapter 35

LOST

That summer when I'm back in Mountain View, the weather is warmer than we're used to. Temperatures hit the low 100s on the Fourth of July weekend. Wildfires are raging in the Santa Cruz mountains and getting dangerously close to homes in the hills just fourteen miles away.

One early Saturday morning, I'm in the kitchen, brewing coffee. Wesley's already up and on his iPad in the family room.

"Mom, there's ash everywhere."

"What?"

"Look outside."

We step outside onto the patio. A fine gray chalky layer is on everything. The patio table, the chairs, the barbecue. The sky is a smoky amber. It feels surreal just like my life.

I write Mark a letter:

My beautiful man,

I'm crushed and beyond sad that we won't get to enjoy our time together, free of the preoccupations of our jobs. We were looking forward to spending more time together, with family and friends. I'm strong like you said I was so many years ago when my dad died. But being strong doesn't mean I'm not sad. I feel so much grief for the special stage in life we were about to enjoy—just you and me, the boys launched. You were at peace about your life before the accident. I'm sorry you suffered so much. I hope you are no longer in pain.

Perhaps the greatest gift we gave our boys was to show them the kind of love like a river current that runs deep and true. You always loved rivers didn't you? I hope they'll find the right life partner one day. I want to live long enough to see them find their beloved. I'll do it for both of us, okay?

Love,
Jenny

What will the rest of my life be like? I become closer to my single friends or friends who married or remarried more recently. They remember what being alone was like. Now that I'm more comfortable asking for help, I want to be a good friend back by offering help whenever I can, knowing they don't always have a partner to count on. I message my single women friends after our night out together to make sure they make it home safely. I never used to do this.

Anita Moorjani, an NDE-er, says that death is not a failure. It's not like they lost the battle. She reminds us that this is our cultural lens. Death leads to a transformation back into something bigger and greater. When we grieve, we're grieving for ourselves.

I read somewhere that grief is love looking for a home. *That's exactly it.* I don't know where to put all that love I have for Mark now that he's gone. It builds up inside me like a dam with nowhere to go, except to remember our love in the past.

My longtime friend Mara, who struggles with depression, tells me that she tends to reject and stop any emotion she feels is negative because she judges it as bad, and instead of vanquishing the feeling, it hangs around her like a black cloud.

I realize that I don't have a voice in my head that judges whether what I'm feeling is good or bad. It just is. In the past, I tended to unconsciously brush aside a negative feeling, not realizing how anxious I was. I'm not sure why I did that. Was it laziness? A lack of awareness? I've changed. Since Mark's accident, once I recognize an emotion—sadness, anger, envy—I face it. I don't fight it and instead let it flow through, and magically, it dissolves like water absorbed into the ground I stand on. I can't push aside my feelings as I might have in the past, because I have to face Mark's sudden disappearance. Every single day.

There were times in the past when a situation made me depressed for a while. Feeling like a fish out of water, living in a New York suburb after growing up in big cities. Overwhelmed with juggling a demanding job, marriage, and motherhood after Adrian was born.

The Buddhists describe how life and the world around us are constantly changing. Look at the cycle of nature. I understand it in a way I didn't before. My grief ebbs and flows like the tide. I have hope that if I feel sad now, I'll feel okay tomorrow or the day after. Having been through the worst time of my life, I realize that I'm unlikely to be depressed again when I remember that life is in a state of constant flux. Bad things happen but good things also happen. Believing that life is static is a recipe for depression.

I feel unsettled in my life. I desperately want to move out of Mountain View. It's like wearing a favorite jacket that doesn't fit anymore. I've become more sensitive to how a place makes me feel. The go-go energy that was great when I was working full time in an exciting, fast-paced career now makes me feel out of sorts. I think of the beauty of the mountains, but Tahoe's a four-hour drive away and I'm unsure about untethering from my Bay Area friends who have become my support group.

I need to rework the plot of my draft novel, but it feels overwhelming without some ongoing feedback and structure to motivate me. I struggle to find any in-person classes to meet other writers because COVID caused all programs to go online. I need to find my tribe. While I know I'm mostly intact after Mark's death, I'm not sure where I'm going in my life. The picture of my future with Mark has shattered into a million pieces and I need to find a new picture.

I read a book titled *Awakenings from the Light* written by Nancy Rynes. Nancy was bicycling in a roundabout in Boulder, Colorado, when a woman driving a large SUV hit her. The driver was unaware that her car had struck anyone. Nancy and her bike were dragged under the SUV for fifty feet. She died on the operating table but came back to life and wrote a book describing what she learned when she went to "the other side"—mostly that she experienced a beautiful landscape filled with love energy and spoke to a loving guide. She understood that we're in this life to learn about love, how to give it and how to receive it. She went from being an atheist who grew up Catholic to believing that we live in a universe filled with a powerful, loving presence in us and around us. It changed her life.

Because my parents died on the younger side, I had read about personal accounts of near-death experiences years before Mark's accident. They were described by people like Anita Moorjani who had died in the clinical sense. While they were dead, many of them experienced a powerful and transcendent state of consciousness. Sometimes they left their physical bodies at the hospital or they saw and talked with loved ones who had died, and/or they experienced the omniscient presence of love greater than anything else they had felt in their lives. Often they came back to their physical lives with significant reorientation of their own purpose and priorities. It was life-changing. Anita was one of them. Nancy was another.

I had been writing almost every day in my journal, a habit our grief support group recommended as a way to process our pain. In one of her presentation videos, Nancy recommends a daily reflection exercise to answer five questions:

- What three things am I grateful for?
- What went well today?
- How did I make a difference?
- How were my actions perceived by others?
- What can I do better?

I find this daily reflection helpful. It makes me more aware of how I'm going about each day rather than living life on autopilot, as I had done just before Mark's accident.

I notice on Nancy's website that she offers coaching sessions. For some time I mull over the idea of talking with her. I'm not used to asking a stranger for help. I had turned down the idea of meeting with a grief therapist after Mark died and instead joined my grief support group.

I think, *Why not? What do I have to lose?* My mind is driving in circles thinking about where my life is going—a mental cul-de-sac—and COVID keeping everyone home isn't helping.

I reach out to Nancy for a coaching call. She responds quickly to my request and asks me to send her a photo of myself and to describe my intentions for our session.

I tell her that I'm looking for some direction in my life, explaining that my husband, Mark, had died after a plane accident. Rather than getting into a detailed description of what happened to him, I suggest that she Google his name and the city of Phoenix to find out more. I also explain that while I have some thoughts about my life's purpose without him, I'm interested in any insight she might offer.

After taking some time to decide whether to request a session with Nancy, I'm now suddenly excited about meeting her.

The first thing Nancy tells me when we get on our call is that like Mark, she's a recreational pilot.

I'm surprised because it's a fact that's not mentioned in any of her books, her website, online interviews, or articles.

Nancy says, "I clicked on the first article I could find about Mark's plane accident. Before I could read it, I looked at the photo of you and Mark."

I know exactly which article she's referring to. It's the one that has a large headline photo of Mark and me on a ferry in Zurich, the summer we saw Adrian off to his ETH program.

"I didn't even read the article, so I didn't know the details of what happened."

I'm not sure where Nancy's going with this.

She continues, "When I looked at the photo, I was immediately transported into the cockpit with Mark. He turned to me and said, 'Nancy, I wasn't afraid. All I cared about was saving people's lives.'"

Something inside me bursts open and I'm shaking uncontrollably. I wipe my eyes with my hands. I didn't expect to hear this. All I can think about in the moment is how brave my beautiful husband was—and how proud I am of who he was.

"He wasn't thinking of his own life at all," Nancy says.

"He was such a good…good person," I say, my voice cracking.

I think of how contented Mark was right before his plane crash.

Rene, his sister, told me that on his last visit to their little town in Illinois, she found him playing in a meadow with his little nephew David. Mark was lying on the grass with David giggling next to him. He turned to her and said, "Isn't this just the most perfect moment?"

Gradually Mark had evolved from a provocative young man out to convince everyone of his point of view—to the thoughtful listener he had become, more subtle in persuading others. He had made peace with his career challenges and was content with where our life was headed next. He told me he looked forward to a life full of family, friends, travel, and plenty of time to hike and ski.

And now, on that terrible day, he had saved others' lives without regard for his own. Cynthia, the driver of the first car on Deer Valley Road, told me she locked eyes with Mark when she saw his plane approaching her as he attempted to land. She said she was sure she was going to die—but Mark then swerved his plane to the right, away from the road. Cynthia said to me, "He was a hero, Jenny. He saved my life, as well as the people in two other cars behind me."

Mark saved the drivers' lives without regard for his own, and I now think of his actions that day as *love in action*.

Nancy and I then discuss the transition I'm in with Mark gone. She offers some wise advice about how to find inner guidance about my situation. She also encourages me to keep up with my writing. I like that she doesn't tell me the answers but rather coaches me to figure out how to discover them for myself.

After our call, I break down crying. Great big heaving waves roll throughout my body. It's one of the few times I completely lose control. I thought I did when they told me Mark had died. Looking back, I realize I couldn't lose it the way I do now because I had to hold it together enough to tell the boys their father had just died.

I lose all sense of time. When the tears slow down and my body stops its convulsive shaking, I have a moment of clarity. I think of Mark's singular focus on trying to land the plane safely and without harm to others.

I think of how he was always there for me. In the thirty-one years I've known this incredible man, I never doubted, and I was never left wondering, if he would show up for me. Mark was my rock.

Around this time, I become obsessed with the question of why I lost my parents and Mark prematurely. I write in my journal:

Dad died at 58.
Mom died at 61.
Mark died at 60.
Why, why, why?

I feel incredibly sad that my family keeps shrinking. For the first time, I understand what my mom must've felt when she also lost my dad so suddenly. He had died in his sleep of a stroke. She had been away visiting family and came home to find him in bed, unable to wake him up. He was only two years younger than Mark. *Is this some awful pattern in our family that I was doomed to repeat?*

I wonder if it's time for me to meet with a therapist. My grief group continues to be a great support, but after my call with Anne, the woman from Maine who lost her pilot husband, I think maybe I need help with the trauma of Mark's accident and death. I find a referral through my friend David who went to therapy after he lost his wife, Margaret. My therapist and I spend the first few sessions discussing what happened to Mark and me, where I am in my grief journey, the back-and-forth progress of finding a few steps forward only to fall back at times.

I tell her how much I miss my dad and Mark, who were the two rocks in my life.

My therapist turns to me and says, "I've gotten to know you now, Jenny. You are someone who makes lemonade out of lemons. Did it ever occur to you that you, too, are a rock?"

I shake my head. *No, I've never thought of myself that way. I'm not sure what I think of that.*

Instead I want to scream, *Don't I get to need someone too?*

Chapter 36

REBUILDING AND FINDING LOVE AGAIN

"We don't need to go anywhere to obtain truth. We only need to be still and things will reveal themselves in the clear water of our heart."
—Thich Nhat Hanh, *Touching Peace: Practicing the Art of Mindful Living*

When Adrian's home for the holidays, we decide the resting place for the other half of Mark's ashes will be somewhere by Mount Rose summit near Lake Tahoe. Mark and I had hiked a loop around this very summit the summer before his accident. He had a confident grin and rugged good looks in the photo we took on that hike, hands on his hips at a scenic lookout point. Behind him, the gentle sloping peaks of rocks stretch out, surrounded by manzanita bushes and purple lupine flowers. It was where he felt most at home.

The boys and I arrive in Incline Village after a giant snowstorm. The roads are treacherous. Thankfully, the day we're to scatter Mark's ashes turns out to be clear.

Because there's so much snow on the ground, we rent snowshoes. Adrian carries Mark's ashes in a sealed bag as we slowly make our trek up the ridge near the Mount Rose summit.

It takes a while to reach the top of the ridge from the parking lot. Adrian's the fastest. I'm next, with Wesley bringing up the rear, stopping frequently. When we reach the top, Wesley arrives after me, bends over, arms on his hips, breathing heavily from the higher elevation. I turn my face toward the views below us, take a deep breath, and close my eyes. The air is so fresh with a faint pine smell, the sun warm on my face. When I open my eyes, I can see Mark's favorite ski resort visible across the winding mountain road.

A strong wind starts to pick up here at the top of the ridgeline. Adrian and I walk around, trying to find the right place to scatter the ashes so they don't fly in our faces. We finally find a good spot so that the ashes can scatter away from us off the mountain.

"We love you, Dad," Adrian says as he stands on the edge of the ridge. We can see Washoe Valley; Washoe Lake looks tiny in the distance. He opens up the bag and shakes the ashes out as the wind scatters them out. Fine gray specks are flying and swirling around us.

He hands the rest of the ashes to me. I take it from his hands quickly so the bag doesn't blow away. I take a slow, deep breath.

"Mark, we're returning you to the mountains that you loved so much." I pull open the bag and allow the rest of the ashes to pour out into the air, the wind carrying them.

We're setting him free.

That evening, Laila texts me:

> *"Remember that special energy in Mark's hospital room? I didn't know what it was at the time. I now know that energy was love."*

I spend the next ski season at my new home in Lake Tahoe. The inner stillness I feel inside mirrors the silent beauty of the snow-covered trees surrounding the house, each tree dressed in its branches of intricate white filigree. It creates a feeling of peace, like a gentle stream of water flowing and filling each crevice of my heart. Content in my solitude, I spend my evenings reading a book about soulmates.

I lost my soulmate. Dear God, is it possible to have more than one soulmate in a lifetime? Could I be so lucky a second time?

One morning it's snowing steadily outside. I'm nursing my coffee, sitting in my kitchen, mesmerized by the fat white flakes falling like small cotton balls from a blank sky. The tree branches are rapidly turning heavy and white with snow. It's so beautiful.

I'm reading an article by Oprah on meditation. *I should try meditating*. Without the pressures of a full-time job, there's no excuse. I reflect on how badly my past attempts at meditation have gone. I have a monkey mind, unable to turn off the endless mental chatter. I had a good experience with a guided meditation app that helped me get desperately needed sleep during my marathon days at the Burn Center. But the idea of meditating without help feels daunting.

The article suggests starting in January with meditating for only one minute. For every successive month, you add another minute so that by December you are meditating daily for twelve minutes.

How brilliant! How achievable! I love it and decide immediately I should try meditating for two minutes. It's February.

I close my eyes and place my hands over my heart. I take a deep breath in and slowly release it. In and out a few times. I picture myself breathing from my heart, a steady rhythm.

My mind wanders. *I've gotta remember to take the garbage bin out tomorrow for early morning collection.... What should I have for lunch today? I'm meditating for only two minutes.... That's not too long. I wonder how long it's been...*

It's very still. The refrigerator is humming. I think, *How lovely and quiet it is in the kitchen. I feel so peaceful.*

Suddenly in my mind's eye I see a white owl flying toward me, surrounded by a bright, white light.

I'm startled. I've never seen images when I've closed my eyes to meditate, let alone that of a white owl. I blink. The owl and the light are still there.

My astonishment quickly turns into a feeling of reverence. This is some kind of special moment I can't explain.

As if telepathically, I hear a message from the owl in my thoughts: *You'll meet your soulmate once you establish a daily spiritual practice.*

Who's saying that to me? Is it really the owl? Or is it my intuition, God, or the universe? I have no idea where it came from, but I'm in awe of both my white owl vision and this message.

I answer back, *I've already decided to meditate daily*. I feel a twinge of satisfaction that I had committed to doing that before this message.

Another thought pops into my mind: *I'm going to let go of trying to control my life*. It's not that I won't plan. Suzie and I had talked about a summer trip to Italy. But I'll loosen the reins by which I was used to running my life. I'm not a control freak, but I do have strong opinions and interests. Mark did too. He and I were both very organized and good at planning. It was an occupational hazard from being business leaders. We were paid to have opinions and a point of view and to make things happen quickly.

For the first time in my life I really let go. What allows me to do this? As I recently explained to a friend, after Mark died I was like a baby bird in free fall from its nest. It wasn't my choice that I was pushed out of the safety of my nice, tidy, autopilot life. I had nothing to lose. *Why not experiment with new ways of thinking about my life?* When Mark died in Phoenix, I came home to California with an urn of his ashes. He's truly gone. I don't have a partner to negotiate life decisions with anymore. I'm free to do whatever I want. It's not what I wanted but this is my life now.

Reading Eckhart Tolle's book *A New Earth*, about focusing fully on the present moment, is helpful as I begin to release control. He explains on an Oprah-hosted show for students, "Life is an adventure. It's not a packaged tour." His concept of living in the moment, not dwelling on the past or overthinking the future, brings hope into my heart, while also acknowledging that the reality of our lives can change in an instant—for bad but also for good. Why can't my life turn into something good, even wonderful again? I get that now.

Bring it on.

I think of what Nancy told me—to trust my inner guidance and how to ask for signs.

As I stepped through the burning coals of what was the worst time in my life, a funny thing happened. I discovered I was okay. It's not some Pollyanna belief that only good things will happen in my life but rather the confidence that through life's ups and downs, which none of us can predict, I'll be okay. Until I lost Mark, I never knew that love and beauty could coexist with deep sorrow and loss. I wouldn't have understood that before.

By giving up control, I won't become a totally passive person. I'll still make plans but I'm going to stop obsessing about the future. I'll keep it loose, open to changing plans spontaneously. I would plan to ski all ski season, but I wouldn't try to pin down all the details of what I would do after that. I thought about moving out of Mountain View. With the boys and Mark gone now, I didn't belong here anymore. It's a great place for jobs and raising a family, both of which no longer matter. My big questions are *Where should I move* and *Will I meet my next soulmate?* I let go of obsessively checking house listings on Zillow for places that seemed attractive: Sausalito, Sonoma, Phoenix, Austin. I received an affirmative answer about a soulmate, so now I need to stop thinking so much about how I'll meet him.

I finish the book about soulmates, concluding that I'm wired for partnership and that I shouldn't feel any less of an independent woman to want a life partner. My marriage to Mark was an example of that. We were each our own person and we also enjoyed being a couple. There are many definitions of what a soulmate is. What I meant by *soulmate* is that Mark and I really "got" each other. When we started dating, we both felt as though we had come home. I loved who he was—his fiercely independent streak. He was a lightning bolt in my life who made me feel alive. Mark had an unconventional way of thinking. He loved reading everything he could get his hands on, and he enjoyed all the fun things that life had to offer. He loved that I had a core that was calm and strong—a tree with deep roots. Like him, I was a prolific reader and loved learning about personal growth, people, culture, history, and world affairs. I had no need to control him. He felt free to be himself with me. Neither of us wanted the other to change.

When the time is right, I want a life partner again. It feels healthy to realize this after having spent the last year and a half discovering who I am without Mark. It's reassuring to find that 80 percent of who I am is intact. I love skiing even though Mark was the reason I learned. I still love to travel. It was my idea to go to Italy our first time, and it was Mark who fell in love with the country after I talked him into going.

When I finally open my eyes from meditation, they're moist, and I blink from the bright morning light streaming in, illuminating the table where I'm sitting. I've lost track of time. While I was caught up in my magical moment, a silent blanket of white powder has softly fallen on the ground and the tree branches. It's so pure and beautiful outside. I'm not sure why I'm crying.

I pick up my phone and Google *white owl meaning.* A long list of descriptions comes up from many ancient traditions—Christian, Celtic, and Native American, among others. The white owl symbolizes purity, sacred wisdom and insight, keen vision, and transformation. It is a sign that something significant is ending and something new is beginning—that if we can embrace change and embark upon new paths, life will be made better through growth and self-exploration as we step out of our comfort zone.

Transformation, change, insight. These are the words that stand out to me. No question—something has ended and I'm heading into some kind of new beginning, the shape of which I can't see yet. In practicing my newfound release, I say out loud to myself, *Let my life unfold.*

Over the next two months, splitting my time between Mountain View and Lake Tahoe, I read more books. Since Mark's death I've become hungrier than ever for books and podcasts that stretch my mind and heart. I read additional books by NDE-ers like Nancy Rynes and Anita Moorjani. I read more of Eckhart Tolle's books. My future with Mark now gone, I understand how powerful it can be to focus on the present moment, not dwell on the past, and not overthink the future. It becomes my personal mantra.

I also read books by doctors and psychiatrists who had patients with extraordinary stories of surviving against all odds because of the power of hope. Of patients who leave their bodies and watch the medical team operating on them. Of a patient near death who experiences a vision of his future, yet-to-be-born granddaughter. I like reading books by authors from a medical background—Dr. Laurin Bellg, Dr. Allan Hamilton, and Dr. Brian Weiss. I read with a critical mind and open heart, grabbing the gems that resonate for me.

That summer, I'm back in Tahoe hosting friends from out of town. Suzie and Lil fly in from Colorado and Tish from Santa Rosa. Wesley drives up on the weekend to join us. Lil's a gourmet cook, so she has big plans to cook a delicious seafood paella on the Weber grill. We stop at the local fish counter and buy some beautiful-looking jumbo prawns and fresh cod steaks. Tish, an Italian wine merchant from Sonoma, brings an abundance of wine to host tasting sessions for us. Suzie and I break out my new inflatable kayaks that try our patience as we attempt to inflate them at the beach. Wesley and Lil are neck and neck with each other during our marathon Scrabble sessions. It's a picture-perfect vacation so far.

One afternoon, our little crew squeezes in time to just relax at the beach. We're enjoying a lively conversation about who we'd cast for the novel I've been working on. It's a coming-of-age story about Nicole, a woman who moves to Milan to launch her new fashion brand, only to discover that her father, who she thought had died many years ago, was in fact, leading a secret life she never knew about. She has a great sidekick girlfriend, Maddie, who spices up the dialogue with a lot of sassy talk.

"Nicole's a very strong woman, but a bit too obsessed with her career. Men take a backseat in her life," I explain.

"I feel like she's a brunette but someone who conveys strength," Lil ventures.

"Oh yes, I agree," Tish chimes in.

We consider and talk through Gal Gadot, Olivia Munn, and Natalie Portman, discussing their pros and cons.

"I think Sandra Oh should play Maddie," Suzie insists.

I frown. "What about Emilia Clarke?"

"But she plays such a power player in *Game of Thrones*," Lil says.

Wesley nods vigorously. "I agree. Why her?"

"Haven't you seen her in *Last Christmas* with Henry Golding? She's funny," I reply.

Not everyone's seen the movie.

"Kate McKinnon could be hilarious too. She has that wickedly sarcastic humor," Tish offers.

While they continue bantering about actors, I watch a huge family, several generations setting up their colorful oasis of beach chairs, towels, and umbrellas near us. Grandparents, parents, and their children, ranging from teenagers to elementary school–age kids. There's a steady stream of voices filling the air, punctuated by loud bursts of laughter above the background din of jet skis and motor boats on the lake. They're talking loudly about how they want to come back to Tahoe for Thanksgiving, who makes the best stuffing, and that they should order their turkey at Blue Ribbon Meat and Butcher Shop in Reno—they're the best.

They remind me of the big Navajo family I chatted with at the Burn Center. Something grips me hard in the stomach, a dull pain, and my eyes instantly brim. Their abundance hits me at the center of my loss, not just of Mark but my dad too.

My mind takes off, driving an inner vortex, a fast-speaking monologue that I can't seem to stop.

It's not my destiny to have a big family. My parents are both gone. All my uncles and only aunt are gone—an entire generation.

I've now lost Mark. I have Wesley and Adrian but they lost their dad around the same age I did. I still have my sister, Teresa, and her little family, and my cousins Richard and Kent.

Then there's Mark's family—many more of them with their Midwestern upbringing, so different than mine. They're as sensible and normal as families come. But the closest lives 2,200 miles away in Dodgeville, Wisconsin.

"Jenny! What'll it be? You're the author and director. After considerable discussion, the peanut gallery has voted that Maddie should be Sandra Oh," Suzie announces.

I laugh. It feels so good to be surrounded by my posse of family and friends.

I may not have a lot of family but it's okay. My friends ARE also my family.

My shoulder relaxes as I sit back in my chair.

It's a near-perfect moment.

I'm startled one day to realize that it's been almost two years since Mark died. It's just like Suzie had said last year. *Jenny, make new memories.* For every memory I have of Mark, I now have a new memory.

In addition to picking up a six-pack of Sierra Nevadas for Mark, I now remember picking up giant prawns for Lil's paella and an Italian Barolo for Suzie.

In addition to Mark and I stopping at the Village Ski Loft to get our skis waxed, I also recall buying myself a pair of snowshoes.

In addition to Mark and I enjoying our coffee at the beach, I also remember Matt, Jane, and I laughing at Ka'ia's shiny eyes as she made her debut swim, paddling eagerly toward us with an enormous log gripped in her mouth.

I also realize around this time that there's no right time to be ready to date. Grief and sadness ebb and flow. I'm not going to wake up one day and feel that I've overcome my sadness over losing Mark. Adjusting to being single for two years is a drop in the bucket compared to the thirty-one years Mark and I were together. Lately, falling into the dark hole of tears becomes more of a moment than a crying jag. My eyes brim suddenly, the moment falls away quickly and I'm back on solid ground.

Unlike some widows and widowers, I never felt that I would betray Mark by dating others. He had told me years ago that if anything happened to me, he would need love and companionship again. I was too scared at the time to think of losing him to even go there in our conversation. But I knew it meant he'd want me to meet someone again if he died first. Well, here I was in that situation, far earlier in my life than I ever imagined.

Brave new world—I take the plunge. In a strange role reversal, Adrian lectures me on how to be safe online. During this time, I text with a nice, sensitive guy from Santa Cruz who works for a tech company. In the end, he stands me up on our first coffee date. I surprise myself with how much I feel sorry for him, thinking he'd have to be pretty messed up to do this to me. The younger me would've been mortified. After my many years of life and love, I feel secure now, knowing who I am and that in spite of my quirks and flaws, I'm a love-worthy person.

Next, I meet a handsome Israeli venture capitalist on video who admits to lying about his age. I go on two dates with a tall, very funny man—a professional keyboardist. We immediately bond over death—his sister's premature death as a UC Berkeley student and Mark. But he's never really ventured out of his comfort zone in life and I run out of interest on our second date hiking.

I join a widows and widower dating Facebook group. One evening someone posts:

"Would you consider dating someone long distance?"

My immediate response, which I keep to myself is *No way! The traffic here is terrible. I wouldn't even consider someone north of San Francisco.* Since I had been online, I avoided clicking on any guys in Mill Valley, Fairfield, or Larkspur.

Someone responds with a post:

"I'm open to up to a two-hour drive."

A two-hour drive to me is not long distance. That would be Sacramento. I rethink my response.

Someone else posts:

"I'd be open for the right woman."

The right woman. I pause. *What if it's the right guy? Mark had commuted to Reno four days a week. It was a one-hour flight.*

I immediately remember happy family vacations in Carlsbad and San Diego. Palm trees, bright blue skies, red-roofed Spanish-style homes, cute restaurants near the beach, the grand old red-rooftop Hotel del Coronado, and fantastic Mexican food.

Okay, I'd be open for up to a one-and-a-half-hour flight. San Diego, LA, and Portland. That feels doable. It might be exciting to meet someone from those cities. I always enjoyed visiting them.

I post my response:

> *"I live near San Francisco. For the right relationship, I'd be open to a flight that's up to an hour or an hour-and-a-half away. For me, that'd be LA, San Diego, or Portland."*

A week later I check messages I've received on the dating app I subscribe to. A nice-looking guy named Robert sends me a message. Green eyes. Very kind-looking. Handsome. Six feet three inches. Tall. He's from La Costa, California.

Where's La Costa? I've never heard of the place.

I Google La Costa. It's a subdivision of Carlsbad.

Interesting. I think of my Facebook group response about being open to dating someone from San Diego. Carlsbad is just a few towns north of San Diego. I would've taken a pass on this guy a week ago before I saw the Facebook group post.

"You look so happy with your kids," he writes to me. He's viewed profile photos of me with the boys in Phoenix at an indoor food market and skiing in Verbier.

On our first video call I ask him if he skis or snowboards. He's tried but never really took to it.

He asks me where Mountain View is. I explain that it's fifty minutes south of San Francisco, puzzled by why he didn't already know. He explains that, having just returned from the Bay Area to see family, he hadn't realized when he messaged me that the dating app had localized his search to the Bay Area rather than Carlsbad. It's how I showed up in his search.

We're both widowed. I tell him my story; he tells me his. Our spouses died in the same year. His wife died of ovarian cancer. My mother died of ovarian cancer.

He's been through hypnotherapy and read *The Tibetan Book of Living and Dying*. I'm intrigued, having done neither. I tell him about my spouse grief support group and about the spiritual books I've read. We end the call with me blurting out, "You never know who the universe will put in your path." I wonder where those last words I spoke came from. I have no idea.

Over the next three months we go on a series of dates in the Bay Area, LA, and Tahoe. Because of the distance between our homes, seeing each other takes time. We share a love of words (he's witty and funny), live music and dancing (he sings in a band), and the ability to get caught up in the reverie of the ocean sunsets (he lives in Carlsbad).

By our third date in Tahoe, while we enjoy a drink together at the Hyatt lakefront patio, I know he's the "one." It's an idyllic moment. The lake is shimmering in the midafternoon sun, the warm air suffused with the distant purr of motorboats on the water and voices carrying from the beach. Our hands are touching. There's something about Robert that brings out my kinder, gentler self. I like who I am around him. He calls me the *supernova of love*. I call him *my dancing bear*.

When I'm with Robert, a door opens, a powerful ray of sunlight that illuminates all parts of my heart, the pieces of me that lived in the shadows the last couple years. It's the love that had nowhere to go but is now so much bigger and brighter than before. Love that deepened only because I first had to walk the lonely path of loss and pain.

I don't want to make the same mistake as I did with Mark. Mark knew I was the "one" after our third date. But instead of trusting my heart, I made him wait five months after he proposed. Sitting together in this magical moment by the lake, I tell Robert that I know he's "the one." He squeezes my hand.

I mention to him with pride how my dad raised me to be super independent. How my boyfriend before Mark suffocated me with wanting to take care of me. How I found the right balance in Mark because we were both independent, equals, and each other's best cheerleaders in life.

Robert asks, "Are you okay with being taken care of now?"

I'm stumped by this question. I chew on my lip, thinking. *I'm not sure.*

"Yes." I hesitate because this is so new for me. "I think I would be now?"

I'll have to think about this some more.

I'm astonished that Robert is from Carlsbad. When Mark and I decided to move to Tahoe, I had told him, "I grew up on coasts, so for the record, I still want a beach cottage in Carlsbad." I had told no one except Mark about Carlsbad.

It's also interesting that Robert found me by accident with the dating app's localized search algorithm—and that his wife, Jean, died the same year Mark passed away. We discovered that in that same year we stayed five blocks apart from each other in Phoenix. He was there with Jean for alternative medical treatments while Mark was at the Burn Center. *Are these merely coincidences and I'm reading too much into it?*

Mark, did you guide us to each other? It doesn't seem so far-fetched when I remember how Mark had said goodbye to me through the "Sirens" song the morning before he died. How he spoke to me while I was recovering from my first migraine without him. How he made his presence known to friends—Showa, Laila, and me. Those early dates between Robert and me become the start of a journey that would lead to a joyful, loving partnership. Along the way I feel the guidance of Mark, my own intuition, and the loving forces in the universe.

One morning I'm out for a walk by the lake in my quiet Tahoe neighborhood. Robert is flying in that afternoon to see me, a reunion after a long absence between us. I'm anxious and not sure what to expect from his visit. Part of the way into my walk, I hear Mark say to me in his typical commanding voice, "Listen to me, Jenny." It's so loud that I'm startled and take my earbuds off, thinking someone is speaking out loud to me on the trail. There's no one near me. I'm certain it's Mark. It's the same annoyed tone he used to use when we would watch a movie together and I would ask, "What just happened?" because I was distracted, on my phone.

This time I know what he means. Instead of *Get off your phone,* he means *Take your earbuds off.*

"Yes?" I ask out loud. Thank God no one is near me. They would think I'm some crazy hiker lady.

He says to me, "Just love him."

"Okay," I say out loud to him, astonished.

Did I imagine that Mark just spoke to me?

Two blocks later, I pass a sign, *Robert Avenue.* In all the years I've walked in this neighborhood, I never encountered Robert Avenue. *Could it be a confirming sign from Mark?*

Epilogue

"As you walk on the way, the way appears."
—Rumi

Wesley announces that his fan fiction writer partners in Austin want him to move in with them. He's been thinking about it for a while and finally decides it's time for him to leave Mountain View. I tell him how thrilled his dad would be for him. Mark would visit a lot because he loved Texas barbecue and Stevie Ray Vaughan.

Over spicy jambalaya at our farewell dinner at Nola in Palo Alto, Wesley says, "Mom, I decided it was time for me to move to Austin now that I know that you'll be okay."

I'm touched. I had no idea he considered how I was doing in his calculus for leaving.

I reach out and hold his hand. "Thank you, Wesley." My face is wet. Tears are always near the surface these days. He gets up and hugs me.

"Do you miss your dad? How are you doing on the whole grief thing?" *Will he be okay leaving the home he grew up in with all its memories of Mark?*

"Of course I miss him," he says softly.

We're both quiet.

"I think the way I processed my grief was to help you."

My chest feels so full. Adrian got me through Phoenix, and Wesley helped me after Mark died. I'm proud of who they are. *Who was it that said, until you're tested by the trials of life, you don't know what a person's made of?*

"Thank you, Wesley. I'll miss you but as you said, I think I'll be okay."

After I blow my nose, I pivot to more lighthearted conversation.

"How's your Discord group doing?" Wesley's a moderator.

He explains he and others have been coaching a guy who's living at home with abusive parents. They've been trying to help him find ways to move out and build his own life.

I'm proud that Wesley cares enough to get involved.

"He struggles with his own issues. I had my 'tough dad' talk with him recently."

"Tough love, huh?"

Wesley nods. "You know, I showed him unconditional love. I could only do that because you and Dad showed me unconditional love first."

I'm suddenly out of breath; my chest beats faster.

"Really?"

Wesley nods.

Mark, did you hear that? Your son just told us that because of the love he received from us first, he has the capacity to love and care for others.

The more I travel this journey of grief and loss, the more I realize that love is the epicenter of all that matters. It is the great healer. Love is more than an emotion. It's a powerful energy that radiates beyond each of us to others.

It's summer and I'm back home in Mountain View from Tahoe. The YMCA where I used to work out remains closed. I continue to walk in my neighborhood as often as I can, discovering a lot of beauty I never noticed in my suburban community. I note which house has the nicest succulent, zero-landscaped garden, which ones have the most beautiful rose bushes. I pass a house with life-sized bronze sculptures of people in their garden, only the owners have placed blue COVID masks on each face. *What a strange time we're living in!*

Today, it's another one of those brilliantly blue northern California skies. As I walk closer to our house on my return loop, I notice a white bird circling above me. It's flying lower than I've noticed other birds flying. I vaguely notice it while I continue walking but stop when it gets my attention by flying directly above me in circles. Around and around. It makes me think of Mark circling up in the air in his plane.

I've seen seagulls with their white necks and gray wings fly in our neighborhood. We're only four miles from the bay. Looking up, I notice that this bird, however, is completely white. I'm not a birdwatcher so I have no idea what kind of bird is flying so closely above me.

While the bird continues circling in a wide arc, I glance at my watch. It's time to get home for lunch. I head for the last two blocks toward our house.

When I walk in through the garage, I glance at my phone. *My goodness. It's June 12—the same date as Mark's plane crash several years ago.* Then I remember that Mark's nickname in high school was "Bird," because he had such a long waist and short legs and looked like a bird out on the basketball court. It's not the graceful bird image that one thinks of, yet here we are. The white bird makes me think of him.

Was that bird Mark, greeting me on the anniversary of his plane accident?

A tingling, warm wave surges in my chest, overwhelming me with a feeling I have no words for. I catch my breath when I get into the kitchen. The Peet's French roast coffee bag is on the counter—Mark's favorite because he loved his coffee dark and strong. His giant smoker near the deck, in full view out the tall windows, is where he spent hours on weekends, an American Gordon Ramsay in his apron, attending to his brisket. Memories of his loving presence are all around me—it feels so real.

Thank you, God, the loving universe, Dad, and Mark, for taking care of me. I realize my dad and Mark were always there for me, solid, each a rock for me. Meeting Mark right after Dad died represented some kind of cosmic handoff from him to Mark. Thank you that I have found love again in Robert, a love that draws from a deep well that's certain and true. I only now realize that Mark is handing the baton off to Robert.

I don't know what my life will bring next. What I'm certain of is this: Life's an adventure that can bring both joy and sadness, and the inner refuge of my heart and the loving outer sanctuary of all living things—the trees, the birds, the snow, and sunshine—will sustain me, whatever happens. It includes the people who magically show up in my life at the right time and right place.

Through everything I've been through, I've grown from being a baby bird in free fall from its nest to learning to fly, soaring through the open sky, forever free.

Acknowledgments

Thank you to Gretchen Young, my editor at Regalo Press/Post Hill, for her kind and deeply insightful guidance. A very big thank you to Charlie Fusco for her belief that my story was important enough to share and her guidance for how best to bring it to the world.

I wouldn't have gotten started if Janis Newman wasn't the first to believe in the power of my story and give me the confidence in the "craft" of writing. She intuitively understood what I was trying to say. Thank you also to Wesley, my son, a fellow writer, for reading my many drafts and offering valuable feedback and ideas.

My most profound thanks goes to Thomas Hunnicutt for his incredible courage in rescuing Mark from his burning plane. He gave our family the gift of five months with Mark when he would've otherwise perished. Thomas showed us what "love in action" means. He is a true hero and angel.

My deepest gratitude to the Arizona Burn Center team—Dr. Kevin Foster, Dr. Michael Peck, Dr. Marc Matthews, the nurses and the physical therapists, too many to name, whose incredible competence, dedication, love, and care carried Mark and I through some of our family's darkest times. The nursing team truly became my second family. Thank you to Lori Janek, formerly at the Arizona Burn Foundation, who supported our family during our rollercoaster journey with Mark.

I couldn't have survived my time with Mark at the Arizona Burn Center without the daily presence and support of my son, Adrian, and my soul sister, Suzie Oh. Many family and friends visited during my time in Phoenix but the two of you were my constant companions. I'll be forever grateful to you for being by my side every day.

Wesley, Adrian, Rene, Michelle, Steven, Kim, Teresa, Bob, Todd, Dee, Rick, Marcene and Harlow, Richard, Kent and Oanh—I couldn't have asked for better love and support from family. I'm also so grateful to my "on the ground" support team in Phoenix—Jeff Dempsey, Neil and Sue Tessman, Mike and Kathy Lucia.

Thank you also to my Chegg family—Dan Rosensweig, my fellow C-team, and my People team for their unwavering support. They gave me the time and space I needed to fully focus on Mark. I'm so proud that we built a culture that cared about people.

I come from a small family and Mark's family lives far away, so friends are my family too. My special clan of friends kept me going the first few years after my time in Phoenix. Suzie Oh, Showa Sahle, Laila Partridge, Stanka and Branko Radonjic, Matt and Jane Arena (and my bundle of love, Kai'a), Kathy Thibodeaux, Mike Lanza, David Birnbaum, Denis Browne, Maya Lockwood, my Chegg women's group, and my Friday cocktail group. Some of you are longtime friends, others are newer friends who joined me in my journey to help me to grow and become the person who I am today—someone more empathetic, open, and able to let go enough to allow the grace of God and the universe to work its magic in my life. It's been an amazing ride so far!

Thank you Robert Maxwell for being my loving partner. I'm certain my dad and Mark brought us together. I marvel at the deep love and synchronicity between us and how the loving universe continues to guide us every day. You are my soulmate.

Finally, thank you Mark and my dad, Augustus Fung, who created the foundation by which I knew I was always loved. Your enduring love helped me grow like a fledgling, well-watered flower. Because you came first, I could find love again and have the confidence to know what has been true all along—that love is the greatest healer and at the center of all that's good and beautiful in the world.